Ruth & Clive

CW00500380

FOOTPRINTS
through the
Gates of Europe

Compiled by

Steve Lowton

**Grosvenor House
Publishing Limited**

with contributions from Andrea Harrison, Gemma and Dick Bonham,
Justin Thomas, Chris Meredith, Steve Hallett, Paul Wood, Dave Herron,
Kathy Garda, Chris Seaton, Sharon Cooke and Andrew Crump

With thanks to
Debs Robinson, Andy Crump and Paul Wood for the photographs.

Edited by Dick Bonham

Steven Lowton is hereby identified as author of this
work in accordance with Section 77 of the Copyright, Designs
and Patents Act 1988

The book cover picture is copyright to Andy Crump

Cover design by Andy Crump

Lightening over the Parthenon

(For commissioned work email Andy on andycrump@hotmail.com)

This book is published by
Grosvenor House Publishing Ltd
28-30 High Street, Guildford, Surrey, GU1 3HY.
www.grosvenorhousepublishing.co.uk

A CIP record for this book
is available from the British Library

ISBN 978-1-906210-84-7

*This book is dedicated to the households
of faith that are rising at this time.*

*Also to my wife Kathy and
my four daughters,
Hannah, Laura, Chun Zhen and Jin Zhou*

This is a chronicle of a journey that began on the rugged cliff tops of Whitby in North-East England and came to a temporary conclusion in the historic setting of Jerusalem, the most contested city in the world. Walking across seven different nations and through some of the most wonderful scenery in Europe and the Near East, one question was carried by everyone who took part: can nations change through the choices and decisions of ordinary people like you and me?

In between holding down the responsibilities of jobs and everyday life, the team walked through the global gateways of London, Paris, Rome, Athens, Istanbul, Damascus and Jerusalem. Believing passionately in the power of prayer and the redemptive purposes of their Maker, these contemporary journeymen and women pick up the tale of the cities and people they encountered, finding the storyline of their own lives woven into the fabric of the nations they walked through.

So join their journey as, like a modern-day tale of Narnia, they make their way out of their doorways to find stories waiting that link their homes to the landscapes unravelling around them. Be enticed by the beauty of France and the wonder of the coastlines of Italy and Greece; admire the beautiful mosques of Istanbul and Damascus; and linger with them as they make their way through the West Bank, into Bethlehem, and on to Jerusalem. Find yourself asking the question: are we spectators in the course of world events, or can we be partners with the maker of all things in the affairs of nations?

"This book is an adventure story, an alternative travelogue, which takes faith out of the safety of four walls and into creation. Like the hobbits of Middle Earth on an incredible journey, Steve and his companions dare to believe that their individual lives and choices can make a difference across continents. Their interweaving stories connect history and geography, time and place, the grand and the mundane, and so we catch a glimpse of the God of history, making Himself known in ordinary lives in extraordinary ways. Best of all, it is a true story with all the sweat, blisters, cost and risk that goes with such an arduous and daring expedition. It surely demonstrates that life can be lived to the full with a God who encompasses it all."

Sally Ann Dyer, Loughborough, the Midlands.

"The journeys we embark on ourselves, or even through the stories and recollections of others, can be as important as the arrival, for there are treasures to be discovered along the way. Steve and his fellow travellers have brought us journeys and stories that can touch us at the deepest level. Journey with them, read the book and prepare to be impacted. I can give no better recommendation."

Keith Robson, Northumberland.

"This book will need careful attention to get to the story behind it; of how ordinary people did something quite extraordinary, as they made the journey on foot from Whitby to Canterbury, to Rome and then on to Jerusalem. It's not just a story of a modern day pilgrimage; it's also a record of the spiritual journey of Steve and his team as they linked back into the footsteps of history.

We were privileged to be able to pass on the baton of walking and praying across Europe to him, through one of God's co-incidences, and look forward to what he will do next."

John and Yvonne Presdee, Kent.

"'Never doubt that a small group of committed citizens can change the world; indeed it's the only thing that ever did' (Margaret Mead). Here are stories of a small group of nobodies, audaciously believing that their wanderings, fuelled by that imperishable trinity of faith, hope and love, can change the history of cities, nations, and continents. You might not go along with everything they say, but you have to applaud their faith and perseverance."

Mike Love, Leeds.

"Steve weaves his own journey, and the journeys of fellow walkers, into a continuous story of a visionary trek through Europe. Exciting but ordinary, inspiring and challenging, these stories are full of down to earth incidents and spiritual encounters, unassuming but maybe making history."

Linda Harding, Leeds..

About the Author

In recent years, Steve Lowton has given himself to long-distance walking as he has carried across nations a passionate love of the land and its people. Believing that we are inextricably linked to the places we live, he has continually carried questions into the courtrooms of his Maker, daring to believe that there is a God who listens and cares. Married to Kathy, and the father of four daughters, Steve and his wife have committed themselves to discovering a contemporary expression of the monastic way within their own home, seeking to uncover a counter-cultural pattern of living. Editor of a compilation of different life experiences called *Journeys of the Heart and Mind*, Steve puts high value on the power of story, in his own journey and the journey of those around him.

For further copies of this book or others by the same author, visit www.journeysoftheheart.co.uk

Contents

CONTENTS

CONTENTS

Foreword

Martin Scott

Storytelling. The art is probably as old as the human race itself. Perhaps it is an important aspect of what *makes* us human, and maybe it is good storytelling that will help *keep* us human. Enough stories have been told that dehumanise people. The imperial stories that tell of the success of the centre and the benefits that can flow to subservient citizens are ultimately dehumanising. The imagery of advertising, and its story that we are made significant through buying a product, dehumanises us. Stories can destroy and control. But they can also release. If there is much in our world that simply dehumanises, then maybe it is time for storytelling to become one way that helps to humanise our world again.

Jesus was not just fully human (like us), he was also truly human (unlike us). He was the great storyteller. His parables were not just nice illustrations to communicate the truth in narrative form, but were powerful stories that pointed to a new way of living. They were stories of hope and grace. Would it be a fantasy to think that the future could be shaped by simple stories?

Stories can be told for many reasons, good and bad, but in this season it seems the prophets have to learn to tell stories again. I use the term 'prophets' not because I wish to give a title to those who write and edit the following pages, but because the promise of Pentecost was that people would hear those touched by the Spirit speak in their language. Those touched would prophesy. Prophets must tell stories, and the stories will prophesy of a new day of opportunity.

What you will read is more than a journal about a particular set of travels. It is more than the personal chronicle of Steve and his companions. I believe what is written is multi-layered. I am sure you will find yourself being drawn into the journey; sometimes because of a historic or geographic resonance, but more often because what is being told (maybe with a few changes of detail) will seem like your story.

We all read differently, but let me make a suggestion. And this suggestion comes from someone who is not good at reflecting, and hence does not always learn from what he has walked through. So I humbly suggest that when part of the story resonates, make sure you have space and time for 'deep to call to deep'. There is in your life a depth that makes you who you are. There are places, thoughts, desires and potentials that make you unique. Whenever we tentatively discover that uniqueness there will come from God a corresponding affirmation that we are significant. Deep will call to deep. Although we are but one person among six billion, and can easily be lost in the crowd, we are also different to all the others. Through that individuality we are encouraged to tell a story of a new way to live.

I write from the conviction that, once we refuse the lie that we have to be 'successful' and prove everything through some objective measurement, we will find that (amidst our failures) we have become strangely effective.

Effectiveness is not easy to measure, but when we live according to our uniqueness we will begin to infect others. How many will we infect in our lifetime? Maybe only a handful. The greatest storyteller ever seemed to only infect a few as he walked to Jerusalem. Maybe we do not have to do too much, for success is not the goal. Perhaps, instead, it is to be one of the many who walk gently through life, seeking to learn and point the way to a world still to come.

Recently I wrote this prayer:

Lord, give me enough time (whether that is short or long) to see a generation established that is free of imperialism, religiosity and competitiveness, so that there might be some tangible correlation between the people of God and what you called your ekklesia1. I am grateful that you send your Spirit from heaven to earth. I welcome the Spirit of hope.

I know you will read of hope in the pages that follow. I trust that this book will be effective, for some will be infected as they read.

Martin Scott
10 January 2008

---

[1]Ecclesia is a term derived form the Greek root ekklesia which literally means a "gathering" of citizens. It was a name for the popular assembly of citizens in Athens and, in New Testament times, a name for the Church. (www.wikipedia.com, accessed January 2008).

CHAPTER 1

A Deeper Magic

Steve Lowton

I looked around the room. Slowly the horror of what I was seeing began to penetrate the tedious layers of boredom that were resting upon me, like one of those days when clouds sit heavy across the sky as far as the eye can see. Everyone and everything was grey; the décor, the suits, the hair and even the ashen faces belonging to those who have spent too much time shut away in endless meetings, as far from the wind, rain and sun as we were that grey morning. The most shocking part of all was that I felt, and probably looked, just as grey and bleak as the rest of my work colleagues.

Without knowing it I had become grey; if Spitting Image had any interest at all in aging Church leaders then they would have quickly found another outlet for the John Major persona that caused embarrassed chuckles at the expense of a nation's Prime Minister. Grey, grey, grey.

Now you need to know that for someone still in their late thirties this was hugely disturbing, and more than your average mid life crisis. In the pioneering zeal of my

1

youthful days it felt as if I had created a monster that seemed about to consume me; a totally distorted perception, but one that seemed hugely real at that point. The reality was that I could no longer do the corporate church leader thing; either I got out quick or I would go under. The words of a friend echoed round my head when he casually commented to me that "my biggest fear is to give my life to something and wake up to realise that I no longer want to be part of it." An extreme statement, but one that had sufficient elements of truth to make me sit up and take notice.

Something big had to be done. Cutting my hair short and getting an earring was a temporary shot in the arm; a misguided attempt, perhaps, to recapture the days of lost youth. However, deep in my heart I knew that this phase of my life was coming to an abrupt end. Tired of fire-fighting and tired of keeping the show on the road, I knew I had reached my sell-by date. I could no longer believe the vision statement, and was tired of the corporate logo. It is totally legitimate to "knuckle down" and find some way through the struggle when faced with all the responsibilities that litter our lives. But for me there was no more grace for that. If the God I had chosen to give my life to was worth anything at all, then this had to be a moment when I discovered the reality of what that meant.

Over the next two years I fought like a man possessed as I made my way out of the centre of responsibility, seeking to find a way in which I could pass on the fruit of fifteen years of labour. As I emptied my desk and tidied away the last bits of debris, I noticed a newspaper article that I had, somewhat prophetically, pinned to the notice board years before. It was dated 1989 and showed a map of the Soviet Union, with the headline "But will the centre hold?" As long as a decade ago I was already asking questions that took a whole ten years to work their way through. For me, the discovery, like that of the early desert fathers, was that the God I followed could no longer be found in the centre of institutions, or even in guitar-playing, flag-waving churches, but only in the wilderness, the margins of life and the uncharted paths that hold the unknown round every corner. It is surely here that the richness of life and faith grows and the reality of what we have is measured, far away from the trappings of a successful career marked out along well-trodden paths.

Roll the calendar on a couple of months. Imagine one of those cold October days on which winter seems to have come too early. The rain is driving down and I, along with my faithful friend Jonathon, am sitting under a bridge alongside the Liverpool to Leeds Canal in the north of England. We are cold, soaked to the skin, aching from head-to-toe, and wondering what on earth we were doing attempting to walk the breadth of the country from Liverpool to Hull. Looking back I have more understanding. Without doubt I was in need of some sort of cathartic experience, away from the creeping greyness of recent years. I was out looking for new pathways, those wild and untamed tracks where I could rediscover an edge to life and allow the drab colours to be reinvigorated. However, to be sat in the mud underneath a motorway bridge, alongside a dreary canal was hardly the adventure I was looking for. Surely those early Celtic wanderers never felt like this? Yet this was my reality; no career, no real shape to the future, just a hunch that there was something out there for me to discover.

All of us know moments when dreams go into the ground and die. For those of us who tune into so-called reality TV it's there for every voyeuristic viewer to see; the shattered hopes as one contestant after another faces the reality check of decision day. For me this was that kind of season: the winter season, where death is everywhere and spring so far away. Yet without the cycles of death and life that nature so wonderfully models, the processes of creation would short-circuit. We would probably be left with some plastic substitute, no different to the shopping malls and TV shows that present such a shallow view of who we are. Death is essential and can be good! In fact, it's vital for life, and it is those who have the courage to allow cherished dreams to go into the ground that really find new birth.

Maybe the ancient patriarchs understood this far more than us. If you were to visit Hebron on the West Bank you would discover that even before it was the site of David's anointing as King, it was the place where Abraham first owned a piece of the promised land. However, it was not land on which he celebrated a new conquest: it was a burial plot for his wife, Sarah. The entry point for the land of promise was in fact the place of death.

In the ground, the natural processes of decomposition work away at us, separating out that which is dross from that which is real. Flattery and self-delusion are quickly found wanting, and space is given for refining and purification.

In the ground, could it be that a deeper magic unfolds? Is it possible that the storyline of our lives can become interwoven with the storyline of the land itself? Could it be that when our protective coverings are gone it allows the reality of who we are to find a synergy with the depths of the towns, cities and nations of which we are a part? Can the prayers and hopes we carry begin to capture something of the substance of the land itself?

Far fetched, I hear you say: too much wine and not enough real life. However, in the western world we have such a shallow understanding of the land. We buy our pre-packaged food from the supermarket and have no idea at all what it means to live close to the soil; or to have to run in fear of our lives from the land our forefathers farmed for generations.

This came home to me strongly when I had the privilege of visiting a refugee camp during the Kosovo crisis in the late 1990s. After wandering through the jam-packed rooms, trying not to appear too intrusive on the misery unfolding before me, I came across a woman who said these words to me, words I will never forget: "I have lost my husband and I have lost my two sons, but give us back the land, give us back the land." Indeed, as I walked from the room she kept repeating those last words: "Give us back the land."

Could it be that there is a story waiting to be told that connects not just the ordinary lives of you and me, but also the towns, cities and nations we are a part of? Could it be that what goes on in our living rooms can shape the destiny of cities just as much as, if not more than, the politicians and power players of our time?

This book is full of those questions. It charts a trek across the M62 corridor in the north of the UK that became, in time, a journey from Whitby to London, Paris, Rome, Athens, Istanbul, Damascus and on into Jerusalem. Here we attempt to tell the tale of the journey, woven together with the story of some of the major cities we walked through.

The imagination is deliberately given space to roam as we transcend the realm of ordinary human beings into the realm of angels and the unseen. Clear historical narrative gives way to sweeping brush strokes of the imagination as the life and personality of each city finds artistic expression, and the sound of feet walking through the gates of Europe echoes between heaven and earth. That Damascus and Jerusalem lie well beyond the boundaries of Europe is no matter, for their influence upon this continent and the western world is huge and befits the title of this chronicle.

Peppered through such a tale of adventure and discovery are the ordinary living room experiences of my own household, as together we stumbled into a journey of discovery of our own. Common currency is found between that which grounds us in the realities of babies and sleepless nights, bank balances and earning a living, and the wonder of life on the road. Time and time again we ask the question, which is where this book starts: can nations turn because of decisions made in our own front room, or are we in fact pawns in the hands of those selected to be the power brokers of our affairs?

So turn the page, let your imagination roam, and see what possibilities open up for you in this tale of discovery. Be slow to form conclusions, but let the journey encircle you and take your mind and heart through the stunning scenery that makes Europe one of the most wonderful of places to live. Smell the aromas of the bazaars of Istanbul and imagine the storyteller as he sits in the eastern gate of Damascus. Hear the crackle of thunder over the Parthenon in Athens and catch sight of the Bedouin Shepherds along the roadside in Syria.

To begin our journey we must first go back in time nearly 3000 years, to a mysterious tale of famine and hardship, soldiers and outcasts and - yes - the living room of a strange, mystical man. I let Chris, one of those who walked with us, pick up the tale.

CHAPTER 2

Living Rooms and City Gates

Chris Meredith

Chris is currently involved with postgraduate research into the Hebrew Bible. The following chapter is a direct retelling of a story from the book of 2 Kings (6:24 – 7:20).[1] It explores some of the Biblical narrative that helped provide the backdrop to our journey. Chris walked with me down through England to London and was a key part the walk out of Athens, up past Mount Olympus and into Istanbul.

Usually on a clear afternoon Samaria's watchman would be able to see across the fertile valleys and flatlands below the city, over the Plains of Sharon to the

---

[1]The contents of the story itself remain almost entirely unchanged. Descriptive qualities and some background information have been employed to bring relevant elements to the surface. Historians be warned; I have not been overly focused on the likely fashion and technology of the age! No dialogue has been added and what there is remains almost entirely unaltered; a handful of terms have been modernised or had elements stressed to tease out the likely original emphasis. Supplementary elements, such as voice-tone or descriptions, have been added only when they are not critical to the plot.

foamy ribbon of wave-marks, and to the blue of the Mediterranean beyond. They would watch the road running between the mountains Ebal and Gerazim, mind the communication corridor out to Syria and Phoenicia, and look over the Northern Kingdom with a watchful eye. Perching itself as an urban crown on the high hill over everything below, it was a city for watching[2]; a city with a firm, resolute gaze, unassailable by force, its eyes susceptible only to siege and famine. Samaria – the city of the Kings of Israel; the city of their tombs; the capitol of the tribes of the north; the city that watches...

Slowly, the moon appeared for the first time that evening, its regal silver fingers escaping the cloud and teasing the tops of the city walls. Hunger gnawed at Samaria, and the soft, innocent shafts of lunar light played across her empty streets, stables, and aviaries, before sheathing themselves once more in the carefully rolling envelope of cloud far above. The streets were empty; too full of fear, too full of shadow and the darkest sides of life to allow the starving much room. The animals had been dead for some time, eaten unceremoniously; everything from the vermin to the palace horses had been plundered for survival, and the carcasses picked clean. This contributed heavily to the silence. Dove manure – were you to have found a dove with a functioning digestive system - could now be purchased for as grand a sum as five days' labour per quarter pint.

---

[2]The word Samaria comes from the Hebrew root Shamar meaning 'to keep, watch, observe' - there is obviously a Hebrew play on words, and possibly some irony, in the story where Omri buys the land for the city from a gentleman called Shemer and names it after him.

The head of a working animal, a donkey or a mule, would earn you perhaps sixteen times that; though the calculations were academic. Money had long since become useless and labour an impossibility. The thought of finding food was laughable; selling it, merely suicide.

The king and his first officer[3] padded the tops of the city walls in the night air, briskly looking, I suppose, for news from the Syrian army encamped in their siege positions far below. Whether there was any news of Ben-Haddad's troops or not we cannot know, because her voice tore through the muggy quiet of the evening. "Help, my Lord O King!"

She half-shouted, half-shrieked the words, which echoed as they bounced between the narrow stone-worked streets up to where the King and his first officer walked on the parapet. Their strides shortened, eyes peering into the lonely gloom below. They could see no-one in the streets. Only the cry hung in the air.

"If Yahweh does not help you, where can I find help for you; from the breadbin or the off-licence?" The king's voice was fuller, deeper, and swam through the space more imposingly than hers, though with far less feeling.

She emerged into the flickering torchlight; thin and filthy, grime covering her weak, doubled body, hair tangled and matted, narrow, fleshless fingers pulling her shawl tight around herself, cold despite the relative warmth of the summer night. The dust clung to her cheeks, giving way only for the tears that ran from her dim, tight eyes to her overly visible jaw-line, dividing once or twice along the

---

[3]The original term for the officer is literally 'man of the king's right hand', from which we get the term 'right hand man'. 'First Officer' seems an adequate translation here.

way in testimony of more than a moment's weeping; of more than a passing sadness. The king, looking down to the woman, lowered himself slowly into a crouch, sword point prodding against the flagstone beneath him with a metallic clink. His movement threw a little more light onto the trembling subject of his furrowed gaze. "What is troubling you?" he asked, more gently.

She opened her mouth and paused, unable to continue, face contorting as she desperately searched and re-searched for words. What came was the answer of a dying woman, trapped in a dying city, alive now for the sole reason that her body, even as she spoke, was awkwardly digesting the boiled flesh of her son. He had travelled such a little distance; from belly and back again, a body turned against him through hunger and terror and persuasion and fear. Eventually the words rushed out of her: "This woman said to me 'Give your son that we may eat him today and we will eat my son tomorrow'; so we boiled my son and ate him and I said to her on the next day 'Give your son that we may eat him', but she has hidden her son!"

The king didn't answer. Raising hands to his robes, thick war-ridden fingers felt the creases formed across his chest as he crouched on the towering wall. Palms met fingertips, catching small swathes of cloth – and he pulled. Stitch left expensive stitch and the unexpected and unkingly sound of public, mournful garment-tearing spilt into the silence. In one movement he was on his feet again, striding quickly and purposefully along the wall, pulling on his gloves as he rumbled forwards. His officer hurried quickly behind him, eyeing the soft flaps of cloth that rippled as the king walked. The eyes of every guard they passed darted to the same thing; the thick, coarse

Hessian shirt, which the richer, brighter robes had concealed; the sackcloth garb of a man in secret mourning, the deeply troubled spirit of the king displayed for all on Samaria's walls to see.

Perhaps it was the shock of rife infanticide which so troubled him in that instant; perhaps the question of whether the woman's upset sprang from the ugly death of her son, or because her next meal had been denied her. Perhaps instead of one generation sacrificing itself for the sake of what was to follow, tomorrow was falling under the knife for the sake of prolonging yesterday, where all that could be, all that might be, dies unheeded and unfulfilled; consumed because yesterday demands it.

That would mean a troubled city indeed.

The King's mind raced, as did his first officer's. Long, heavy strides quickened as anger and frustration mixed with the fear rising in both of them. Their deliberations, I am sure, were remarkably similar. I have little doubt that if we took the time to peer into the many other thoughts and conversations lurking in the city, we would hear the same things oft-repeated. A renowned prophet rested within the city walls – Elisha son of Shaphat, no less - the man who had parted the Jordan, raised the dead, healed foreign lords of their leprosy; the man of God who had fed whole armies with only twenty barley loaves and a knapsack. But there was no deliverance; no weighted words or divine bread; no ceremonial actions. Rocky outcrops had not been commanded to gush with a plentiful supply of water, as in the old stories. Scorching chariots did not emblazon the eastern sky tonight. They had not emblazoned any of the city's long, torturous evenings. Waiting was simply not working.

The king turned to his first officer as they walked, eyes resolute and unflinching, and through clenched teeth and a hardened jaw he growled beneath his breath, "God do so to me and more also if the head of Elisha, the son of Shaphat, remains on him today." The order was as blunt as it was obvious. The officer broke away from the king, hand on hilt, powering into the night. The streets stood open before him, and the prophet's lodgings were only a short distance away. Somewhere across the other side of the city, the watchmen were changing shifts. The warm evening was beginning to lose its thickness as the night deepened, and the officer marched into the waiting shadows, disappearing as he did so.

In those moments he began the last twenty-four hours of his life.

Slowly, the moon appeared for the first time that evening, its hopeful silver fingers escaping the cloud and teasing the tops of the city walls. Elisha, son of Shaphat, sat looking out of his window, watching the soft, innocent shafts of lunar light play across the streets before sheathing themselves once more in the carefully rolling envelope of cloud far above. Sighing, he turned his attention back to the room, and the troubled group of men sitting with him. Here were the elders, the great and experienced men of Samaria, those who sat in the great gateway of the city of sight.

As with all ancient cities, where Samaria's walls gave way to her gateways, civic courtyards opened up. Here people would be funnelled as they entered or left the urban malaise and in these open spaces the populace would buy and would sell. It was also beneath the towering doors that the elders would come together, discussing and shaping city-life, sitting in judgement over disputes, meeting, talking, proclaiming. At the gate, the place of crossing over, the place of economics, and the place of decision were all rolled into one, and was presided over by the city eldership. This same group of men now gathered in Elisha's Samarian living-room; looking, apparently, for answers. Thus far they seemed not to have found any.

The house was simple and uncluttered, and there was no fire. Had there been one it would have thrown light onto the room's empty table and its woefully empty water jars. But there was little else to light and even less to cook. Elisha sat at one end of the room in silence, banishing the deserted streets from his thoughts and beginning to focus once more on the faltering expectations of the men before him. They stared at him; for a man perceived as living in the presence of the answers, he was being remarkably unforthcoming. He shifted his weight uncomfortably where he sat. After all, he was hungry too.

Then suddenly, in one swift, uncomplicated movement, Elisha was on his feet. The men opposite blinked, taken aback at the abrupt and unprecedented display of energy. Something had stirred him instantly and without warning. He drew breath. Nothing in the room dared compete with the sound. His head turned slightly as though a thought had simultaneously invaded and shocked him. They waited. Then his voice filled the room, carrying with it his characteristic edge of sharp annoyance: "Do you see how this son of a murderer has sent someone to take away my head?"

The elders looked blankly back at him and blinked again in unison. "Look, when the messenger comes shut the door, and squeeze him in the doorway[4]." The short, sharp, staccato words of Elisha's Hebrew commands met unresponsive faces. "Is not the sound of his master's feet behind him?" But while he was still speaking, and before this final sentence had even fully left the prophet's terse lips, the door opened.

Moments later the king's first officer was standing, slightly embarrassed, and squeezed amid the collection of ageing men who pressed him firmly and harshly against the door. He could not help but rail: "This calamity is from the Lord! Why should I wait for the Lord any longer?" He shook, struggling against the grip on his shoulders slightly, managing a couple of inches of movement before the gaggle of elders restricted him yet further. His anger rang in the room far louder than the saliva-flecked words, however, deftly outlasting them and prompting Elisha to turn and face the sandwiched man, meeting his glare head on.

Elisha spoke simply and directly: "Hear the word of the Lord." The elders turned as one to face him, eyebrows aloft. "Thus says Yahweh: tomorrow, at about this time, eight gallons of flour shall be sold for a day's wages, as will sixteen gallons of barley, in the gates of Samaria." Elisha turned back to the window. The room stood stunned, some eyebrows landing while others tunnelled. The officer spoke first. "Look..."

He exhaled the word harshly, half sniggering it in the prophet's direction. There was more than a mild

---

[4]The word I have translated here as 'squeeze' is an important one, as we shall see in due course. The original Hebrew term is 'lahats' and means 'to squeeze, press or crush' The old King James version, 'hold him fast' doesn't really do this justice.

incredulity as he spoke, shaking his head and smiling, though with no hint of humour.

"Even if Yahweh were to open the windows of the heavens, could this thing be?" His sentiment was real, pragmatic, and singularly terrifying; that even if Yahweh Himself were to intervene, this city would not, could not, turn.

Elisha remained still. Looking out for a second he bowed his head, chin almost resting on his chest, hands fastened loosely behind his back. "In fact," he said softly, "you will be the one to look: you will see it with your eyes." He paused, turning back to the room of people, serious, commanding, sobered. "But you will not eat of it."

Slowly, the moon appeared for the first time that evening, its simple silver fingers escaping the cloud and teasing the tops of the city walls. Outside Samaria, at the foot of her imposing gates, four figures slept in the open air, neatly curled into the meagre shelter provided by the meeting of foundation, rampart and door. All of them were leprous[5]; all of them outcasts. Their skin, disfigured and diseased, having propelled them to the edge of their social world, now ensured their abandonment there. Perhaps they lay at the gates as wanderers from home, arriving at a distant city at precisely the wrong moment; refused entry while a siege began around them. Or perhaps they were Samarians ejected as the siege set in, a contagious liability in a city barred and bolted. Either way they lay unnoticed. All

---

[5]The term 'leprosy' in the Bible actually refers to the whole range of skin diseases, not simply our modern understanding of a very specific illness.

that dared to touch them was the soft, innocent shafts of lunar light that played across their sleeping forms, before sheathing themselves once more in the carefully rolling envelope of cloud far above.

Despite the presence of kings and elders, of armies and their officers, heaven has found four sleeping outcasts living in the margins; and in twenty-four hours the fate of this city will rest in their delicate fingers. Their words and actions will echo in the corridors of power, prophetic fulfilment will hinge upon their hidden lives and on this - the humblest of fulcrums - a broken city will turn in a moment, because four forgotten lepers find themselves beneath the gates, in the place of legislation.

Behind the doors the watchmen changed shifts.

Most of the following day does not speak across the ages to us, but it would be hard to believe that the power of rumour was not alive in Samaria; hard to imagine that elders did not report the prophet's words to their wives and children, or that such reports only travelled the length of a household in a world of extended families and a claustrophobic city. In short, it is difficult to imagine that expectation didn't leak into the crumbling world of Samaria's sons and daughters. If so, the morning must have passed slowly, with many heavy lung-fulls of baited breath. The afternoon must have come painfully, feelings of foolishness inevitably pressing against the anticipation as the sun turned from its lofty apex to begin the slow descent home. Hour after eventless hour would wear on with waxing disappointment, families eventually returning hungry to bed, the sunlight gently fading, as with much else in the lofty city.

If Samaria was sitting amid weighty apprehension, such feelings did not lay their hands upon the four uninformed figures sheltered in her gateway that afternoon. Aware only of the Syrian army pointed towards their makeshift shanty-spot, the leprous men looked up at the unrelenting doors together as the same wheeling sun rolled across the sky. They had propped themselves against the wall, backs meeting rough stonework, now shaded from the heat as the shadows turned in their favour. And they said to one another, simply and plainly, "Why are we sitting here until we die? If we say 'we will enter the city', the famine is in the city, and we shall die there. And if we just sit here, we will die also. Now, therefore, come: let us surrender to the army of the Syrians. If they keep us alive we shall live; and…" The weight of the pause would probably have passed us by had we crouched to listen on the other side of the doors. The words following it would not, perhaps, have grabbed us as they did the heavens that day. Simple as they are, they have proven themselves vast enough to overturn empires in the long years since: "And if they kill us, we shall only die."

Maybe this is the way to truly begin a journey; in search of life and having shed the fear of death. To go without commitment to destination, dedicated instead to the way, to the going itself, to the search; to face the winding up of all things in the hope that a tomorrow might be grasped which may otherwise pass by. Just such a journey began one evening, sanctioned by no-one, on the edge of this dying city; and almost no one watched them go. It was twilight when they did so.

The approaching evening seemed already to have dipped the hilltop air with translucent blues; and though it was not yet fully dark, the hue deepened, beginning to breach the daylight. Soon the western sky would also be marked out in purple, but for now the final rags of yesterday's cloud passed into the horizon, still dripping with the setting reds of the dusk and staining the sky's tattered canvas brilliant crimson. Twilight: one Hebrew day becoming another[6], today slipping into yesterday with Technicolor precision; tomorrow breaking in and seasons changing; ending and beginning meeting for a few short instants before falling away from one another as the new moment rolled inevitably on. Yes, it was twilight when they left.

And twilight still bruised the sky when the Syrian camp heard it: the noise sent by the Lord.

Yahweh's sound-making suddenly raged at them from all directions; deafening, bellowing, howling across the plains with a heaven-borne fury. Horses thundered, snorted and shrieked from beyond the darkness. The sound of ten thousand stallions with riders, hooves hammering, bridles stammering, relentlessly battered down on Syrian ears. From the south captains roared and their legions roared in answer. Thumping shields and hungry blade noise flogged the air behind a crescendo of feet, and across the unbroken rhythm of the drums foreign war-chants rode the malevolent winds. Western chariots clattered. Timbers groaned. Wheel noise pummelled the earth, imagined joints creaking with duress as unseen whips snapped back and forth, demanding speed. From all sides, Yahweh's cacophony broke

---

[6]In a world without clocks or the Greenwich Meridian twilight was the switch-over point between one day and another; Hebrew days ran from evening to evening rather than from midnight to midnight. This crucial part of the story, then, which facilitates so much change in fortune, is placed at the official starting point of a new day.

hard against the Syrian troops, crashing threats bearing down on the camp as the darkness swelled unremittingly about them. And they ran, fleeing the empty plains, fleeing the lonely hill, and babbling to one another of Hittite kings and hired Egyptians as they scattered into the distance, leaving all behind them.

Meanwhile, somewhere on that empty hillside, surrounded by those quiet plains, four diseased men hobbled onwards toward the camp, amid the silent twilight. Unnoticed footfall is sometimes the loudest.

It was with trepidation that they made their final approach to the outskirts of the encampment. Scouts or sentry-men should have stopped them well before they reached the first cluster of canvasses, at the very least with questions. A silent arrow from behind the blackness was always half-expected. What the four men certainly didn't expect was what they actually found; an empty camp, with its banners flapping in the breeze.

The horses and donkeys still stood tethered to their posts, gently pawing the earth and braying to one another with mild nonchalance. Tents remained untouched, beds made, weapons intact. Most of the untended cooking fires had consumed their wood, reducing themselves to embers. Wobbling oranges danced across the remains of ashen logs, while their stove pots boiled dry. Spoons still lay patiently in empty bowls; it would have been a shame to keep them waiting any longer, so the four ate and drank, sinking starving teeth into meats, oils and breads, into dates, figs and raisins and stores of wild honey. They drenched their tongues with water and, one shouldn't wonder, with some of the finer wine. Then they set about storing some of the gold and silver, not to mention abandoned clothing, from each of the tents they visited, before coming, simultaneously, to their overwhelmed senses. "We are not doing right!" they said. "This is a day of good news, and we remain silent." Looking at the deserted camp around them, and up at the blinking summer stars, concern set in. "If we wait until the morning light, some punishment will come upon us. Now, therefore, let us go and tell the king's household."

Four nourished voices were soon hollering up from the roots of Samaria's now familiar gates to the shadowy men standing above them. The city was engulfed in darkness by the time they had returned with their news, and the guards, grinding stomachs and all, were nearly at the end of their watch. "We went to the Syrian camp," the four men shouted, provoking no small reaction from the growing cluster of onlookers. "And, surprisingly, no-one was there; not a human sound – only horses and donkeys tied, and the tents intact". This time the reaction was considerably larger, and the wall-mounted guards were at once bustling, passing messages along the perimeter of the wall, waking royal servants and hurriedly relaying reports to the king's household.

With this excitement one watch of the night ended and another began.[7] In the gatehouse, shifts changed. Drowsy men went to their beds and fresh ones emerged, blades polished, sleep banished. And in charge of the

---

[7]The Biblical narrative doesn't tell us when the first officer is posted on the city gates. It also doesn't tell us he was one of the men the lepers met, nor does it tell us he was present at the king's briefing. So while we cannot say when exactly the story puts him at the doors, now seems as likely time as any, perhaps more likely given his stark omission from both prior and ensuing events. In any case, the significant issue is that he is the gatekeeper this evening.

gates this evening was the king's first officer, a day since the grip of the elders on his shoulders, a day since Elisha's stern gaze, on duty now in the doors of a weary city.

Elsewhere, the king was being woken. Screwing up the covers of his bed, and dumping them on its edge, he swung his bare feet onto the cold, stone floor, snatching the torch from the nervous herald as he stuttered the final words of the momentous message. By now the royal residence was fully awake with rumour; corridors bustled, and the spreading news had brought a number of servants, advisors, and messengers to cautiously hover at the open door. The king, torch in hand and muttering, strode into the adjoining room, where open maps covered a large table. The throng of advisors swept in behind him. Pushing the torch back into the nervous young page's hands the king turned, putting his finger on the mapped location of the invader's camp as he did so. Internally, he congratulated himself on his own sense of drama.

"Let me tell you what the Syrians have done to us," he announced sardonically, head tipping slightly to one side as though addressing children. "They know that we are hungry." The page's stomach growled in confirmation of the fact, winning him a number of accusatory glances from around the room. "Therefore, they have gone out of the camp to hide themselves in the field, saying 'When they come out of the city we shall catch them alive, and enter the city.'" He had adopted a Syrian accent for these final words and nodded decisively as he concluded, eyes flitting to each of his advisors, the apparent logic of the statement and his impatience at having been woken by so obvious a matter welling up behind them.

But one of the servants at the back of the room answered: "Please..." Those around him sidled gradually away as he began, though this didn't seem to perturb him. "Let several men take five of the remaining horses that are in the city. Look, they may either become like all the multitude of Israel that is in the city, or indeed they might become like all the multitude of those spared." The young man's request reverberated around the room to a background of murmuring.

We must note that his sentiment, which alone dared to hope, is not first sown into the city here, in this grand room and among these grand people. It is, of course, unknowingly lifted from a conversation sown into a gateway the day before, a conversation re-sprouting now in a very different context. The lepers' heaven-moving words, enacted into the twilight moments of the day, now re-organise themselves through the mouth of a servant, echoing in the heart of Samaria's corridors of power; echoing in her king's bedchamber; echoing in the company of his advisors. Because, really, the servant's sentiment makes the same proposal: 'Make the journey and maybe we will live; at worst, the riders shall only die with the rest of us.' Hidden decisions for life, sparked in the margins, now ring in the centre.

Hanging his head, the king squeezed the bridge of his nose as the onlookers waited for a response. Finally he spoke and, so as not to lose his air of irritation, he motioned abruptly to the door as he did so. "Go and see!" The assembly briefly stared in disbelief before the extended arm of the king seized general attention, prompting a swift and immediate return to the bustle of the passageways. Men made ready, stable boys

appeared, and in rooms far below two chariots were carefully exhumed.

⤳

The moon that evening suffered none of its predecessor's patient, cloudy obscurity, hanging large and clear
over the events, which unfolded at some pace below.
From such a vantage point there was much to see. Two
chariots, for instance, burst from Samaria's gates,
charging past four lepers as they went; lepers who now
leave the story in the same way they entered it - without fanfare or epilogue, nameless in the gates. There
was the chariot journey itself to witness; the driving on
of gaunt horses; the astonished faces of arriving chari-
oteers; the following of the Syrian equipment-trail,
which littered the road as far as the Jordan; the turning of the speeding steeds; and the foam-flecked,
bloodshot journey back to the teetering city. There
were the watchmen's faces to observe; the relief; the
joy. There was the spreading of the news, the sight of
lights appearing in room after room, house after house,
as family upon family awoke and spilled into the
streets, looking for confirmation.

Reports broke quickly and the ensuing frenzy came
suddenly. Feet trampled across the city to its gates.
Whole households, following the rumours of food and
open doors, raged across Samaria in pursuit of famine's
end. This eruption converged on the gateway from all
directions: a whole city shoving, calling, groaning,
reaching, storming, pressing at their gates. And then the
pricing-cry came through, stoking the tumult yet further.
A shekel could now buy you eight gallons of flour or else
sixteen gallons of barley - as Elisha had predicted only

twenty-four hours before. He too, having disappeared with no epilogue, now hovers over the story by implication only; taken, presumably, by the blowing of the wind in some heretofore undiscerned direction. Regardless, the crowd continued to press.

Finally, in the rising crush, there was the king's first officer to watch, the man in command of the gates; the man struggling to make his voice heard as the crowds descend; the man unable to hold back the expanding throng, soon fighting against the tide of limbs and gasping for breath as people funnel tightly through the gateway; the man loosing his footing in the midst it all; the man lying motionless once the hoards have passed, mortally trampled in the gates; the man whose eyes saw; the man who never tasted.

And so the circle closes, and the threads are drawn together. Twenty-four hours ago this officer burst into a meeting of elders. Tonight the city bursts upon him, where those elders usually meet. Yesterday he was held in a domestic doorway; tonight in the doors of a city. Last night he was 'squeezed' against Elisha's door in a room full of elders; today, the same soldier is crushed to death in the doorway of the city, in the traditional place of eldership. Elisha's living room prophesied the officer's fate before the words had ever left the prophet's lips; squeezed in the doorway.

The very doorway where, unbeknown to the city, the journeys which would lead to its rescue were secretly carved out by the least likely of men; men finding the grace of twilight, of fearlessness, of Yahweh's journey with them, their words reappearing in the strangest of places. A city which rejected them, reopening on the strength of their story.

What if signs enacted in the smallness of the living-room could be transposed in the city? What if heaven were not watching courts and castles, but tiny homes? Where the issues of life are fought with: here is the place of the prophetic. Here are the signs. Here is the word of the Lord which, finding space and expression in the meekness of an individual address, leaps to fulfilment in the midst of a people. What if decisions, however small, however unnoticed, could shape conversations in the king's bedchamber? What if the nameless marginalised could make a decision for life and shed the fear of death? What if four diseased men could become four conquering armies in the midst of the turning between the days and seasons? Might sieges break, might famines wither?

What if we were told a story where tomorrow hinged on a living-room and a reckless journey? What might that mean for our households of faith? What might it mean for the horizon?

These are questions for our living rooms, perhaps. And for the road.

SECTION 1

WHITBY TO ROME

The framework for the story of our journey is the reports that I sent out whilst walking. These are almost entirely unchanged from the originals. Interspersed between these are some personal reflections, which I have worked on as I have looked back on the synergy and dynamic that existed between life in the home and life on the road. These sections I have entitled *Reflections from Home*. The stories of thirteen of the major towns and cities that we went through also provide colourful and heart-stopping exclamation marks to the whole journey, as the question is posed: can cities and nations change through the decisions made in the living rooms of ordinary people?

Whitby to Rome

CHAPTER 3

Whitby:
The Turning of the Tide

Andrea Harrison

Andrea is a teacher, who lives in Blyth, Northumberland and has given herself to understanding and imbibing the ancient pathways of the early Celts. She joined the walk as we left Whitby, and again in Northern Greece.

The wind is a mighty element. It cannot be seen, though wherever it blows it leaves a sign that it has been there. It has the power to brew storms and whip waves, it gives the gift of flight and brings a sense of freedom to those who have stood in wide open spaces and felt it gust around them. It is wild. It is untamed. It is uncontrollable. The wind blows where it will, irrespective of time, place and circumstance. Many times I have observed as it has rustled the tiny leaves of the moorland heather, giving the impression of purple waves sweeping and receding across the desolate landscape surrounding Whitby; I have been mesmerised, gazing towards the heavens, as it has effortlessly pushed heavy clouds impregnated with rain around the skies; and I have watched as it silently guides ships into safe harbour. It is the wind entices the autumn leaves on the trees to leave their place of rest, wooing their delicate frames to rise, fall and swirl as they embrace its invitation to dance. The birds of the sea gracefully soar on its gentle thermals and I have also stared as it has streaked across the ebb and flow of the tide producing white, crested ripples upon a sea of brilliant, blue glass.

Today, however, I stand on the headland and there is no wind. The air is damp, and unusually still. Even the sails of the ships in the distance fail to inflate as their life-less carcasses try blindly to find their way into the harbour below. Behind me, the cold and empty abbey stares out towards the dull sea, its grey-green stone reflective of the sombre mood hanging in the air. What transpired yesterday within its walls has brought confu-sion, betrayal and devastation. It would be fruitless to call for a second chance to be heard. Time has run out. Though the decision made is final, it makes me want to scream out at the top of my voice. The words uncontrol-lably project from deep within me as though I have no power over their release. "Where are you, God? Come on! Where are you? Show yourself!" As the words leave my core I have the sense that they are unheard and have merely been swallowed up and absorbed by the dense, misty air that shrouds the coastline. I shout again into the void before me: "What now?"

Silence. Waves of disappointment rise and fall within me and break on the inner shore of my spirit. Silent tears well up in my eyes and stream uncontrollably down my face. Frustration burns my throat and I am forced to breathe more deeply in order to keep myself composed. If I let go, let myself fall apart, I will have given it more control than it has right to. But if I hold onto it I fear it will slowly and painfully suffocate me on the inside. I never actually thought it would come to this. Yes, I had considered the possibility, given it a fraction of my time, but deep down I thought it would merely be a formality. I could not have been further wrong, for the unfolding of yesterday's events lift a horn that could sound the death knell for a movement which has been gaining strength and momentum for the last three hundred years.

The movement obsessively and undeniably loves Jesus and lives to worship Him. He is the centre. Its followers are not confined to dwelling in large, ornate buildings or required to offer empty sacrifices on stone altars. Jesus Himself dwells within each of them. They are mobile like the wind, and they carry the light of Jesus in their hearts. They wander wildly with God, following the prompting of the Holy Spirit. The Followers of the Way are free from religion and materialism. Onlookers stare at these nameless, faceless individuals and wonder at their unusual existence. They are free, yet they are bound to God; the hungry, the hurting, the lost and the dying. Their desire is that others know and love Him.

I have heard numerous stories passed down through generations about the Followers of the Way. The stories have woven together in their fabric the elements of work and prayer, community and the arts, worship and mission. I have been inspired by them. They have shaped my own journey. They tell tales of men and women with true apostolic passion. One of its fore-runners, Columba, travelled from the rolling green hills of Ireland to the island of Iona to pursue the conversion of souls for

Christ. He was a man dowsed by raw, holy passion. It was beneath the sun-bleached skies, and beside the wind-swept, silver shores of this solitary island that the Followers shared in the working of the land. Some led worship and others copied the scriptures. The Iona community was characterised by purity of life and love of God. As the community grew so did its influence; kings and princes sought Columba for his wise counsel. When he died sixty-seven years ago Columba left a rich inheritance of peace previously unknown in the kingdom of Scotland, the tiny sparks of which fanned the flames of the wild fire of the Holy Spirit that have spread from the rugged highlands and islands, to the desolate moors and sleepy valleys of Northern England.

It is stories like these that have shaped our past. There are too many of them to mention, but they are stories from my culture, and for that I am truly grateful to God. The Followers of the Way travelled long distances shar-ing their faith, and as they journeyed they baptised those who became part of their Jesus movement. They gath-ered communities and trained others to continue their work. Many of the names of these individuals have long been forgotten, but their legacy is sown deep within the land on which they lived, worked and prayed.

It is at this point that the stories I have heard others tell weave their silvery threads into my own. I was brought up in King Edwin's court after my father was murdered. As my father was the nephew of King Edwin, it was my right to stay in this place. I was later baptised. It was 12 April; springtime, a time for new beginnings. This was significant for there was much of the past that I wished to leave behind, even though I was only thir-teen years of age. Being fatherless since infancy, I had found Him; not my earthly father, but my Heavenly father - the One who watched over me, and guided the path I would walk.

The next few years were an unnerving time, veiled by the dark reign of Penda and Cadwalla as they attempted to stamp out Christianity in the lands in which we lived. Fortunately in later years Oswald, Edwin's nephew, returned to fight the violence and injustice of Penda's reign. The site identified for battle lay beneath a towering stone barricade that divided England and Scotland, the construction of which was ordered by the Roman Emperor, Hadrian. Under the immense shadow of the wall, the two armies engaged in their sword-yielding game.

Against all odds Oswald won, and it was upon the golden shores of Bamburgh that he set up his residence. As the wide-open skies and turning tides of Northumbria embraced the new landscape, another chapter in its history was about to be written. Having been educated on Iona, Oswald sent there for a missionary to carry the light of Christ to the rest of his kingdom. It was then that God began to stir the heart of a man named Aidan; a man who has greatly influenced my own journey of faith. Aidan travelled from Iona with twelve companions and established a monastery on the holy island of Lind-isfarne, the shapely outline of which could be traced through the lead framed windows of the castle at Bamburgh. There was an unusual connection between these two places, something in the land which relied on the other for its timely existence; mainland to island, past to present, present to future.

It was at this time that I felt the hand of God steering my own life in a different direction. When Aidan arrived in Northumbria, I felt there was a need to set aside my royal heritage. The large, lifeless castles, wealth and centralised power didn't do it for me. There was a simpler life; a call to the margins, a call to be a Follower of the Way. I lived first as a nun by the fresh, flowing waters of the River Wear; later as an abbot at the monastery in Hartlepool; and seven years ago I moved to Whitby and founded the monastery here. I have seen the hand of God at work and I have witnessed many miracles. Such a heritage, such a journey; though I ask, what now? What will become of the new way which is to seemingly rise in the land?

Standing on the cliff-top the damp air has succumbed to the change in the evening temperature. Where previously delicate mists weaved their way intricately across the coastline, now their fronds fuse together and condense to form droplets of rain. As they descend hastily from the emptiness above they gather volume and weight, their fragile beads falling like tears onto the earth below. Currently, I can only make out the periphery of the headland as the dusky twilight creeps in silently around its weathered edges. As the light fades further dark, indistinguishable shadows bob lifelessly on the surface of the sluggish ocean below. I have stood here countless times, gazing at the mirrored reflection of purple skies streaked with golden tones as the sun has set behind me. Each time the promise of tomorrow has been framed in its graceful light. Though I know tomorrow will arrive, exactly how much promise it holds this time I do not know.

Seventeen years before my birth they came to re-evange-lise England, sent by Gregory the Great, the Bishop of Rome. As they moved out north and west they discov-ered to their surprise that they were not the only missionaries operating in Britain. They assumed that the supposedly pagan lands of the north were spiritually barren, though on their journeys had exposed trails already broken, suggesting that the spread of Christian-ity had already begun under a different guise. Apparently the movement they uncovered was different. It raised heads, because it lacked structure and organisation. Some suggested that it needed to be controlled. I have heard on the grapevine of meetings held with Followers of the Way, their inviters urging them to join Roman missions in England. I guess there was an underlying motive to try and make individuals conform to their practices. No wonder conflict emerged.

For years now, two streams of church have co-existed, each encouraged by different royal houses. Many years ago, my great uncle had established Roman practices; however, when Oswald defeated Penda he had encouraged the practices of the Ionan monks. Oswiu, now concerned about the religious differences that are threatening to destabilise his family and his kingdom, has decided to call a meeting of church leaders to resolve things, as he put it, "once and for all". I find it a bizarre twist of circumstance that I end up hosting this gather-ing, given that history places members of my family on opposing sides of the argument.

The Synod held here yesterday did not discuss church doctrine, but centred on more trivial matters; the date for Easter and the style of tonsure to be displayed by a monk. Part of me wondered what the point of sitting around the heavy wooden table of the Abbey actually was. Surely there were more pressing things to be involving ourselves with. As heated voices exchanged in the air waves, I couldn't help two words springing into my head: mountains and molehills!

On one side there was Wilfred, representing the Roman Church. His quandary was that the two different streams of church celebrated Easter on different dates, and was adamant that this should change. Due to the way the different calendars operated, and with his clever words, he argued that while one royal faction was celebrating Easter, the other would be still fasting during Lent. Strangely, this had not been a problem when Aidan was alive, so I wondered why it had come to the fore. The answer seems to lie in the fact that Aidan's successor, Bishop Finan, found himself challenged by an Irish bishop, who had been trained in Rome. It is now only in the time of Colman, the third Ionan monk elected as Bishop of Northumbria, that the conflict seems to require royal attention and resolution. Why? My own guess is that Colman is Ionan and not Roman. Three letters can make such a difference.

There were a number of us sat around the wooden table inside the Abbey; Bishop Colman and members of his Irish clergy; Romanus; Agilbert; Agatho, one of his priests; and James the Deacon. The set up was completed with the presence of Wilfred and King Oswiu, who would give his royal authority in support of one side or the other. The small room of the monastery must have appeared simplistic and bare compared to what many of the delegates were used to. Most of us had heard about the happenings in Rome. Some had even been there and experienced its splendour first hand. As the necessary introductions ensued bright sunshine warmed the cold room, whilst the golden light from its beams cascaded over the stone floor creating swirls and eddies in its corners. There was no way in which this spectral show could match the glamour and sophistication of Rome. Its beauty was simple and yet, at the same time, deeply profound. The combination of light and movement reflected the journey so far. What I observed was a metaphor in itself. I watched, mesmerised, as angelic shapes danced around the room.

On the other side of the table Bishop Colman sat rigidly. He was a quiet man, but sure and steadfast in his faith. I had great respect for him. I watched as he picked nervously at each fingernail in turn. I wondered whether he knew what the outcome of our time together would be; not because I thought he was involved in any back door dealings, but because I could see the way in which the light in his eyes had begun to fade. I also observed how his elbows supported his weary body as he sat. His line of reasoning regarding the calculation of the dates of Easter was austere and uncomplicated. It was the practice of Columba, the founder of our monastic network; a saint of unquestionable holiness, who had followed the teachings and traditions of John the apostle and evangelist.

By now the evening light was beginning to approach, and the tide turned once more. Skies etched in pink and blue rested high above the cliff-top as once again the day entered its latter half. Where bright rays of sunshine had streaked through the small windows of the abbey just a few hours ago, candles were now needed to ward off the darkness. Their flames danced and flickered, illuminating the dusky corners of the room. As I watched

I remembered the significance of the light and the wild fire. My hope, or rather my prayer, was that the light would not be darkened or quenched in the coming days.

Once our case had been heard, conversation and reasonable debate continued to give way to a spiral of clever arguments dowsed in grandeur and self-importance, as Wilfred presented the Roman view. The dates that he suggested for the celebration of Easter were common practice in Rome and in the Church generally, even as far away as Egypt. Wilfred continued by assaulting Columba, arguing that he had done his best considering his limited knowledge, but now that others had found the calendars were in conflict, the present Ionan monks did not have the excuse of ignorance. It seemed as though things were becoming personal.

I glanced up in an attempt to free myself from the muffled conversation. Around the table the other delegates appeared motionless in their stance, an elbow propping up a hand, propping up a face. Others sat poised with folded arms resting on the grained wood beneath their limbs. I wondered what they were thinking. Where at the beginning of the day I was confident of the outcome, I now squirmed inside, wondering whether we had done enough. Our case could not match the intellectual debate now echoing around the walls of the room.

Then came the final argument put forward by Wilfred. The Roman ways stemmed directly from Saint Peter, who was holder to the keys of heaven, a superior authority to the Irish monk Columba. Wilfred was a clever academic, though I quietly wondered at the secret motives I saw flickering in his eyes and the lust for power that bubbled beneath his words he spoke. Whether King Oswiu had taken leave of his senses, or whether he felt backed into a corner, I do not know. The words he spoke to determine the outcome of the Synod, however, still resound in my head like the beating of a drum: "Do you agree that Peter was given the keys to the kingdom of heaven by Christ, and was pronounced to be the rock on which the Church would be built?"

Technically we could only find agreement, as this is indeed written in the scriptures.

Oswiu then declared his judgement in favour of the holder of the keys. His words, though, communicated much more than agreement over the calculation of Easter. From here Roman practices of being church would be established as the norm throughout England. I imagine that it will not be long before the Episcopal seat is transferred to York, and Wilfred asserts himself as Bishop of Northumbria.

The decision made yesterday is devastating. How can something as wild and free as the movement be contained? It is like damming a rushing river. Once the great slabs of stone are put into place, there is nowhere for the water to flow; eventually the flow is curbed, and the waters are forced to deepen. Deep waters become still. It is like forcing back the sunrise by human hand, or trying to trap in a wooden box the wind I have seen blow over the moors.

I have heard that there are those who will not tolerate the decision made by Oswiu, and that they may even consider returning to Iona and their homelands. They worry that the movement will be quashed, and that the spirit of the wild goose will be caged. I am inclined to agree; both Wilfred and his father have clearly nailed their colours to the Roman mast. Unlike the others though, I am not in a position to return home. Northum-

bria is my home. I must look at the present like I have never seen it before and try to find a way forward. However, finding a way forward means stepping into what is to come, and presently I find myself stilled.

Amidst the many doubts I have, there is the certainty that all I have ever known, and all I perceive to know, will change over the coming years. I have heard of those who have travelled to the continent and seen for themselves the tall spires of the religious buildings which adorn the skyline. The Roman Church is gaining imperial power as it dresses itself in grand robes and fine insignia. I remain unimpressed. The spirit of God cannot be trapped within structures of stone. I fear that the new way will bring restriction. What we recognise as ordinary and spontaneous will be forced to conform to ritual practice and abstract piety. Perhaps the movement will find life underground. Perhaps it will be somehow redefined. How, though, do you even begin to redefine something that from the outset never really had a name?

I turn my back on the ocean and attempt to walk towards the dimly lit monastery ahead. Behind me the tide turns again and with eyes closed I breathe in the moist night air, infused with the rich, cloudy aromas rising from the green grass and brown earth beneath my feet. I am cold, wet and hungry, but I stand stationary, despite the shelter of the abbey just a stone's throw away. Inexplicably, I find my inner self transported to the muddy battlefield upon which my ancestor, Oswald, fought over thirty years ago. The space in which I find myself is vast. As I lift my head towards the heavens I hear the rustling of the sweeping grass around me, the gentle breeze weaving between its long blades. I stand completely alone. There is nobody here but me. However, there is a Presence; a Divine Presence. Prior to battle, Oswald raised a high, wooden cross above this very site and prayed for divine intervention in a contest he was overwhelmingly expected to lose, his army clearly outnumbered. Against the odds he won, a breakthrough born out of faith.

It would appear that upon this very evening my family's past, my present and the movement's future entwine as I pray for breakthrough, the outcome of which appears to be against the odds.

As the rain intensifies and soaks both myself, and the headland on which I stand, I reach forward and lift the unyielding latch of the abbey door. As I turn to close it, I catch sight of the ocean and I am reminded of the wind that at one time majestically and powerfully swept over this very coastline. My prayer is that it will blow once again.

The wind is a mighty element. It cannot be seen, though wherever it blows it leaves a sign that signifies that it has been there. It is wild. It is untamed. It is uncontrollable. The wind blows where it will, irrespective of time, place and circumstance.

CHAPTER 4

Whitby to London

Steve Lowton

WHITBY TO YORK: 24 AUG 2005
Team: Chris, Sally Ann and Martin, Jenny
and Alan, Andrea, Debs, Marv, Sharon, Chris,
Mel, Jayne, Dave, Chris and Hannah, Tim,
Francis and Sally, Val, Lizzie, and myself.

Let me describe our starting point for the walk to Canterbury and Rome. Whitby is a small fishing town on the edge of the North Sea on the north east coast of England. Tucked away behind the purple moors of North Yorkshire it is an evocative place. On the cliff-top overlooking the harbour lie the ruins of the Abbey that hosted the Synod of Whitby fourteen centuries ago (664AD), a momentous occasion when the unruly, passionate Celtic Church of the northern lands was brought under the subjugation of Rome. With the wind whipping in from the east and the waves crashing against the cliffs below, it does not take much imagination to picture the scene when the simple monks of the north encountered all the finery, splendour and sophistication of Rome.

The bitter taste of treachery, greed, betrayal and fear was the backdrop to this Synod. Such seed is the foundation of empires worldwide, whether in the church, the commercial world or the nation state. It was poignant, therefore, that as we gathered to pray we did so on the back of a day during which these ancient roots of poison were addressed in a very specific way by members of the Northumbrian Community; a wonderful context in which to be sent out at the beginning of the walk to Canterbury and, eventually, to Rome.

York was our target for this first weekend of walking. This city is second only to Canterbury in the ecclesiastical hierarchy of the Church of England. It is also the place where Constantine was first crowned when his father died. Many would therefore say that this is the birthplace of Christendom, for it was the Emperor Constantine who first legitimised Christianity and hijacked the faith in the cause of the Roman Empire. Whilst persecution ended at that point, so did the growth of the church as it found itself increasingly became a servant of Rome and nationhood, rather than the sharp, prophetic voice that Jesus so modelled.

We were a motley crew as we trekked the 46 miles over the sun-kissed moorland into York. With young and old taking breaks in the support vehicles, this walk is not about making some super-human effort to cover every mile, for that would be in the spirit of the killing machine that was the army of Rome. No, this is about mobile church expressing something of community and the wonder of the body of Christ whilst walking and praying with intense purpose and focus; for these are truly days of emergency for the church in our nation. We have to emerge to a new place of standing and authority as we embrace the scalpel of the living God into our own hearts and lives. Standing in the place of intercession we are calling not for some false mercy that prolongs the inevitable, but for the clean and pure judgement of the Lord; for in the pathways of judgement, oh Lord, we wait for you.

Kneeling in front of the statue of Constantine outside York Minster we repented once more for the sin of empire within our own hearts, the heart of the church and the heart of the nation. Some of the youngest amongst us then rose up with incredible passion, declaring an end to the days of the high seat and a quickening of the wild wind of the Holy Spirit that was so crushed in Whitby.

Now we are pressing south onto the Midlands, and eventually to Canterbury; there are big miles ahead, but joy, excitement and sobriety in our hearts. This is not the time for "peace, peace", but for declarations of war and intent.

THROUGH MIDDLE ENGLAND: AUGUST 2005

Team: Chris M, Jonny, Gill, Debs, Andrea, Sharon and myself

As I prepare to get back out on the walk this morning I was struck by the absurdity of all that we are doing in walking to Rome; for this is no pilgrimage. Rome is no Mecca that we are looking to. Quite the reverse! Yet what is this walk? It is, on the one hand, so huge; and yet on the other so ridiculously small and fragile. One puff of wind and our tiny, Hobbit-like group could be blown away, such is our insignificance. Yet never have I carried such a sense of the urgency of our times. We cannot afford to ignore the paths that are opening up to us.

We are now about to leave Nottingham and head through Leicester, which lies at the heart of the Midlands. The Midlands is the power house of England. Everywhere along the length of the River Trent are power stations that supply most of the country with electricity. Late on Sunday we will arrive at High Cross, the place where two of the major Roman roads that straddle the nation of England cross over (Watling Street and Foss Way).

Our paths these last few days have been haphazard and have not gone at all to plan. We have wandered into the Midlands almost like the early Celts; sometimes losing our way, sometimes simply standing at a junction and making a snap decision as to which way to go. Soon we will be back on the Roman ways, calling for the ancient power lines across our nation to come up, whether they are lines of witchcraft, freemasonry, unjust trade routes or the paths of marching armies and blood that still calls for sacrifice. One thing is sure: the ancient centres of power cannot hold. There is a huge sign of this in Britannia coming off the coinage in the UK. What must concern us is what replaces her; a responsibility we cannot deny as church.

During these next few miles I expect the God of heaven and earth to be releasing the possibility of continuing beyond Canterbury and onto Paris this Autumn. If the door continues to open we will walk further, with the target of walking through to Rome before the end of this year, 2005. If you pray for us I we would be grateful that we would know how far we are to go, for in the words of Bilbo Baggins, "When you walk out of the door who knows where your feet will take you."

MIDDLE ENGLAND TO LONDON:
EARLY SEPTEMBER 2005
Team: Sally Ann, Chris M, Stew, Lionel and
Christine, Tim, Emma and myself

Stirred and provoked by the appalling images from New Orleans there has been fresh urgency to the 150 miles that have taken us from the north of the Midlands through to the capital city of London. Whether it is 9/11, the terrorism that rocked the UK in July 2005, or the events of the last two weeks, if ever we in the west needed a reminder that we are not immune from either man made acts of terror or awesome acts of nature, then we have it plainly before us. For the window of grace within the UK is undoubtedly narrowing. This is why we are out on the road, giving ourselves to intense prayer and intercession, mile after mile down the backbone of England. I and many others walking with me cannot be passive at this time. Neither must we hesitate in the face of the giants of unbelief that hold fast the church: for as Jesus said, "We must work the works of him who sent me whilst it is still day; night is coming when no man can work."

Our passage through the Midlands was tougher than expected, as was our entry through the northern gate of London into the capital city. Gates are places of contesting. They are also places where battles are won and lost. It was the northern gate through which the terrorists came from my home city of Leeds two months ago. It is also the northern gate that has seen two terrible train crashes over recent years, at Potters Bar and Hatfield. So it is at these points in a prayer walk that we particularly press in with strong intercession. At a point such as this I often see the contesting being worked through in the physicality of our bodies. Injuries are picked up that mysteriously disappear just a few miles later. Exhaustion sets in when the day is still young. That is the richness and the challenge of prayer walking, as we drag our bodies and the testimonies of our lives across the land.

We finished this section of the walk once more back at the Tower of London. For those of you who have been following our walking this year you will know that this is the third time that we have either started or finished a walk at the Tower. Once more our focus was to call creation out of bondage to big business, to the powerful and the mighty, and to those who think themselves more than they are. Instead, we call for creation to be free to serve not the purposes of nation state, but the purposes of God.

As we got off our knees after concluding prayer, the first drops of rain began to fall that heralded a deluge upon the city that brought chaos and flooding to much of the centre of London. Whether this is a sign I do not know. I do know that is was spectacular; and that God is in heaven, so let the whole of the earth be silent.

We get back to the walk in six days' time, when we will be journeying into Canterbury and then on into the heart of France. Rome is calling; the Lord is calling; this is our response.

REFLECTIONS FROM HOME

The wonder of the walk down from Whitby to London felt like to me the fulfilment of a five-year journey that I had been on since abandoning the tried and tested paths of organisational church. To leave behind those certain paths had been one of the hardest decisions of my life. Taking to the open road in pursuit of something fresh was exhilarating, but hugely challenging.

In these years I had to discover a fresh level of trust in the shepherd of my soul. In our western culture, where the self-made man is elevated and idolised, it is an alien concept to deliberately position oneself where we have to discover whether there is a God who can truly provide. This was the testimony I knew we were taking to Rome. We had no statement to make against Catholicism, for we owe much to the ways in which our Catholic friends have held onto the mystical aspects of our spirituality. However we do not need Prince Charles, Constantine, Mother Church, or anyone else as defender of the faith, and for that reason Rome represented much to us. Nor indeed do we need a Christian state as Islam so pursues an Islamic state. We have a Father in heaven who knows our needs, and that is enough.

The storyline of my newly adopted daughter Chun Zhen was intimately tied into all this, even as I look back on an earlier walk through to the Tower of London in March 2005; a walk that opened up the door for our later journey to Rome. At that time, provoked by my household companion and friend Stew Thomas, we had stumbled out of our home on the day of Zhen's birthday. Chun Zhen was born in China on 16 March 2002. Her name means "spring treasure" or "new beginnings". It was during that time that circumstances conspired to bring to my attention the possibility of a walk through to Rome, not least of which was the death of the Pope. Knowing that this was not a time for the straight and predictable paths of the Roman ways, my imagination was stirred as to a walk that could take us right to the heart of Christendom.

Here we were, daring to believe that the storyline of one family could, along with that of many others, begin to speak into the fault lines of the continent of Europe and call for a new beginning that carried something of the DNA of those early Celtic fathers; the ones who inhabited the margins of the Roman Empire of the day.

CHAPTER 5

London:
A Sign of the Times

Gemma and Dick Bonham

*Gemma and Dick have given themselves to working in
the arts for all of their eight years of marriage. Living in
Leeds, Dick writes, performs and directs for Imprint
Theatre Company. Gemma currently works at the
Carriageworks Theatre and is also gifted historian, with
roots in London. Joining us as we walked into her home
city and then into Rome a few months later, together
they are well qualified for this illuminating documentary
on our first city: London.*

The timing was perfect. As we strode into Greenwich,
it was to the sound of cannon fire: a sound that marked
the 200th anniversary of the death of Nelson at the Battle
of Trafalgar. We couldn't have planned it better.

How could a group like us resist? Walking, as we
were, to pray for change and renewal in the hearts of
ourselves and our nations, we loved these sorts of signs.
They seemed to spring up from the earth itself. They gave
hints that our trek was not in vain; that, in some small

way, the God of the land might be taking notice of the journeys being undertaken by our broken, blistered feet.

And in this particular event the major themes of this part of our travels were tied together in one, beautifully symbolic moment: the immaculately timed entrance into the home town of time itself; the marking of a naval history which allowed us to place our hopes on the might of our military vessels, rather than in the hands of God; and the connection of our personal histories to seasons and forces beyond our immediate perception or control.

Could you imagine living a life not governed by the clock? However easy going we imagine ourselves to be, these simple devices have come to dominate our affairs. We might arrange to meet a friend at a particular time, and face their wrath if we leave them waiting. Catching any form of transport would be a tricky process if we had no idea when it was due to depart. And our boss at work would be quite upset if we showed up at an hour of our own choosing.

This way of thinking is only possible because time has been standardised. And, by gosh, if it wasn't the jolly old British who managed it! In the 1800s, the line of longitude that passes through the Greenwich Observatory was made the Prime Meridian: the point from which time was calculated. It was a potent emblem of the spirit of Empire. Other countries might have different time zones, but these were determined in relation to the English centre. The use of this particular longitude is actually entirely arbitrary; but Greenwich Mean Time served as a powerful reminder of our civilising dominance and prestigious learning.

(The French, of course, were somewhat upset by the imperialism of their arch-rivals, and for several decades refused to recognise its legitimacy. Instead, their maps used a meridian passing through Paris.)

Without the widespread adoption of these systems, my life might have been very different. Around the same time that I joined the team for the walk, I became obsessed with tracing my family tree. It was an attempt on my part to understand the chronology from which I emerged. With a weird synchronicity, I found that I came from a line of watchmakers. My great-great-great grandfather, Cornelius Richard Woodcock, owned a clock-making shop in Salisbury. His son (also, somewhat unimaginatively, called Cornelius) moved to London and made his name working for Benson's in Ludgate Hill, looking after time pieces at Big Ben and Buckingham Palace.

Perhaps it is this heritage that gives me an ongoing interest in discerning the true meaning of the times and the seasons. My family prospered through serving the British time industry. Yet here I was in Greenwich, wondering if our obsession with measuring and calibrating history had actually helped us lose touch with the true rhythms of creation. Was the inheritance of Britain's era of Empire an inability to plot our future course as a nation?

The seasons weren't put in place so they could govern and bind us. We weren't always supposed to be trying to beat the clock; particularly not in the service of that contemporary empire, consumerism. Instead, they are a way in which God attempts to help us make sense of our lives through the ability to create narrative (this thing happened, then this, and then another); through reminding us that some things are bigger than us, and we are not in full control (the cycle of years, of spring, summer, autumn and winter, carries on regardless of our labour); and through helping us look forward, believing that specific periods of endeavour can be guided by the Lord – indeed, that during particular times he has a call and a plan for our lives.

Months after our walk through London I find myself back in the capital, staying with old friends. Our conversation ranges over a vast array of topics. We are all believers, though over the years our ways of understanding and expressing that faith have taken different paths; sometimes your history together is just more important.

Eventually, the topic of debate flits upon the creation narrative. As believers in a "literal" seven day story of the Earth's formation, my friends claim the world is somewhere between 6000 and 10 000 years old. Of course, in opposition to this, evolutionary theory suggests a scale of millions, not thousands, of years.

This isn't the place to rehash such arguments. Considering that none of us really knows what happened it's a topic that can get people surprisingly hot under the collar. Interestingly for us, though, these disagreements emerged at much the same time as the creation of GMT - there must have been something in the air. The importance placed on the debate shows that the study of time is never an entirely objective, scientific pursuit. Just as the Empire claimed its capital as a centre for the global calibration of clocks, our understanding of the seasons is often shaped by our attempts to fit them into particular stories or narratives.

Proponents of a literalist interpretation put humankind at the centre of God's activity. They wonder why He would bother to take any longer than was strictly necessary to get to the really important bit; though for me, this represents a God who is a bit of a clock-watcher and doesn't enjoy the job of creation for its own sake. Meanwhile, evolutionists have often told a story in which God simply never existed, our rational nature allowing us to move beyond such primitive concerns. Neither solution seems entirely satisfactory.

My point is this: the stories that shape us are contested. We need to grapple with them; to journey with them; to keep going if we are to find something that approaches the slippery, elusive entity we call 'truth'. Standing in Greenwich it seemed to me that our small trudge across the land was an attempt to understand, re-interpret and re-tell the stories that had formed us. We were trying to align ourselves with narratives that emulate the ways of Jesus.

A farmer must know the optimum time of year to plant his crops, so that they are not destroyed by frost or scorched by the sun. Trying to seed stories of restoration and hope into creation can also be successful only if we partner with the seasons emerging from heaven.

Some of the knotty narratives that we were trying to untangle were forged in this very place by that master naval strategist, Vice-Admiral Horatio Nelson. Heralded as one of Britain's finest heroes, countless thousands converged on Greenwich for his three day lying-in-state in 1806. Some reports say as many as 20 000 mourners were turned away on the first day alone (Jennings, 1999).

He had become an icon of Britishness; a representative of the Empire's divine appointment. Even today he is well loved. In 2002, he was voted as being among the 100 greatest Britons in a BBC poll.

For the British Empire, naval might was one of the main ways of asserting power. From the time of Nelson until the middle of the twentieth century, our fleet was the envy of the world. But then, you don't need me to tell you this. Every school child knows that "Britannia Rules the Waves". Did such a spirit of domination and violence truly arise "at Heav'n's command", as the lyrics of the song suggest? I would say not. Our nation's tendency to place its trust in patriotic invincibility has often caused us to miss a more righteous path. Our insurance should be in God, not our ships. And true victories, as Jesus showed on the Cross, are never achieved through military oppression, but only through sacrifice and love.

As we walked through this historic port, it seemed the nation was clinging to the supposedly illustrious achievements of a season that had passed, but was hesitant about where it wanted to go next. Was this the real legacy of Nelson? Greenwich is now the site of a Maritime Museum. Even the Observatory, which once told the world the time, is disused for any practical purpose, standing only as a monument to former greatness. As one writer observes, "Greenwich has become a place that deals with memories, rather than actualities" (Jennings, 1999).

Standing like some vast, squat toad on the opposite bank is a symbol of this current uncertainty: the Millennium Dome. Built to mark a thousand years of shared history, it was a hugely controversial project. From the moment it was announced, the media and public frenzy revealed a deep-seated anxiety that the inheritance we are leaving for the future is inadequate.

Chief amongst the complaints was that the exhibition contained within would be temporary. Its useful life would be limited to just one year, and the building itself would last only twenty-five. Critics slammed the sinking of vast sums of money into such a transient project. Surely, they claimed, this was an opportunity to lay down a more meaningful bequest to future generations? Yet no-one could agree what that might look like; no-one really knew what story we wanted to tell about ourselves.

Whatever the relative merits of the Dome, the uproar proved one thing: concepts of Britishness and its representation were up for grabs. Tony Blair and the team responsible for the project just didn't seem to have that "Nelson Touch". No longer could they expect "that every man will do his duty", as had been the case in Horatio's day; and no longer would we stand behind the Union Flag, agreeing what that might mean.

In the years since the opening of the Dome such questions have only intensified. In the aftermath of 9/11, the 'War on Terror', the heated debate around issues of immigration, and rising concern about fundamentalist religion, there is a constant call for us to return to the spirit of Empire; of self-interest, self-protection and self-promotion. As we walked, we were praying that a more Godly heart might emerge; one of peace-making, generosity and a call to the margins rather than the centre.

In the months after we stood in Greenwich, a number of bizarre things happened.

Firstly, a whale swam up the Thames and got stuck. (Honestly, you couldn't make this stuff up.) Could a real life Jonah have come to judge our unjust ways? Was this a signal, smack bang in the middle of "Old Father Time" itself, that we were supposed to be entering a new season?

Then the Cutty Sark caught fire as it was moored at dry dock in Greenwich, awaiting restoration. A tea clipper, this legendary Victorian merchant ship is emblematic of the unjust trade practices that were a natural extension of our nautical domination. The inheritance of such traditions is with us today, both in our unfair treatment of producers in poor countries and our general lack of engagement with how the food on our table is produced. For the West, this has resulted in increasingly processed, unhealthy diets and, some would argue, greater numbers of allergies and intolerances.

At the same time we were in London, modern-day prophet Jamie Oliver also launched a highly publicised campaign for better school dinners. Was time being called on wrong practices? Had the famous chef unknowingly caught something of the flavour of what God was preparing, and with it a taste of the real meaning of communion? Eating together allows communities to share the essentials of life, bringing with it a mingling of the physical and spiritual, of heaven and earth. It seemed to me this campaign, whether its figurehead realised it or not, was based on a very holy principle.

Finally, our good friends at Pointed Arrow Theatre Company toured the south coast of England in a big, red postal van. As they travelled they sought to embellish the myth of seafaring rogue Leonard-Le-Bec, performing pirate tales to impromptu audiences in pubs and on windswept beaches. Their technique was to plan as little in advance as possible. They would simply turn up and ask around, giving a free show to whoever wanted it.

Arriving in Portsmouth (still an important naval base) they made their way to the dockyard that now houses a number of historical ships including, amongst others, the Mary Rose. They were surprised at the welcome they received. One of the pieces they put together for the tour was 'Adoring Horatio', a playful re-imaging of the Admiral's life and achievements. Before the day was done, they found themselves performing it in front of HMS Victory, the ship that bore Nelson home to London after his death.

A rag-tag group of strolling players, they were speaking into the heart of a nation, re-telling its history as they did so. They drifted in and no-one was sure where they came from. They carried no flag, and bore no insignia. Their only armaments were stories. Their very way of working and being stood against the spirit of empire. It seemed like God Himself had appointed the moment for this tale to be told.

What was required from them (and us, as we walked) was the confidence to set out in all uncertainty, not trusting to clocks and maps, but to the ebb and flow of something unseen; something that can break through with sudden clarity into our humdrum, everyday lives.

At the moment I realised this, cannons fired in Greenwich.

After the walk I made my way home, to Leeds. I was in reflective mood. It was exactly a decade since I had first come to the city's university to study. I was suddenly closer to my thirties than my teens. In some ways I was happier than I had ever been, but the ghosts of the past, and of wasted opportunities, weighed heavy on my mind.

I wanted to find a way of celebrating what had happened to me in the last ten years, but also moving on from it. If I was going to criticise Britain for being stuck in a bygone era, then I also needed to get my own house in order. The writer of Ecclesiastes says there are seasons in our lives for 'everything under the sun'. If that was true, I needed clues about the one I was leaving and the one I was about to enter.

On 31 October – Halloween – a group of us met together for a very different kind of celebration; different, at least, to the one practiced by the neighbourhood kids in their witch and devil costumes as they went round trick-or-treating. I had brought along ten years' worth of my diaries. They didn't contain my deepest thoughts and vast streams of consciousness. They were just appointment diaries, containing the briefest of notes about the places I had been to, the people I had met and the projects I had been involved with. I had never been able to throw them away. It would have felt like I was throwing away my memories. But now seemed like the right time. We all have to learn when it's right to let go.

As we gathered in a friend's living room, I began to rip out the pages. Many just fell to the floor. Some I presented to people as a gift; a record of a day or a week that had been important in our lives. As the pieces fell, pandemonium broke out. I had been worried that people might find the evening a bit odd – what was this strange behaviour all about? But my fears quickly disappeared. Memories flooded back as we waded through the days, months and years that had gone before.

Some people had known me since university and could remember pretty much all the major events of my life. Some I had met only recently, which probably made them look at what I was doing very differently. Most of them, though, were very vocal, freely sharing sudden recollections and emotions in a way that soon passed out of my control.

We took the fragments that had come from the diaries outside. Then we built a fire and burnt them. As we stood around the flames, we paused for a moment to bring a prayer to God. It was a prayer not of loss and mourning, but of hope for times to come.

A few days later, one of my friends contacted me with an interesting parallel for our activities. Unintentionally, our act of remembrance mirrored an ancient Celtic ceremony that was also traditionally held on this day. It was another piece of excellent, if accidental, timing.

I was pleased with this. I had been greatly inspired by Celtic Christianity over the past few years. Its anarchic spirit seemed to chime with our post-modern times. The Celtic Christians would often adapt customs of the pagan people around them, re-interpreting them for use in the worship of the one true God. It is in this tradition that our celebrations of Easter and Christmas first emerged.

With my diary burnings, I was also given the chance to re-invent some old customs. In pagan Celtic belief, the season in which I held my bonfire was the Festival of Samhain, a forerunner to the modern practice of Halloween and All Saints Day. This was a celebration of New Year, a time at which the gods were said to come near to the earth. Sacrifices and gifts would be offered up as the community gave thanks for the harvest, the defining event of their lives and work. Personal objects symbolising the wishes of the supplicants or illness to be healed were cast into the fire. In the flames the people would see the kindling of a new beginning – dreams, projects and hopes for the year to come.

Our prayers that night echoed this call for the best of what the future might hold, while never forgetting to celebrate the guiding hand of God in all our wonderings. As we gathered in the dark, was there something springing up from the land that pushed beyond the imperialism left by Nelson? Was there hope, however fragile, that Britain could throw off the shackles of her past? Perhaps. I remain uncertain as to what it will take this nation to gain a sense of true identity, allowing the values of Christ to flourish. Of one thing, though, I feel sure. God used that evening to help me reconcile where I had come from with where I was going.

I paused to look at the fire, and pressed on.

FACT FILE: GREENWICH, LONDON

At the time of the Roman occupation of Britain (circa 60AD), Greenwich was a small fishing community based around the river.

Its name comes either from Saxon invaders of the sixth and seventh centuries ("Green Town"), or the Danes of the ninth century ("Green Reach").

Greenwich's ties to royalty began in 1417, when the brother of Henry V, Duke Humphrey of Gloucester, took residence in the manor there. It became the principal residence of Henry VII.

The architect of the Old Royal Naval College and the Royal Observatory was Sir Christopher Wren, one of the greatest British designers; his other buildings include St Paul's Cathedral. The Royal Observatory was the first purpose-built scientific research facility in the country.

Today, Greenwich is a world heritage site and home of the National Maritime Museum. It will provide one of the sites for the staging of the 2012 Olympic Games.

The National Maritime Museum displays the uniform that Nelson died in; his personal connection to Greenwich, however, is actually quite slim.

BIBLIOGRAPHY

Jennings, Charles (1999) *Greenwich: The Place Where Days Begin and End* London;

CHAPTER 6

London to Paris

Steve Lowton

**LONDON TO CANTERBURY: MID-SEPTEMBER 2005
Team: Gemma, Ally, Sharon, Val, John, Sally Ann,
Alan, Chris and Hannah, Rob, Adam, Jane, Nancy,
Claire, Stephen, and myself**

On leaving the Tower of London we headed east along the Thames. Before long we found ourselves in Greenwich, walking to the sound of canons being fired amidst the celebrations of the 200th anniversary of the death of Nelson. For those of you who don't know English history so well, Nelson is a huge symbol of our past as a sea-faring nation. The British Navy protected the trade routes that were the life blood of the Empire. They were our insurance policy, protecting the fruit of unrighteous trade upon which much of the wealth of England was built.

Issues of covering and insurance dominated this section of the walk, for if Canterbury symbolises anything it is our failure as church to care for the poor and position ourselves for the sake of the nation. It is symbolic of our desire to find covering in the context of the nation state, rather than in childlike trust of the Father. Church is not our life source, our insurance policy against disaster, or our place of covering. Jesus is! He is our strong tower and our kinsman redeemer. Jesus is the person to whom we run; the Lord is our Shepherd, we shall not want.

Once more therefore the Lord had orchestrated our paths to provoke repentance for the ungodly foundations that drove so much of the British Empire, which at its peak painted nearly a quarter of the land mass on the world's maps red.

As well as the British Navy, Greenwich is symbolic of time, for it from here that Greenwich Mean Time is calibrated. Should the Lord give us grace we will arrive in Rome on 21 December, the shortest day of the year. The days are indeed short. London, the UK and Europe are on hold as the Lord prolongs the period of grace that is there for us to lay hold of. These are truly our days if we can seize the window that has been given to us[1].

Kent was not an easy county to walk through. The welcome was wonderful, but the ground was hard. There will be many others, however, better equipped, that will follow on after, carrying further whatever we have opened up. We concluded the walk at Augustine's

---

[1] At this time the European Parliament was in disarray over the proposed new European Constitution. Here in the UK, the announcement of the successful Olympic bid was followed the day after by the 7 July bombings; incredulous joy one moment; appalling tragedy the next. Many of those who believe the living God speaks through the circumstances of life were saying that these were signs showing that London, the UK and Europe were indeed in the balance.

Cross, which marks the original point where this papal emissary came ashore prior to the establishing of the ecclesiastical stronghold of Canterbury. Once more we thanked our Maker for the bold, pioneering zeal that he undoubtedly carried, while also acknowledging the unholy mix that is typical of so much of our lives and the life of the church within the UK. Together we looked back to our starting point in Whitby, calling with all our strength for the wild fire of the Holy Spirit to break across our land, taking with it all double-mindedness and half-heartedness.

Tomorrow just four of us get the ferry across from Dover to Calais, before continuing our walk into the heart of France. To all of the forty or fifty people who at different times have walked, laughed, groaned and cried our way through England I want to say a huge thank you. The last 325 miles would have impossible, and certainly a lot less fun, without you all.

REFLECTIONS FROM HOME

It was wonderful to be able to spend twenty-four hours relaxing near Dover prior to another team joining Sharon and I, and leaving for France. My only disappointment was that my wife Kathy was not able to be with me, due the responsibilities of our household. However, I knew things were secure back in Leeds, having made the decision to share our home with Stew and Beci, two friends from Wales. The sense of covering for Kathy was strong, and over the next few months there was rarely a moment when I had to look back over my shoulder to see what was going on in my own back yard; a huge contrast to what was to follow after Rome.

For now, these were magical moments, and Sharon and I prepared for the next few months of travelling together as we committed to the responsibility of the journey.

CALAIS TO PARIS: late September 2005
Team: Andy, Val, Sharon and myself

Coming out of Calais onto the northern plains of France was one of the most wonderful mornings of walking that I have ever experienced. Swept along on a sea of prayer, the open spaces of France unfolded before us as we dipped down into the wooded valleys, fully alive to the wonder of being caught up in the purposes of God. For everything turns! Whether a marriage, a household, a city, a nation or indeed a whole continent, there is always a turning point with Jesus. Never have I experienced such a release of faith and joy.

REFLECTIONS FROM HOME

Two things happened as soon as we were off the cross-Channel ferry, both of which were challenging to my credentials for walking into Mainland Europe. Firstly, I completely got my bearings wrong, and rather than heading south out of Calais was soon on my way to Norway. Much laughter was had when the support car finally tracked us down. What hope did we have of successfully making it across Europe?

The second error related to my poverty of skills when it came to bi-lingual negotiations. Never have I experienced such embarrassment as when I committed my greatest error of translation. Having set off by myself on the day's walking I quickly lost my way, doing further damage to my faltering reputation for a good sense of direction. Hitching a lift back to where I started I was picked up by a local French builder. In my best French I tried to say "France is very beautiful". A bemused expression came across his face as he pondered what I had just said. It began to dawn on me that I might not have communicated quite what I intended, and before long my fears were confirmed. As I later found out, instead of praising the French countryside, I had commented that "French men are very beautiful." His reply was revealing; with eyes glinting he said, "Avez-vous une famille or êtes-vous gay?"

In horror I pretended not to understand, jumping out of the car at the earliest opportunity in a ridiculously embarrassed and shamefully homophobic way.

My reports take up the story:

Five days of walking into Paris left me with many rich moments. On one occasion, a cyclist passed us from England. When asked where he was going his reply was simply "I don't know!" How cool is that? The day is coming when many will set out walking and praying, following the finger of God; they will simply pick up the wind of the spirit, not knowing quite where they are going, but knowing they have to go.

On this occasion we have a clear mandate: Rome. Something has to shift over the UK and Europe. When it does there will be a release of those called to wander, exploring the storyline of scripture through the arts and the media. In the meantime we walk, knowing that, as scripture says, "we have the word of the prophets made all the more sure, and we do well to pay attention to it".

This is exactly what we are seeking to do. Ten hours of walking between the team each day is an unmistakable way of paying attention. We are allowing the Holy Spirit to interrupt our schedules so that we can walk, pray, and pay attention to the word of the Lord. Europe is on hold so that we, the people of God, can arise, as a fisherman called Peter once said, 'Until the dawn breaks and the morning star rises in our hearts.'

We are now in Paris. Walking in through the African quarter in the north opened up to us the reality of life in the city beyond the boundaries of the tourist routes. As ever, entering such a global city is energy-sapping and full of demands.

We have been given some wonderful accommodation on the Isle of St Louis, a good place to take some rest before we set our faces to Orleans. This city is not quite on our route but we feel compelled to go there, having witnessed the scenes unfolding in New Orleans in recent weeks. I will write more of that on my return in a few days.

REFLECTIONS FROM HOME

It seemed like a dream to be in this city of romance. To simply hook into the storyline of those who have graced this city with their creative talent would be wonderful enough; to arrive carrying our own story in the making was more wonderful indeed. When the doorway to Rome began to open up it seemed at first that the sensible thing to do was to plan for the following year. Thank goodness I listened to the growing generation of believers who are learning to live lightly and make room for spontaneous and what some would call foolhardy decisions. There are moments in all of our lives when we have to throw caution to the wind and grab the opportunity with both hands. This was one of those times. Somehow my former life of endless meetings and grey cardboard cut-outs seemed a dim and distant memory in contrast to the beauty and wonder of Paris in the September sun.

Back home I was glad to know that Kathy was doing well. With Stew and Beci around I knew the load of a young family, as well as the household chores, would be spread more evenly. Perhaps there are pathways we can all find that give room for the extraordinary, and contradict the unspoken decrees that say our lives should be conducted according to the rule book of social norms.

CHAPTER 7

Paris:
The Great Feast

Steve Lowton

It is impossible for one story to encapsulate the many themes flowing through the life of this wonderful city and most beautiful of nations. However, when a nation of culture and taste is interrupted by riots and lawlessness, as happened in the autumn of 2005, maybe it is time to look back at the less savoury aspects of her past. This, therefore, is one attempt to do that.

It was as dark a night as he had known. Even the huge, imposing buttresses of Notre Dame were hidden from sight as the mists rolled across the swollen waters of the Seine. The chill of winter cut deep and Vito huddled nearer to the watchman's fire that blazed at the foot of the steps. Soon, the last of the guests would be here, and he would go inside to take up other duties. Above him he could just make out the celebration of the Feast of Martin de Tours in full swing. What he needed right now was to warm himself on the mulled wine. The date was 11 November 1788.

Letting his mind wander from the noise above, he remembered the story that his Grandfather had told him of his flight from Marseille, and the terrible plague a generation ago that killed thousands and thousands of people. He was glad of his Grandfather and those nights when he would sit at his feet and listen to those stories; stories of lands far away, of terrible hardships and appalling injustice as his forefathers laboured on the sugar plantations of some distant land. Gently, he allowed the words to curl around his tongue as he rehearsed the place name his Father had told him never to forget; the Kingdom of Khasso, where the blood of his own family had once mingled with the soil of that land. With time, his imagination was able to colour in the scene he had nurtured for so long, of family and friends sitting round the warm fire under a start lit sky, the whip of the slave master far from sight.

The sound of boots on cobbles brought him sharply to his senses. There, coming towards the bridge, were a group of bedraggled travellers, making their weary way through the late hours of the night. Calling gently from the shelter of the doorway he beckoned them to warm themselves by the fire. Grateful for the opportunity they lowered their few belongings to the floor and made their way over. Running his eye over them he quickly realised that these were no ordinary travellers, but pilgrims returning from the long journey to the south-west and the shrine of Martin de Tours. They were pale and thin; the famine was biting hard and bread was in short supply. Rumours abounded of intentional plans of starvation by land owners; the most destitute in the land were at greatest risk. Whether this was true or not, Vito did not know. What he did know was that the new tax called the Dime, introduced by the Church, was hated with a vengeance. Never had France groaned under such a weight of injustice, made worse by the many wars that had been fought at royal whim.

Despite their obvious poverty, this little band of pilgrims seemed somehow elated after their long journey. As he began to ask them of news from afar, their stories started to tumble out, momentarily lifting the gloom of the night. There was talk of a torn cloak with magical powers, mysterious ramblings about the dead coming back to life and exuberant debate about the cave-dwelling habits of the most simple of saintly figures that was Martin de Tours. Prayer, hospitality, friendship, laughter and love of life seemed to be strong in the code of these humble journeymen and Vito was, even in this brief encounter, drawn to their gentle ways. He was not too sure of the talk about miraculous powers, but he knew a tender heart when he saw one, and that was all too rare in the people who came through his master's home.

The laughter and companionship of this brief encounter was suddenly interrupted by the sound of horses' hooves, as several mounted riders clattered across the wooden bridge over the Seine. Dismounting in a swirl of cloaks, Vito quickly returned to his duties as the last guest arrived at the feast being held by his master. Rising to his full and impressive stature, the ebony-skinned doorman welcomed the new guest with a loud voice that echoed through the mists and sent the pilgrims scurrying. "My Master Lamenie de Brienne welcomes Maximilian Robespierre to the feast of St Martin de Tours." The doors were flung open and, without so much as a sideways glance, the cloaked figure led his small entourage up the flight of steps into the warmth of the party that was, by now, in full flow.

Turning to look over their shoulders, the pilgrims caught a brief glimpse of the great feast; the light from a thousand candles cascaded through the open door. As they made their way up the gentle incline towards the poorer quarters in the north of the city the sound of singing and dancing was soon lost. A mournful cry of a dog in the distance and a sudden gust of wind made them draw their cloaks even tighter around their shoulders.

In the warmth of the banqueting room, Vito stepped back into the shadows to observe the all too familiar surroundings. The effect of Maximilian's entry was immediate for already, as some were drawn to him, it seemed as if others shied away. Vito replayed in his mind the conversation he had had earlier with one of the servant girls who once worked in Maximilian's household. A prim and proper master she had called him, always so neatly turned out, yet forever a tinge of sadness about him. With his mother dying when he was just six and his Father abandoning him and his younger brothers and sister soon after, he was, to all intents and purposes, an orphan. Now an established lawyer he didn't tolerate fools, and the advice was always to steer clear of his foul tempers. Vito noted that this was one such moment; the lawyer's furrowed brow searched the room almost as if looking for some easy prey. Vito shuddered.

To the far side of the room were the artists and musicians. Totally at ease in their surroundings, they were laughing, holding hands with both men and women, and gesticulating in the way that only those used to the dramatic gestures of the stage are able.

Behind them stood the street girls, dressed in the provocative ways of their trade, leaving little room for the imagination. Plunging dress lines and seductive displays of slim, stocking clad legs were neatly displayed for the customers-in-waiting to peruse. To one side of the group, however, stood a young girl who looked different from the rest. Her dress was the same and her beautiful figure was something to be admired, but there was a sweet demeanour to her face, a gentleness that belied her trade. As Vito watched, he saw her fingers carefully tracing a carved brooch that hung delicately round her slender neck. He could not be sure, but over her wrist he thought he caught sight of a letter, or at least some form of rolled parchment, resting in a beautiful laced bag. Every detail of her was worthy of debate and conjecture.

He realised that he heard about this young girl. Brought to Paris by her peasant father she had been cruelly abandoned, left to wander the streets and fend for herself. Yet the rumours were that many a homeless person was grateful for her kind heart and understanding word. Possessing a wisdom beyond her years, her reputation somehow carried a dignity into the most undignified of trades. Though distant and aloof, she was undoubtably one of the girls waiting for the invitation to dance and her eyes swam with warmth and welcome. It was said that no man had lain with her, such were the spell binding qualities of those eyes, which carried an authority that made men wither before her.

Standing near the large fire that now burnt in the hearth were the military men. Dressed in all their finery, there was something supremely confident about them.

Their swords hanging to one side, illuminated by a thousand dancing flames that reflected in the lethal metal of each blade. Looking to the far recesses of that corner he saw the Corsican; a man who started his life as an islander and a free man, but would end it confined to another island, St Helena, a prisoner of the hated English. Bronzed through many a long hour in the sun, Vito had never spoken to him, though rumours were rife as to the General's intentions. Certainly he did not seem to be the sort of man to be crossed.

To the left were the men of the Church, but Vito spared them little time, disgusted as he was with their greed and selfish ways. Dressed in the full garb of the priesthood they seemed out of place, ill at ease with the hilarity and natural Parisian grace that lit up the lavish room.

Then to his Master, Lamenie de Brienne, the Finance Minister for the King. Normally his entertaining would be done in the Palace of Versailles but, tired of the overbearing presence of Marie Antoinette, he had asked leave of King Louis XV1 to celebrate the Feast of Martin in his home on the Isle St Louis.

It was as if the whole of Paris was somehow represented in those who were gathered together that night, except of course the famine-stricken underclass. Anyone walking in would have seen a tableaux of the hopes and tensions that weaved their way through the life of this cosmopolitan city.

The sound of raised voices brought him back from his observations. Turning towards the far end of the room he saw Maximilian in full flow, standing squarely in front of the most senior Priest present. Maximilian Robespierre was someone who did not need to raise his voice to be heard across a room full of people. Used to addressing courts, this man of just thirty years was regaling a man of cloth at least double his age.

"Is it not He whose immortal hand, engraving on the heart of man the code of justice and equality, has written the death sentence of tyrants?" said Maximilian. The musicians had stopped playing and all attention was drawn to the spectacle unfolding before them. "He did not create kings to devour the human race. He did not create priests to harness us, like vile animals, to the chariots of kings."

Vito's master, Lamenie, was almost running across the room such his fear, for no such words should be uttered where there are many ears to hear. But before he could get to them, the lawyer turned and stormed towards the door. Flinging both doors wide open he tumbled down the steps onto the bridge over the Seine. Standing squarely in front of the imposing skyline of Notre Dame, he looked into the swirling mists that all but enveloped him, crying out with a loud voice, "I damn the God of the courts of St Louis and I damn the God of the Priests of this city." As if addressing Gargoyles that stared down on him, he continued, "Liberty, equality and fraternity. Let that be the tyrant of tyrants." With that, he strode off into the darkness, leaving the spectacle of a hundred pale faces gawping after him.

If you had looked closely beyond those shocked and trembling faces you would have seen the Corsican General carefully make his way across to the embattled host of the party. With handkerchief in hand, words of consolation flowed easily for someone of his obvious military prowess.

I don't know whether the cry came from high above the dark skies of Paris, or from deep down in the bowels of the earth. Maybe it was its terrible rawness that made it so difficult to determine the source. For it wasn't a scream, neither was it a groan. Rather a deep stirring, almost as if something dreadful and dark had been awakened on this night of feasting and celebration.

This was not meant to be.

The terrible curses uttered from the lips of someone who understands the power of words should not be underestimated. His measured voice had pierced deeply, cutting through the layers of human debris and destitution that marked out the dark side of this city of the night. It seemed as if even the Gargoyles, sitting on the heights of the towering cathedral, pricked up their ears. Growing in strength, cat-calls and ear-piercing screams added to the cacophony of noise, as all across the city dogs began to howl with terror.

Then a new sound, more terrible than before. The sound of metal on metal, of sliding or sharpening, accompanied by a lustful cry that can only rise to the smell of blood. The noise was now so loud it was as if the city itself would haemorrhage. But this was not the end, for what followed was a drum roll of terrifying intensity, rising to a mountainous crescendo. A great cry went up; then silence, the howling of dogs fading into the background.

It is reported that someone venturing out later than anyone should on such a night saw a hunched figure running from the shadows of the cathedral and across the courtyard that sits to the fore of the West Rose Window. Whether this is true or not nobody knows, but many a Parisian awoke in the early hours of that morning, troubled in their sleep with dreams of human heads rolling along the floor and cackles of terrifying laughter from those gloating nearby.

The flames licked their way along the roof of the bus as the riot police sought to carve a way through the mob before them, giving space for the fire fighters to attend to the burning cars that blocked the road ahead. Angry faces searched out new missiles to hurl at the baton-wielding police as they sent in snatch squads to pick out the ring leaders. There was a loud bang as the petrol tank of the bus exploded, sending flames shooting across the road in all directions. A peel of delight echoed round the crowds. It was a moment of satisfaction amidst the endless monotony that marked out the average day of those living in these northern suburbs. Then, almost as quickly as the crowds had gathered, the youths, nearly all of North African origin, began to disperse down side streets and pull back into dark corners. Weary from many days and nights of such troubles, the police leaned on their riot shields and stopped to catch their breath.

It was then that one of them caught the most fleeting of glimpses; a shadowy figure. Many had said she was stunningly beautiful, others had commented on her shapely figure. Indeed the beauty described was such that it would have been easy to have dismissed the talk as the fantasies of men looking for solace from the stress of each day. But there she was, standing at the end of the alley across the way, watching purposefully and gently stroking a brooch or pendant that hung round her neck. He couldn't be sure, but in her hand it appeared as if she was holding a scroll. His training would have suggested that it might be a gun, but that was so incongruous a thought as to be dismissed immediately.

As if drawn by some hidden force, the policeman put his shield to one side and crossed over the road towards her. In that moment she started to move herself, gracefully gliding along the pavement and down the Rue du Turenne towards the banks of the Seine. Entranced, the policeman continued to follow, over the Port Marie Bridge and onto the Isle St Louis. Entering an apartment building, she climbed the three sets of stairs that twisted their way to the top floor, gently pushing a door that was ajar at the summit of the steps. Forgetting now about the troubles of that evening and the fear that had gripped him and his colleagues these long November nights, he continued to follow, slipping through the doorway and quietly sitting down to watch expectantly.

Unfolding before him was the most tender of scenes, a stark contrast to the hours of naked fear that he had felt night after night in front of the angry mobs. The woman stood to one side while in the centre of the room a young Algerian and older Caucasian Frenchman wept in each other's arms. There were no words, just the gentle sobbing of someone whose heart had been deeply touched.

How long this went on for is hard to tell, such was the magic of the moment. At some point others entered the room, unnoticed. Some carried whole racks of wine and lavish hampers crammed full of sweet pastries, exotic fruits and grapes. Others carried musical instruments. Still others arrived in white dungarees, splattered with the brightly coloured oil paints of someone accustomed to standing before a canvas. One or two walked in with pencils behind their ears and note books in hand, lost in the world of their imaginations.

At first the conversation was gentle and measured, but within a short period of time laughter and singing began to echo around the room as, with incredible passion and Gallic flair, the musicians picked up their instruments and began to play. By now the wine was flowing and glasses were being raised. The air was full of the intoxicating presence of something the policeman could not even begin to adequately describe. Transfixed, he sat resting against the wall and allowed the fear and awful scenes of the day to fade into the background.

He awoke to the rich words of a woman, who was stood in the centre of the room. He couldn't be sure, but it seemed like she was reading from a scroll not too dissimilar to the one in the hand of the woman he had followed, though she herself had disappeared.

Not able to quite make out the rich accent, he moved closer, hearing mention of the seven spirits of God and those clothed in garments of white. He leant back against the door frame, moving to one side a curious pile of walking boots that had been left nearby. Seeing a tattered newspaper underneath the shoes he noted the date of the day that had just broken: 11 November 2005. "France at a Crossroads" the headline proclaimed. Beneath it was a brief mention of the Feast Day of Martin de Tours.

Paris was once again stilled. Feeling almost drunk, though he did not know why as just one glass of wine had passed his lips that night, he slipped quietly through the door.

FACT FILE: PARIS AND FRANCE

Martin De Tours

Martin of Tours is the Patron Saint of France and lived from 316/317 to 397 AD. He established a monastic community in Marmoutier on the pilgrimage route to Santiago de Compostela. Many miraculous deeds were attributed to him and he explored the disciplines of monastic life well before the Benedictine rule.

(www.wikipedia.com, accessed February 2008)

The French Revolution

During the French Revolution and the Reign of Terror (1793-1794) at least 16 594 people met their deaths under the guillotine. It may have been as many as 40 000.

(www.wikipedia.com, accessed February 2008)

The Slave Trade

France was one of the leading nations trading in slaves during the seventeenth and eighteenth centuries, with several colonies in the Caribbean. Over half a million were working the plantations of Haiti alone. However, France also became the first nation to abolish slavery during the French Revolution of 1794. Furthermore, on the 10 May 2006, France became the first nation in Europe to hold a national day of remembrance for the victims of slavery.

(Journal of Turkish Weekly May 2006)

France and Algeria

France has a long history of immigration. During the period from World War II to the mid-nineties, immigrant workers in France rose to 6 million, with the majority being North African, principally Algerians. However, exact figures for ethnicity are difficult to track as it is not included in census material.

(Middle East Quarterly, March 1997)

During the Algerian War of Independence, 1954-62, over 1 million Algerians were killed in what has been described as one of the most brutal conflicts France has ever been involved with.

(Fisk, Robert (2005) The Conquest of the Middle East, Harper)

In October 1961, it is alleged that an unreported massacre of 300 Algerians took place in Paris as they protested about a night curfew imposed against them, their bodies being dumped in the Seine.

(Fisk, Robert (2005) The Conquest of the Middle East, Harper)

The Riots of Autumn 2005

The French riots of autumn 2005 started on 25 October and run at their peak through to 14 November, spreading right across France. Many commentators blame a society that has marginalised the children and grand children of North African immigration.

(www.CBC.news.ca, accessed February 2008)

During the riots nearly 9 000 cars were torched and 200 million Euros of damage was incurred. The French police arrested 2 900 people and 126 police and fire fighters were injured.

(www.ssrc.org, accessed February 2008)

CHAPTER 8

Paris to Marseille

Steve Lowton

PARIS TO ORLEANS, Late September 2005
Same team as walked to Paris: Andy,
Val, Sharon and myself

Joan of Arc is perhaps the most famous historical figure linked with the history of the French city of Orleans, 80 miles south of Paris. Like the English heroine Boadicea, she is a folk heroine who drove back the invading armies, whether they be the Roman garrisons in Colchester or the English in France. Fighting women evoke something of the underdog we all love; the one who, against all odds, runs against the tide and lays an axe to the bullying and dominant forces of imperialism. A good reason, therefore, to walk the extra 50 or so miles demanded of us.

However, there are also more current reasons to walk to Orleans, for all of us must have been deeply moved to see America staggering under the effects of hurricane Katrina[2]. As in 2001, with the appalling destruction of

---

[2]Hurricane Katrina hit New Orleans on 29 August 2005. The effect was catastrophic and long lasting. 1464 people lost their lives and 80% of the city was under water. The city is currently being rebuilt. www.wikipedia.org, accessed February 2008

the Twin Towers, we are once again forcefully reminded that here in the western world we are not immune to disasters that are commonplace elsewhere. There are some who would go further, saying that the atrocity of 9/11 and the natural disaster of New Orleans is a forceful reminder that the sin of empire touches even the depths of these world shaping events. So within four years the symbol of western capitalism and economic imperialism, the Twin Towers, is destroyed; followed by the destruction of New Orleans, a city built on the scourge of the slave trade. The fruit of imperialism within economics and the trading in life and misery that is the slave trade is there for all to see.

Yet we in Europe are not immune to the sufferings of America. In the names of New York and York (UK), New Orleans and Orleans (France), there is a reminder that what happens in the USA patterns the future for Europe. If there is the sin of imperialism within America it is only because of what we in Europe have sown into the foundations of that vast, dynamic nation. We walk, therefore, and we pray. Our prayers are really not very good. As one day flows into another, so the cumulative effect of eight days of successive walking builds up and the energy levels drop. However, when the body is weak the heart is strong, for there remains an urgency about these days.

Whilst walking, we heard news of the final terrorist to be captured in the aftermath of the bombings in London this July, being returned from Rome, the place to which he had fled. Tracing the route of religious imperialism as marked out by Constantine, so we retrace the route of this fugitive suicide bomber and modern day crusader of death. Despite this we take courage, for the giving of ourselves is not at the price of the life blood of others, as with terrorism, be it inspired by nation states or a few individuals. The way of Jesus was to overcome through the laying down of his own life rather than the lives of others.

Hidden, sometimes weak, ridiculously small and insignificant, we add our prayers to those of many others, believing that this is a time when whole continents can line up and nations turn around.

We are off the walk now for a fortnight before returning to Orleans in mid-October. Huge thanks to everyone who is standing with us in prayer. There remains a window of grace that we must lay hold of.

ORLEANS AND THE LOIRE VALLEY:
A birth canal in Europe
Team: Sharon, Dave, Sarah, Dave H, and myself.

I write this just as we set out again to France to pick up the walk through to Rome. We are 20 miles north of Orleans and, with the help of two different teams, hope to be 350 miles further down the road by the time we come back in two weeks' time.

It's always massively exciting to get back out. At the same time it's often at this point that I can feel daunted by all that we are walking and praying for. The mileage alone would be sufficient reason. Since leaving Whitby in mid-August we have walked over 550 miles, and yet we are still only one-third of the way there. The pressure of being away from home for so many weeks is also very real, and all that we are praying for can seem beyond us. It's at these times that I reflect on the many ways in which our paths have been clearly marked. Let me share just one such way.

On **16 March** this year, the day after the Ides of March (a day which marks the assassination of Julius Caesar), my friend and household companion Stew Thomas and I set out to walk to the Tower of London. We simply walked out of our front door one Wednesday morning and headed south from Leeds. There was no planning, no great trumpet fanfare, just a crazy prophetic desire to get up and go. As we walked to the Tower, so we carried with us the testimony of our friends, Sue and Martin Scott[3]: that in the face of the death of Sue, there is a place of no fear that, if we allow, the One who has overcome death can open up to us. This is the overcoming cry of the church in Smyrna in the book of Revelation and it marked, we believe, a change of season in the UK. We also carried the narrative of Elijah and the ravens; calling the ravens, as a symbol of all creation, into liberation, free from the tyranny of imperialism that plagues nation state, big business and every other potential manifestation of empire within the UK. It was this walk to the Tower that opened up the walk to Rome that I am now on. Little did we realise what was going to open up as we walked out of our front door[4].

Now stay with these details, for in the little time I had to plan for this walk through mainland Europe, I pencilled in a finishing date that was no more than a few

---

[3]Sue was the wife of Martin Scott, a friend and fellow journeyman, who is a strong prophetic voice in the UK and beyond. Sue died on 14 February 2005.

[4]The mythology surrounding the ravens that are kept in the Tower of London is that the nation is safe as long as they stay within the walls of the Tower. If they fly away then the nation is in danger. Their wings have therefore been clipped.

days away from Christmas. This gave me time to maximise the walking days we had, but also time to avoid the Christmas travel rush. As I have already shared, this date is **21 December**, which I have subsequently realised is the shortest day of the year. What I hadn't realised until recently is that this date is exactly, to the day, forty weeks from the day when Stew and I stumbled out of our front door to walk to London. In other words, ever since that moment we have been in process, in a heavenly birth canal - forty weeks being the normal length of a pregnancy. What confidence that gives when unchecked thoughts come to despise or ridicule. This is not some random idea for a few people with nothing better to do than to take themselves off on holiday, wrapped up in mumbo jumbo prophetic language. Neither is this a diversion from the real agenda. No. This is a clear assignment from our Maker that I cannot and will not ignore. The giants are not that big. We can see this continent turn.

So we will resume the walk first thing Monday morning, the 17th, concluding this section on Sunday 30 October. After travelling out, we will pick up a schedule that will mean there is someone out on the road praying from 7am in the morning through to at least 6pm at night. In the evenings we will cook some food on our camping stove in the motel car park before getting to bed boringly early, too tired for much else. Prayer walking is work. Good work, fun work, but work. We go to work each day in prayer and between us cover 30 to 40 miles. There will be moments when the flow is strong and clear; other times when we will wonder whether there is an articulate thought left in our heads.

If you want to follow us on the map we will be walking up the Loire Valley, then over to Lyon and, hopefully, finishing down near Valence. Huge thanks to everyone who would want to walk but cannot, and to everyone else who is standing with us at this time.

REFLECTIONS FROM HOME

It gave me such a buzz, looking back, to know that this walk was not birthed round some meeting table, fuelled by big finance and glossy leaflets advertising how we could change your lives for sixpence. No, this was a walk birthed out of a home somewhere on the east side of Leeds; a walk that others had sight of for many years. We were given a grace that we were able to enter into because of that, but the credentials we carried were crafted through the tough choices made in the intimacy of our own living room: choices to stay true to the covenant of marriage even when the grass seemed so much greener elsewhere; choices to die to the natural instincts of self preservation within us and allow the hand of the Lord to put our lives through the fires of his altar; choices to risk livelihood and sound financial reason to discover afresh that there is a God who provides.

The early Celts were not power players in the Machiavellian politics of their time. They refused the seat of power in order to occupy the lowly places at the table. It was that same spirit that the living God had to work into my own life; a willingness to step out of the centre of my own little world in order that others might rise to shape and influence, even if it be at my own expense and at risk to my own livelihood. It's a grace that, right now as I write and reflect back two years on, I do not carry too well. We all love to be in control of our own worlds and we all love and hate the unknown. Being willing to embrace death is a life-long journey; death to our own ego and yes, sometimes death to our own dreams. It is this that gives space for the living God to work a deeper magic; a magic that begins to allow our lives to line up with that of whole cities and nations. It is a truly awesome prospect.

THE LOIRE VALLEY AND RHONE VALLEY:
Orlean to Lyon and beyond, October 2005
Team: Vito, Rosita, Tim, Sharon and myself

It is impossible to put into words the kaleidoscope of memories and intensity of emotions surrounding a fort-night of intense walking and prayer. I could talk about the breadth of history, cultural and geographical splen-dour that we walked through as we made our way from Orleans through the Loire Valley then on into the gate-way city of Lyon. I could rehearse some of the stunning scenery as we moved further south of Lyon, down the eastern side of the Rhone Valley with the backdrop of the Alps always with us. On this occasion though, I simply want to write about three members of the two teams that accompanied us over the 550km of this last leg. Our prayers are of little consequence without the testimony of our lives behind them, for the testimony of Jesus is the storyline of his followers. With their permission, let me share some of their story, for they stand as wonderful metaphors for all that we are walking for.

Sarah is in her mid-twenties, and up to two months ago was in a wheelchair suffering from a disorder that at times left her in so much pain she couldn't even wear jewellery. I know this because over the last couple of years she has been up to our home in Leeds on a number of occasions. No more than two months ago any thought of walking more than 10 miles a day would have been laughable. Yet her story is that, within the space of 36 hours, God completely healed her. I know this because it happened whilst she was in our home! The truly remarkable part is that nobody prayed for her and nobody laid hands on her. She simply began to find the confidence to speak to her own body and call through the healing that was there. As strength began to flow, so boldness grew and further faith was found.

What a testimony to declare across the land of France, so rich in the grace of healing. What a testimony to declare out of the heart of a home rather than yet another meeting. This was not the testimony of the healing evangelist laying hands on all and sundry. Of course there is a place for that. But this was simply a young woman finding the courage to believe again; that after five years of huge disability there was grace and hope. Sarah didn't need to utter one prayer as she walked her ten miles each day, though she did in fact pray all the time; and laughed all the time, too. Her testimony was, and still is, all that was needed to touch both heaven and earth.

Secondly, I want to mention Rosita. She is a young French woman from Martinique. She is of Afro-Caribbean origin with her ancestry rooting back into the slave trade. She came to live in Paris when she was eight, before moving to England in her late teens. Brought up by her mother, her testimony is a wonderful story of the adoption of the Holy Spirit. Coming to terms with her history has been wonderfully redemptive and she stands

as an incredible trophy of grace for the orphaned continent of Europe. All the social statistics reveal the huge
search for identity amongst the young people of Europe.
As the blood of Jesus speaks a better way, so does the
testimony of Rosita. When our praying each day from
noon 'til night does not seem too good, I take huge
encouragement from such amazing people. The
orphaned continent of Europe can come free from its
legacy of slavery, empire and all that disinherits. Rosita
is a living example of that.

Lastly, I want to speak about Vito, our French guide
and gatekeeper who led us through Lyon and the heart
of France. All heart and passion, it was wonderful to see
him running down the roadway, staff in hand and strong
in prayer. Involved in French/Anglo reconciliation in
Canada, it seemed as if (and I know this will seem
strange to many) the echoes of prayers prayed were
reverberating back to the continent of North America
and the indigenous first peoples of that land. On two
occasions after leaving Orleans, our Maker underlined
this strongly and clearly, for there is a lining of up of the
prophetic voice to come through across Europe and the
Americas that cannot happen without the voice of the
indigenous people of both continents. To think otherwise, I would suggest, is hugely arrogant. Now is the
time for the lining up to happen.

We pick up the walk in a couple of weeks time just
100 miles north of Marseilles; a city known in France as
the most northern city of Africa. Sitting on the Mediterranean coast, its current life is dominated by the legacy
of the slave trade as it was the largest slave port in
France. It was also the place where Augustine came
ashore from Rome during the seventh century, on his

way to the UK to quell the unruly Celts and bring them back into line. This journey, in turn, led to the Synod of Whitby, and our starting point some ten weeks ago. No surprise, therefore, that as we the church have sort to enslave each other, so ground is given for the sins of nations to follow.

Huge thanks for all the interest and support. It means so much.

ALTARS IN THE LAND, November 2005

Once more it is that time when, with mixed feelings, I'm packing my bag for the next section of the walk to Rome. Great excitement on the one hand, but also great sobriety also at the scenes of violence that have once more dominated our TV screens, this time from across the wonderful nation of France.

In late 2004, I found myself declaring that 2005 would be a shocking year. The riots in France are yet further evidence of that. Deeply disturbing, it is as if a zip is being drawn back across the breadth of France, revealing that (as in New Orleans earlier this autumn, and down the backbone of the UK with the bombings in mid-July), the legacy of slavery and the fruits of colonialism, both in Europe and the USA, are still very real. Without in any way excusing violence, it would seem that as we as historic colonial powers have orphaned whole nations, so the cry of the angry child is beginning to be unleashed against the parents.

Yet prayer walking is not some form of jet stream spiritual warfare, where we parachute in to deliver a cruise missile-type blow to make everything right. It is a process marked out by each and every mile. Indeed, the mile after mile of walking determines that no clever prayer is going to unlock anything, for if we carry any clever prayers at all, they are used up in the first half-hour. It's after this that maybe, just maybe, the Maker begins to work.

These are wonderful days for us as the people of God. For me, this was clearly marked out at the end of the first 40 days of this 40 week season of the walk to Rome. On that day, 25 April 2005, exactly 40 days from the start of the walk to the Tower of London on 16 March, I found myself at the home of John Presdee, the father of prayer walking within the UK. It was there that I was commissioned for this walk as John and his wife Yvonne laid hands on me, and one generation stepped aside for another. That was remarkable enough, but what a way to underline the days of destiny we are in when I realised that the home they now live in, and where we actually met, sits on the road of my birth, 48 years ago. Nobody could have orchestrated either the timing or the location of that incredible meeting. Yet the living God was declaring not just to me, but for all of us who are willing to journey beyond the well-worn paths, that our destiny is indeed calling; one that can shake whole nations and call forth the true purposes of God across Europe.

There is one other aspect to the sign that this meeting at my birth place signalled. Not only was it 40 days from the start of the walk to the Tower of London, it was also 70 days exactly from the tragic death of Sue Scott on 14 February (70 being the number universally recognised as that belonging to one generation). Sue was married to Martin, a good friend of mine and a man who has inspired many across the UK. I do not claim to understand this fully and I speak carefully and cautiously of such tender times. What I do know is that everything about Sue's life stood for the generations that are yet to rise. That is where she invested her time and where her hope truly lay. I also know that in some of the most intimate details of the battle for her life, the contesting that was there was not just about the life of Sue but also, and as she would want it, for the life and the freedom of those yet to come. Nothing else mattered more to her. Maybe her God was marking out through that 70 day period the generation that is rising who, as with the lepers of Samaria, are truly free to walk into their destiny because they have lost all fear of death. Ignored and overlooked by many, true lepers outside the gates, laying hold of the twilight moment and embracing the incredible promise of the future that befits those who are called people of The Way.

So the Lord marks out our paths, from one holy altar to another; from 14 February and the death of Sue, to 16 March, the birthday of my adopted daughter, Chun Zhen, and the start of the walk to the Tower. From 25 April and that remarkable sign-post of destiny that was the home of John and Yvonne Presdee, through to 21 December, our planned arrival date in Rome. As we walk through the place of death so we gain entrance to the place of our destiny. How awesome is our God?

Our next big marker is Marseille. As we walk into this ancient slave port over the coming days, our focus will be the sin of Europe rather than that of Islam or anyone else. We will be seeking to own our sin, praying that the legacy of imperialism that runs through so much of Europe's relationship with Africa will begin to find healing. We will take encouragement that, over these very days, there is an historic gathering taking place in Berlin, looking to address some of these issues with representatives of the followers of Jesus within both continents.

We will then head up the coast to Genoa, before turning south to Rome. There remains 1100 km left to walk, and just 21 walking days to complete what has been marked out. During this period, I will be away from home for three and half weeks out of four and a half. I would particularly appreciate prayer for all that this demands, particularly of Kath, my wife, as she, along with others in our household, manage the affairs of home.

At this point I also want to mention Sharon Cooke, from Preston, who has walked with me all the way from Whitby. She has been awesome throughout; strong in prayer and able to keep pace with the fastest or quite happily walk along with the slowest. Always looking out for the team, she is undoubtedly one of those rising to go with the wild wind of the Spirit.

Once again, huge thanks for all those journeying with us. I am praying for us all that sight will come and ground breaking faith will be released in the remaining weeks of this window of grace that we are walking through. We start walking on Monday 21 November.

REFLECTIONS FROM HOME

This was a hugely emotional part of the walk as we began to see the full measure of how we were being positioned. My gratitude to Kathy during this time knew no bounds for her willingness to give space for such crazy adventures. Yet I also knew she drew strength from knowing that the life of our own household was so completely caught up in the wonderful paths that were being woven as we walked down through the beauty of Southern France.

This was also a momentous part of the walk for very personal reasons, receiving as I did a phone call from my eldest daughter Hannah, telling me of her engagement to Chris. Hannah has always been a sign to us of the workings of the heavens in our lives. She came back to a place of faith in 2002, the year the prophets were speaking of reversal, for 2002 reads the same forwards as it does backwards. It does not take much to realise that her name "Hannah" also reads the same way backwards or forwards. I found myself wondering what else was in store for us, and for Hannah and her husband to be. What might be marked out through her marriage and what would He have to say to us through that? Little did I realise that I would be walking through the awesome high pastures of Southern Italy and the mountainous beauty of Western Greece, pondering those same questions some eight months later, with Rome far behind me and fresh challenges pressing in.

For now however, there was simply delight that Hannah was finding such happiness. God is very good.

MARSEILLE, November 2005
Team: Hannah, Chris, John, Sharon and myself.

The three days walking into Marseille were challenging, to say the least. Carrying injuries and contending with both snow and rain, it was good to arrive at this gateway port with such strong African connections. Prior to walking in, we prayed together on the outskirts of the city. As we looked at the ground, there on the floor was a ring lying in the mud, speaking so clearly of sonship, for undoubtedly there are huge issues of sonship over the orphaned continents of Europe and Africa. To be reminded of our inheritance as followers of Jesus was good indeed.

To have lingered longer in Marseille would have been wonderful. However, the kilometres stretched out before us in a seemingly never diminishing way. Coming as far south as Marseille had added considerable distance to our journey. We now had to head up the coastline as quickly as we were able, through to the French Riviera and all the wealth of that area.

CHAPTER 9

Marseille:
The Ring of Identity

Steve Lowton

This is a story that seeks to bring alive the wonder of the gateway city of Marseille. Standing there, it didn't take long to begin to imagine all those who have passed through its harbour entrance and some of the hopes and dreams they carried.

Should you wish to tell the story of Marseille then there are many who in such a dark and mysterious place would wish to rise to the task. However, should their trade be any other than that of the Harbour Master then they would be ill equipped to do justice to such an expansive tale. When browsing through the log books that have kept detailed records of every passage in and out of the deep water harbour cut into this rugged coastline, the imagination is easily stirred by many an adventurer in pursuit of new horizons and fresh opportunities.

Of course the earliest records dating back to the times of the Romans have not survived. Long before museum curators could get their hands on such priceless items they have faded and withered under the assault of the elements. Encrusted in salt, the gnarled pages have disintegrated to keep their secretive tales locked firmly away. We need not fear however, for in the tradition of seafaring folk the tales of long forgotten days have always been trusted to safer custodians than that of simply parchment and quill. It is up and down the twisted alleyways of the harbour area that these men of the sea have gathered to tell their stories and pick over the lives of those who have come to look for safe passage within the sheltered coves of Marseilles.

Admittedly if we were to venture down some of these dark alleys today the talk will be of far less savoury subjects; of gun running, drug dealing and the appalling trading in lives that every sea port is blighted by, with tales of human misery and depravity to make even the most stout hearted wretch with disgust at the failings of mankind. To look for more noble tales is at best to invite ridicule and at worst to draw a knife to the belly, for sadly Marseille's reputation for rebellion and skulduggery has travelled far and wide. No doubt the thousands of slave ships that found anchorage here have stirred this dreadful pot of wretchedness and murderous intent. It has always been the task of many a King therefore, in the comfort of Versailles several hundred kilometres to the north, to keep a wary eye of Marseille, for trouble often simmers deep beneath the surface.

Some would no doubt want to tell the tale of the 500 men who set off to Paris to take their place in the bloody rebellion that was fermenting on the streets of that city. With precious little understanding of such words as liberty, fraternity and equality they nevertheless knew the taste of the twisted anger within their own hearts and the deep pain of injustice that had to find a route to the surface. Others would no doubt recall the momentous days of the legions of Rome as they used this southern port as their beachhead for the successive campaigns against the wild men of the north. Such tales sound grand in their delivery, but little space is given for the carnage and blood letting that lurks beneath the romanticism mighty armies conjure up.

However, if we persevere then there are those willing to dig deep into the more noble aspects of story telling and indeed the more noble aspects of this city, for to sit down with the harbour master is to drink at the well of mankind; to know for sure that for every dark deed of the night there are other deeds that bring strength to the weary. It is also to discover that deep within the bowels of this city lay the secrets of safe passage. Many have come with noble intentions, only to fall at the threshold of this point of entry. It is as if the demons that lurk in the tide of human detritus that surround these ancient gates are too strong for the human heart to overcome.

One such person was a noble man called Wilfred. Returning from a life shaping time in Rome, along with his mentor and friend the Bishop of Lyon he may well have lingered in this port too long. For somehow on his journey north the noble aspirations he held as to the fate of the embryonic church in his homeland became tainted. Maybe the seduction of Rome could have been left behind as he stepped off the boat and headed north. Somehow however, this was not to be, and the humble convictions of an honest man began to take on a different flavour. Could it be that the pathway was already tainted, indelibly marked by the self important footsteps of the newly crowned Emperor Constantine, as he journeyed this way three centuries earlier? Possibly it was the influence of the Bishop Augustine whom he had met in Rome some months before. Soon to be the Bishop of Canterbury, was it the tale of land and power that slowly eroded the simple ways of his Celtic heritage? Whatever the reason the gates of Massalia, for that was how Marseille was known, provided no opportunity for safe passage in his journey back home to the north, and eventually Whitby.

So what of these secrets therefore, which even poor Wilfred could not avail himself of? If the demons that lurk are too strong for the Bishops and Emperors that have passed this way then what hope for the simple man, as indeed Wilfred discovered? What is the secret of safe passage that enables the heart of a man to walk freely through such places of entry, coming out the other side with integrity unscathed and conscience intact?

Sadly, the Harbour Master cannot answer such questions. He can only point us to those who have passed through these gates to continue to walk freely. In the telling of the tale therefore, it is for the reader to draw their own conclusions.

So make space for yourself round the table; shut your ears to the noise of the ships' siren and the grand gestures of Gallic conversation, and let your imagination take you back in time. If you are nervous at the thought of down town Marseille then keep your back to the wall, but let your sight soar as you touch what can be possible for us all in the journey of life.

Our tale begins with an ancient legend surrounding a brother and sister from Palestine, two people amongst the many refugees who at some point in history have found their lives washed up on the shores of Marseille.

Fleeing the persecution that quickly followed the resurrection of their Lord they ventured across the seas, casting their cares upon the wind and the waves. What few belongings they carried were wrapped tightly in the small bag that hung loosely over the man's shoulder, a strange assortment of possessions indeed, including a small bottle of anointing oil, a piece of a white burial shroud, and a ring. Quite obviously to anyone honoured enough to look upon these few treasured possessions, the piece of cloth and the oil were self explanatory. The ring however remained a mystery. Some say it was a ring given to the woman by a former lover, others a ring passed down from her own Mother. Another explanation, and by far the favoured one, was that it was a token of love and friendship from the Master himself.

Whatever its source, nobody could deny that strange powers seemed to accompany whoever was honoured enough to wear this most special of rings. It was almost as if in the wearing an overwhelming sense of belonging and well being rested upon the fortunate soul. All doubt lifted as to the normal issues that surrounded such transient places as Marseille. Questions that drew the weary traveller into unhealthy speculation about what had been left behind in some far off land, or what might be in store beyond the safety of those city walls seemed somehow to matter no more. Instead, the wearer seemed to carry a gentle peace and contentment that belied all the unknowns that accompany those whose future no longer rested in their own hands. Some called this ring the ring of sonship, but the harbour master did not understand that language and quickly moved on.

The legend goes that whoever is in possession of the ring is therefore in possession of safe travel. Somehow in the wearing of the ring is all the endorsement that is needed. No other credentials are required, not even letters of endorsement from the rich and powerful, for apparently the ring is endorsement enough. It is said that the wearer journeys without any need to prove himself; through conquest, violence, cleverness of speech or even natural powers of charm. Rather the knowledge of the strange Master from Palestine seems to be the only currency required; the understanding of what it means to truly belong. It is those who can then be trusted to pass through the gates of Marseilles safely, free from pursuit by demons of greed and self doubt, for somewhat surprisingly these demons are often found together.

That the ring was lost without trace is undoubtedly true, as deep in the catacombs that still mark the cliff face of Marseille, it was uncovered many centuries later. Its rediscovery owes much to old-fashioned luck when, in the late seventeenth, century a slave ship floundered at the harbour entrance. Amidst frightening storms many slaves perished but some found their way to the shore-line, taking temporary refuge in the ancient catacombs. As the dreadful sea came alive to the huge shafts of lightening so our fortunate soul found his way deep into the recesses of those caves. Falling into an exhausted sleep he woke to rays of sunlight cascading through the narrow entrance. Outside he could hear the search dogs barking and he knew his moments of freedom were short, but as he stretched out so the glint of the ring caught his eye. Claiming it as a sign of good fortune he wrapped it tight into his clothing and waited for the dogs to find him.

He acknowledges in time to come that his first thought was that maybe this could buy him his freedom and passage back to the Kingdom of Khasso. As the years rolled by however he became strangely attached to this ring. Somehow, the knowledge of it hidden deeply beneath the earthen floor of his wooden hut kept him strong through the most dreaded of days; times when his Master flew into terrifying fits of temper and he feared for his life. When the longings for home and for all that had been taken from him were too strong, so he would take the ring from its hiding place and hold it tight, almost as if he was trying to draw on some unfathomable presence.

Jacob, as was his name, not only survived but began to prosper, even in this new life of slavery. The dreadful longings of his aching heart were quietened. Never would he accept the appalling injustice of his situation, but neither would he be destroyed by his own grief or anger. An unusual peace kept him, even as he saw his children and grandchildren born into slavery also. Through the dreadful plague of 1720 his heart was stilled, the knowledge of the ring enlarged now by a knowledge of its former owner; a true Master, the storyteller, someone who could really be trusted.

The ring stayed hidden for many years for with Jacob's death so the secret of the ring went to the grave also. During that time thousands of Italians, Russians and Greeks made their way through this melting pot of humanity that Marseille remains. Many more were to follow from Algeria and North Africa, but at the time we rejoin the story early just after the World War I it is an Armenian family that picks up our tale. Heralding from Ismir on the western seaboard of Turkey they came with stories too horrendous even for down town Marseille. Tales of slaughter and the haunting cries of thousands of Greeks and Armenians, driven out to sea and left to drown in a slow spiral of exhaustion. For the Abassian family they were more fortuitous and, with the help of their kindly Turkish neighbours made good their escape before the slaughter began. Passing through the port of Piraeus they continued westward, spending what savings they had on the hope of what lay beyond.

That they found themselves washed up upon the shores of Marseille owes much to the Armenians natural trading instinct that has caused them to prosper wherever the course of their lives take them. So it was that, as their two children played in the patch of dirt outside the Alm House where they first found refuge, the ring came into their possession. Ardak, through his trade as a silversmith, knew instinctively the Middle Eastern origins of the ring. However beyond that they knew nothing, except that with its discovery so the dreadful nightmares that haunted the eldest daughter Marta began to ease until such a time when an incredible peace seemed to come upon her. Grateful for the change of fortune for their first born so they kept the ring and like Jacob before them, turned away from the temptation to make a quick profit, preferring instead to use it night after night to fire the imagination of the two children, with stories of their homeland and those lands of the Middle East that now seemed so far off.

Again the ring fell back into the soil of Marseille. Ardak cannot remember when this was, but through the dreadful days of the World War II and the Nazi occupation, so it lay hidden in the mud and grime of life. As whole populations migrated across Europe so the secrets of safe passage seemed lost to a generation. Orphaned nations gradually surfaced once more. The quest to belong seemed stronger than ever and with no one to wear the ring so suspicion and fear fuelled the tensions that always befall those who fear what might be to come.

Our tale of mixed fortune, continued the Harbour Master, may well have ended here save for the passing by of one small band of travellers, cold and wet from the days journey and foot-sore from many long hours on the road. Wisely choosing to pause and pray before entering such a place as Marseille, so the eyes of one of the travellers fell upon the ring, lying in the wet mud of the roadside. Having discovered through many misadventures the snares and dangers of entering such cities, they had learnt through bitter experience the need to heed such moments. Gathering the ring into their tight circle they spoke to their Master once again. They prayed that once more there would be those whose names are known, who would find grace to wear the ring of sonship again.

Placing the ring back on the ground they continued on their way.

The Harbour Master let the final words linger long as those gathered round the table took a deep breath, wondering no doubt as to the whereabouts of this most sacred of symbols and quite possibly the journeys of life that lay before each of them. Then with what seemed to be a genuine gesture of gratitude each one of the guests slipped quietly out into the November fog that had by now descended on the city. The Harbour Master was left alone at the table. To someone watching, the normal calmness of such a man seemed slightly disturbed, as carefully he searched through each of his pockets. Then, he too, with a deep sigh, also headed out into the night.

FACT FILE: MARSEILLE

According to provencal tradition Mary Magdalene evangelised Marseille with her brother Lazarus. There are also early records of the martyr of Christians during roman times. There are catacombs above the harbour.

(www.wikipedia.org, accessed February 2008)

Because of its pre-eminence as a Mediterranean port, Marseille has always been one of the main points of entry into France. This has attracted many immigrants and made Marseille into a unique cosmopolitan melting pot. By the end of the eighteenth century about half the population originated from elsewhere. The main group of immigrants came from Italy (mainly from Genoa and Piedmont), as well as from Spain, Greece and North Africa.

(www.wikipedia.org, accessed February 2008)

From the 1950s onward, the city served as an entrance port for over a million immigrants to France, many of whom came in 1962 from Algeria. Many immigrants have stayed and given the city a vibrant French-African quarter with a large market.

(www.wikipedia.org, accessed February 2008)

Marseille is currently the second largest city in France, with a population of 1.6m people. It is also France's largest commercial port.

CHAPTER 10

Marseille to Genoa

Steve Lowton

**Team: same as those who walked into Marseille –
Hannah, Chris, John, Sharon and myself.**

REFLECTIONS FROM HOME

Climbing out of Marseille was one of those magical moments in the walk as Chris and I pressed strongly forward. The sky was clear and the frost deep and sharp as we drove ourselves hard for the first four hours of the day. Only stopping for the inevitable coffee and croissants to demonstrate that not every minute was sweat and toil, we delighted in the knowledge of beating the dawn and being able to push our road hardened bodies. There is an incredible synergy that can be found between mind, body and soul that prayer walking encapsulates. Pushing ourselves up the steep inclines that took us back onto the hills drew the life of God through us and prayer flowed. I have seen this so many times with those who, because we might not be gifted orators, think that we cannot pray. Discovering a physical dimension to prayer does away with such nonsense, even as those early Celts stood in the waves for hours at a time to find a new way of connecting with the Lord of all creation.

I am also aware that for too long prayer has been left to women, as men have absented themselves from what can appear to the average male the effeminate ways of so much that calls itself church. This was exactly the opposite: two men out on the road together, finding companionship and purpose before the wonder of those frosty hills of southern France. Jesus is not my boyfriend. Neither, I hasten, to add was Chris!

MARSEILLE TO CANNES
November 2005
Same team: Hannah, Chris, John,
Sharon and myself.

Taking increasing notice of the luxurious surroundings and the opulence of one of the wealthiest areas of Europe, if not the world, we journeyed on into one of the most beautiful parts of the walk. What better place to pray into the issues of wealth and greed that have locked up so much through the annals of history. We knew this would now be our agenda as we walked north up the coast towards Genoa. As many have sown their own finances in order to be able to join us as we walk, so we have called with great fervour for a massive release of finance from the centre to the margins.

Tomorrow one team goes home and another joins us. We will then press on into Northern Italy. Each and every team has brought something unique to the walk. This time it was the turn of my family. Walking with my brother John, my daughter Hannah and her fiancé

Chris was wonderful, especially for this section. Understanding the belonging released by a discovery of Jesus is common to us all; it is a good testimony to declare when our own thought patterns would say the opposite.

Leaving France will be an emotional moment. This is without doubt one of the most beautiful countries in Europe. Something in the land has routed firmly into me and I am the stronger for it. It has also been the first country where I have consistently encountered angels. This was especially so as we approached Marseille. Something I am sure had been released in Berlin, and we were riding on the back of that.

Massive thanks again for everyone who is standing with us. We daily know the covering of your prayers.

CANNES TO GENOA
Team: Sally Ann, Sharon, Justin and myself

We started this week on the shores of Cannes, looking up to the incredible splendour of the snow-capped Alps dipping behind the city of Nice and overshadowing the Principality of Monaco. If we want to live by picture postcards then this is it. Yet even the splendour of such locations is shallow without the purposes of the one to whom we have tied our lives. To be here and also yoked to his purposes was wonderful indeed.

This week was always going to be one of testing and transition; we crossed through three countries; walking out of France, we passed through the Principality of Monaco and into Italy. It was also a week that would determine whether we would discover the grace to keep to the scheduled arrival date in Rome of 21 December.

Every team that has walked with us since leaving Whitby have all testified to the incredible intensity of each and every day. I have heard it said many times that we seem to live a month in each week, such is the variety of experiences and emotions encountered. However, one moment in particular will remain with me for a long time. This was as we entered the Principality of Monaco. This is a tax haven for those who need it least; the playground of the very rich, and a place where opulence abounds. If you have been following these reports you will also know of Sharon, the young woman who has walked with me all the way from Whitby. She is someone of very few possessions, but very many friends; something I know so many of us can learn much from. Ye,t of those few possessions perhaps her CD collection is that which she values most highly, encapsulating for her a whole library of memories and emotions, artistic delight and creative expression. To witness her leaving this prized collection at the entrance to this city was awesome to behold, letting her prophetic action declare that "what does it profit a man if he gains the whole world but loses his own soul". I walked through in stunned silence, knowing that there was little my own words could add to such a declaration.

A further 150 kilometres up the coast lies Genoa. Genoa is an Aladdin's cave for historians, dominating Mediterranean history for many centuries. Flying the cross of St. George, its past weaves a web of intrigue between church, state and finance. In the year 2000 it hosted the G8 Summit, and as a place of incredible legislative grace, many global trade agreements have been founded under its grace. A gateway city of huge significance it was undoubtedly a major marker in our walk to Rome. Indeed, as the city behind the establishment of the jewels of the French Riviera, Marseille and Monaco, it made sense of the many kilometres that had been walked as we made our way up the coastline through these places into Genoa. A place of secret societies and unholy alliances we always knew that there would be challenge as we walked through.

Entering Genoa was the part of the walk where I hit the wall. Amongst so many wonderful moments, the toll of one too many early morning sessions out on the road was very real. The urgency of this six month window that we are in has demanded of us a rigorous schedule, as we have walked most of the length of England and the whole of the length of France. It was so good to know that all through this walk it has been the wonderful diversity of the teams that has brought the grace to fully press in. For the entry into Genoa, therefore, I rested whilst two other members of the team walked through the rain into this pivotal city.

As has been said many times, it is impossible to measure prayer, for it is such a hidden realm. What I do know is that on three occasions during this forty week season of walking we are in, immediately following a period of intense, sustained intercession there has been a spectacular disturbance in the weather patterns in the immediate locality of where we have been praying. On each occasion this was of such a size as to make the national news and bring whole areas to a standstill. The first was as we walked into York during the month of June on our way to Edinburgh, North Yorkshire being hit by serious and totally unpredictable flooding. The second was as we walked into London on our way to Rome during late August. Once more large parts of the city were brought to a spectacular standstill. The last occasion has been in the Bay of Genoa, as huge storms this very day have hit all along the coastline from Nice through to La Spezia, the point which we are currently 35km short of.

I am not sure of the full meaning of these disturbances. What I do know is that there is a groan of creation that has to be heard; that we, as the sons of God, are here to intercede at this point of connection between heaven and earth, lifting these inarticulate sounds to the Father. What I also know is that there was no loss of life, for if we are willing to lose our lives for Jesus' sake, refusing the lure of self-preservation, then we have authority to pray in such a way that the groans of creation are heard without the evil one coming to rob, kill and destroy.

I am now back home for just seven days before we get back to the walk on Monday 12, this time going all the way through to Rome. Huge thanks again for all those standing with us. On two occasions since I started walking I have carried injuries that to all intent and purpose should have stopped me from continuing. Grace has been found, though, and I have been able to continue. Yet carrying a walk is not our target, though prophetic action is always better when completed! The coming up of the ways of imperialism is our aim, first within us as church and then within the nations of Europe. So we walk to Rome, calling for a new apostolic grace into Europe and beyond.

REFLECTIONS FROM HOME

Genoa and the coastline of Northern Italy is an awesome place to be, as the Alps plunge down into the turquoise blue of the Mediterranean Sea. Here all the creativity of man lends itself to the incredible forces of nature as tiny villages and towns cling to the rugged coastline. Tucked in between the twisted folds of the snow capped foothills of the Alps, the intricate vineyards and terraces weave their magical path across impossible gradients; man and nature combining in a wonderful display of harmony.

Yet for me creativity has for too long been a word reserved for others, like my second eldest daughter Laura, now studying for an acting degree. I was full of admiration for those so gifted in life, able to project themselves on stage and perform in front of the most critical of audiences. What courage; what freedom! Or take Stew, my household companion as he was then, able to hold others spell bound by his incredible improvisation on the guitar and his tongue-bending lyrics. Yet here I was, the kid who used to stuff his art work behind the back of cupboards for fear of ridicule and mockery, walking the breadth of Europe; and, while I was doing so, knowing the steady hand of the maker of creation as he used the parchment paper of my life and the lives of those I love to weave a fresh storyline into the history of Europe. Could this really be so? Is there a point where we can so blend with the landscape that we become almost like these little hamlets clinging onto the sides of the alpine pastures; woven into the fabric of the land, our destiny wrapped up with the very groans of creation itself?

Never had I felt more alive.

CHAPTER 11

Genoa (Genova): Trade and Tragedy

Justin Thomas

Justin is in his early thirties, lives in Leeds and works for the Metropolitan University. An aging rap artist he describes himself as a lover of good food and fine wines. A key member of the team that walked through Genoa, this is a story that brings alive the city that taught the world how to trade.

Four dead sailors: almost a tenth of the crew lost, on what should have been a routine voyage. Tunis was hardly the end of the world. Vincenzo mulled over the report from his captain as he oversaw his remaining sailors unloading the journey's cargo of spices, textiles and carpets.

Two dead from sickness, one murdered over a gambling debt, the fourth killed in punishment for the murder. Only the loss of the third mate to pneumonia he counted worthy of real note. Sailors could be easily replaced. A good mate was a precious find.

The cathedral bell tolled three. Vincenzo, satisfied

that his cargo had arrived in good condition, left the remainder of the accounting to his captain and his clerk. He chuckled to himself at their inevitable exchange. His man of adventure turned the full force of his sea-worn wit against the dry, unflappable demeanour of his man of numbers. The captain's eagerness to complete a stock-take before a well-earned rest at a local hostelry never quite managed to overwhelm his desire to score points at the clerk's expense. Perhaps it was the clerk's unequivocal refusal to exhibit any rise to the jibes that so enticed the captain's persistence and enjoyment. Yet the qualities of these two contrasting characters were the foundation of his family's, nay even his city's, fortune.

Genova's success was unique in the annals of history. Every empire that had ever arisen had done so through military might. But whilst Genoese knights could hold their heads high, achieving great renown in the latest crusade, the city's influence was not founded upon conquest or battle. When Genova wished to expand she would simply begin to trade. Such was the acumen of their merchants that very soon the new city would feel it was thriving. Permission for a private harbour would follow, eased into being with bribes where necessary. From here would spring a separate walled city and facilities to build new ships. Over time, though so gradually as to be almost imperceptible, Genova's merchant families would be running the city and taxing it for the privilege.

Vincenzo's chest swelled with satisfaction that, despite the continuous and often violent in-fighting that took place between the great families, there was a common, fierce pride in Genova's financial empire. She now had colonies in all the great cities of northern Africa and the eastern Mediterranean. Tripoli, Tunis, Galata in Constantinople, Caffa, Chios, Corsica and Sardinia all benefited from Genova's reflected glory.

It was said that even proud England had come under the influence of San Giorgio. Some rumours said they had taken to flying his flag to procure his patronage, and with it safe passage to Genova's lucrative harbours. Others claimed that King Richard the First had been so impressed by the Genoese knights that he had called on San Giorgio to become patron saint of England too, adopting his cross as part of their livery.

Vincenzo set off towards his favourite café: the Griffin's Perch. His route cut from the old docks, through the Piazza Caricamento, and up one of the narrow streets that ran off from the Piazza's surrounding porticos. Short as the journey was, it was important he take time to greet the business partners, clients and rivals he met on the way. This seemingly innocuous round of pleasantries was fundamental to the success of his business dealings. A 'hello' here or encouraging word there smoothed the way for later negotiations. Furthermore, a question about family over a discreet handshake identified the shaker as being from the same brotherly society as the recipient. This pretty much guaranteed a favourable advantage next time terms were discussed or a bid was tendered.

Even gushing flattery, lavished on one's enemy, helped fuel the fires of future trade. No matter what went on behind closed doors everyone knew the public face of shining Genova must be maintained. Public duty and religious observance formed the crown that unified the empire. Even the fiercest of rivals understood this as the force that prevented it from descending into a chaos of warring family clans.

Reaching the café, Vincenzo was greeted by his long-term acquaintance and sometime rival, Amadeo. He was the eldest son of a once reputable and wealthy family, who had recently fallen on hard times. A careless marriage by Amadeo's younger brother had insulted a dynasty far more powerful than his own. Amadeo had foolishly given his blessing to the match without full awareness of the facts. A few discreet enquiries in any of the societies or with the senior clergy would have enlightened him to the intention of the family in question: to approach his now sister-in-law for one of their own sons.

The resultant embargo was only the beginning. Expulsion from his society followed, as did disdain from those he had previously counted as friends. Amadeo's fortunes plummeted as he lost rights to the more profitable shipping routes and accepted ever more risky ventures to make ends meet.

Under normal circumstances Vincenzo would not have considered this meeting for a moment. Dealing with a merchant so widely shunned represented a significant risk to his own reputation. These were not normal circumstances. Amadeo had a secret that Vincenzo had discovered via a tractable cook onboard one of his rival's ships. On a recent voyage to the west coast of Africa, one of Amadeo's captains had taken receipt of a hold full of slaves. On the return journey sickness ravaged both crew and cargo. When the ship finally limped into port barely a dozen sailors remained, with no cargo to speak of. Naturally, the tragedy was hushed up. Had it become common knowledge it would have been interpreted as a further sign that Amadeo's current misfortune was deserved and that he truly was under God's judgement for his neglect of the social order.

His companion was under the impression that the purpose of the day's appointment was to discuss the opening of a dangerous, but potentially lucrative new route to the far-most reach of the Crimea. However, it was Vincenzo's intention to use his knowledge to advance his own family's business interests.

At their zenith, Amadeo's family had purchased *Liguria's Pride*, one of the finest ships to call Genova's harbours home. Its size and speed were legendary. Three times it had successfully repelled the attacks of Barbary pirates. And it was this vessel that was the object of Vincenzo's ambition.

The merest hint of a smile was the only emotion his face betrayed as he nodded politely, but without committal, to Amadeo's plans and propositions. The animated salesman's pitch drew to a close. He felt hopeful eyes search his face for any hint of approval or affirmation, betraying all too easily the desperation that lay behind them. With inch-perfect calculation he coughed slightly to clear his throat, casually adjusted his posture and paused to take a sip of coffee. He replaced the cup with exaggerated care, all the while furrowing his brow so as to convey a deep sense of consideration for the matters at hand. When it looked as if Amadeo might actually burst, he spoke.

"My good friend, your proposals are well considered and of great interest to an ambitious merchant such as myself. I am flattered that you honour me above others in the sharing of such plans. However, I am concerned, brother - deeply concerned - for you and your family's predicament. Has not the venerable bishop decreed that you are under God's judgement? Surely a venture endowed with such risk would only serve to inflame His wrath? It would certainly be interpreted as prideful and rebellious in the face of His discipline.

"My friend, in response to such sickness of the soul I would be remiss not to counsel you to a more humble, redemptive path. In your situation I should search my heart and rid myself of any great masts of pride within me or my family. I would show a contrite heart, lest the Lord send further pestilence upon my holdings, in punishment of my iniquity."

As soon as he had uttered this last phrase Amadeo's face dropped, and he could not disguise his sharp intake of breath. He felt a sharp pain in his back, as though a knife of cold steel was being turned, and the sick feeling in his stomach near overwhelmed him.

"At what price?" was all he could bring himself to say, as the realisation of his situation turned swiftly to resignation. His lack-lustre bartering secured only a relative pittance in exchange for his family's most treasured possession. Vincenzo, barely able to restrain a smile, hastily put his seal to the banker's note which secured the transaction, all the while congratulating his companion on a shrewd deal. He gushed with promises of the redemption and restoration of fortune that would follow this sacrifice.

The two men shook hands and stood. Vincenzo paused to leave payment for their refreshments and to watch as Amadeo negotiated several beggars who had emerged from the many alcoves that lined the street. Such a merchant would normally show nothing but disdain for those whose lack of enterprise had sunk them so low. But Vincenzo was surprised to see fear flash across Amadeo's eyes. It was as if he truly seeing these beggars for the first time and realising his own fate might not be so far removed from theirs as he had always thought.

Vincenzo shrugged and strode along the street from the café, toward the portico surrounding the east side of the Piazza Caricamento. He felt satisfied with himself and his acquisition. His heart quickened with excitement at the victory for his family's reputation. As he emerged from the archway and turned to his right, the smile on his lips faded. He was suddenly grateful for the shelter provided by the portico.

What had been, not ten minutes since, a beautiful sky of deepest azure was fast being obscured by billowing grey. A curtain of cloud was drawn west to east across the city and not three mooring rope lengths away he could see rain approaching like a sheet. Confusion bristled in his mind. He had seen rain such as this sweeping across the deserts of North Africa on trading expeditions to the great caravans, but never had he seen the like on his own shores - or anywhere else in Europe, for that matter.

He quickened his stride, hoping to clear the Piazza and reach his family's trade house before the rain met him head on. He dodged the hawkers and marketmen, who were rapidly stacking their goods under the tarpaulins that doubled as canopies for makeshift stalls. As he did so, he was acutely aware of San Giorgio watching over proceedings. From his central vantage point on the Palazzo, the usually magnificent patron of their city looked cowed by the forthcoming deluge. Victorious over the dragon he may be, but today he would be drenched with debt-slaves who were scurrying round the docks like ants, frantically stowing cargo under any nearby cover. Mates, captains and merchants yelled panicked instructions in at least a dozen languages.

Distracted by San Giorgio, Vincenzo failed to notice a crate of oranges that had been spilt in the rush. At the same instant he congratulated himself on a swift move to shelter his leg flew from under him, and he was ungraciously dumped on the cobbled Piazza. Both the spectacle of his tumble and subsequent yelp of pain were lost in the cacophony of activity. The breath knocked from him, it took several moments for him to gain a seated position, let alone consider standing.

Resigning himself to an inevitable soaking, his eyes fell on a strangely dressed pair walking across the Piazza toward where he was seated. Torrential rain seemed to land in their wake, yet never catch them. They had a look of serene and incredible peace. They gave the impression of being completely unaware of the mayhem that surrounded them.

By their beads and bangles he knew they weren't slaves. Their clothes betrayed roots in some corner of England, or perhaps one of its close neighbours. Merchant's instinct told him that these were not travellers of enough wealth or means to be worthy of any interest. Yet, instead of attempting to regain his feet and rush to the dry comfort of the nearby house, all his attention was focussed on this odd pair.

He was confused that the rain so mimicked their path, yet not once had it intruded upon their contemplations. He riled at the injustice of a man such as himself being forced to face this deluge, whilst this pair was spared. Who were they? No-one! So why should be humbled in this, his own city? How dare the tempest show more respect to them than to him! How dare they walk past, indifferent to his impending humiliation! Did they not know who he was? Did they not know that this was the day of his triumph? This was *his* moment, *his* hour. They should notice him and be impressed, not pass by calm and untouched by the outrageous unfairness of his situation.

Anger coursed through him at the scandal. This cruelty would see him humbled in plain sight of hawkers, sailors and slaves. The herald's bugle should be welcoming him home, victorious and with honour. Yet instead he would creep home muddy and wet, a rat swimming ashore from a sinking vessel. Fury gripped him and with it the urge to scream at them, all of them, to make them see, to make them realise, to grab them, shake them, beat it into them if he had to. They must know. They must understand. They must acknowledge who he is.

He glared as the travellers stepped out of sight. Awareness of his surroundings snapped back to the forefront of his mind. The anger dissipated, leaving barely a ripple. It was as if a great wave had been careering violently through his consciousness and, just as it was about to break and ravage the shore, simply ceased to be. His fists were clenched and his teeth gritted. Bombarding rain trapped him. His robes were sodden. Finally, as if recollecting an ancient conversation, it dawned on him that he should be making for the shelter that stood not one hundred yards hence.

Announcing news of his triumph to his family did not ease his turmoil. That night, sleep escaped him. What should have been the restful slumber of victory was fitful and broken. The thunderstorm that raged outside jolted images from the day into his consciousness: the dead sailors from his ship; his tumble in the Piazza; the look of terror on Amadeo's face as he encountered the beggars; and the strange travellers who walked ahead of the rain.

His mind returned to it again and again and with every rehearsal of the scene another emotion seemed to spring up: anger, fear, questioning and longing. Longing? Where did that come from? What on earth could he want of *them*?

His train of thought was interrupted by a clap of thunder so loud it dislodged flakes of plaster from the ceiling. The lightening struck so close that even his wooden shutters failed to keep out the intensity of its glare. Moments later cries and shouts went up in the distance. Fully awake he listened, trying to ascertain where they were coming, but the pounding of the rain obscured any sense of direction or distance. A full five minutes he sat and listened, pondering what possible misfortune might have hit his city.

A feeling of unease provoked him out of his bed and he had begun to dress even before the servant knocked tentatively on his door. Even a cursory glance at his servant's expression informed him, in no uncertain terms, that the news was not good.

"*Liguria's Pride*... Lightening... Gone..." stuttered the servant, clearly terrified by the reaction this report might evoke from his master. With a loud cry, Vincenzo pushed past his servant and ran downstairs, pulling on his boots as he fled out of the door in the direction of the docks. Nausea grew stronger and stronger as he sprinted towards the pier at which his prize had been moored.

Even with the rain the flames reached nearly thirty feet in the air. The smell of damp smoke stung his nostrils. The vessel which was supposed to be the pride of his family's fleet looked like the funeral pyre of some northern warrior, burned in obedience to his strange, warlike god. As he drew closer he saw blackened faces and charred clothes that spoke of a courageous but futile attempt to fight the flames. As he slowed to survey the wreck, those stood by the dock flinched away from his gaze. A mix of sympathy and fear filled their eyes. How had Vincenzo so offended the good Lord that His judgement had visited him in such a way?

Vincenzo dismissed all present, muttering faint words of thanks and praise for their courage, and slumped down on the dock, despair gaping at him as if from a foul-smelling maw. Sniffing at him like carrion, it threatened to swallow him up. The unshakable pillars underpinning his family's fortune and reputation suddenly felt as though they were made of paper and might buckle at any moment.

He knew what he must do. This was not the time to crumble and risk being destroyed by the vultures that circled this city, waiting to strike at the merest hint of weakness. Tomorrow was Sunday. He would rise early and ensure that he was immaculately turned out for mass. He would appear disappointed but unshaken and speak wistfully of the ways of God being deeper than those of men. When it came to the collection he would give generously (but not too generously) and, though seeming discreet, would ensure that others would be able to mark well his offering.

Appearance must be maintained at any cost, if all was to be well.

FACT FILE: GENOA

The Black Death was imported into Europe in 1349 from the Genoese trading post at Caffa (Theodosia) in Crimea, on the Black Sea.
(www.wikipedia.org, accessed February 2008)

Christopher Columbus, a native of Genoa, donated one-tenth of his income from the discovery of the Americas to the Bank of San Giorgio in Genoa for the relief of taxation on foods.
(www.wikipedia.org, accessed February 2008)

Genoa's initial commercial empire stretched to the Western end of the Silk Road and came to spread across most of Europe. Genoese merchants could be seen in Byzantium, in Syria and in Africa, in London, and across to China and the New World, always seeking a business opportunity. Their regular sea routes stretched from the Black Sea to the North Sea, from Caffa and Cyprus to Bruges and Antwerp.
(www.grimaldi.org, accessed February 2008)

Genoa was a leader in the rise of capitalism, slavery, and colonization in the Middle Ages, international public finance in the sixteenth century, poor relief in the seventeenth century, and republicanism in the nineteenth century.
S. A. Epstein (2001) Genoa and the Genoese, 958-1528 University of North Carolina Press

Slave commerce during the Late Middle Ages was mainly in the hands of Venetian and Genoese merchants and cartels, who were involved in the slave trade with the Golden Horde. Genoese merchants organized the slave trade from the Crimea to Mamluk Egypt.

(www.wikipedia.org, accessed February 2008)

In 1156, in Genoa, occurred the earliest known foreign exchange contract. Two brothers borrowed 115 Genoese pounds and agreed to reimburse the bank's agents in Constantinople the sum of 460 bezants one month after their arrival in that city.

(www.wikipedia.org, accessed February 2008)

CHAPTER 12

Genoa to Rome

Steve Lowton

TUSCANY, Mid-December 2005
Team: Sharon, Chris M, Steve W, Paul, Annie,
Val, Gemma, Sheila and myself

There are moments on a prayer walk when, amidst the cut and thrust of life together in the team, it is good to get out on the road by yourself to connect afresh with the Lord. I was able to do this during the afternoon as we journeyed down through the wooded hills of Tuscany. With the winter sunshine on my face it was great to enjoy the freedom that comes from an empty road. Meandering between the olive groves and the freshly painted houses I reflected on all those who have encouraged me over the years and stirred in me the sense of adventure I now live with; these truly are the times for which we were born and a time for the church in Europe to rise into its destiny. To know fully the joy of being alive and yoked to the purposes of the Maker is without doubt one of the most wonderful feelings there can be. My heart was full as we concluded this day and returned to our hostel accommodation.

We are now 200km south of Genoa and 300km short of Rome. A reminder about the urgency of the times we are living in came when we arrived at the airport in Genoa just a few days ago. Coming out of the airport there stands a large digital clock. As we passed, one of the team noticed that it read 12:12[5]. So we arrived for the last leg of this journey to Rome on the 12th minute of the 12th hour on the 12th day of the 12th month of 2005, just a few days short of the 12th anniversary of that incredible outpouring of the Holy Spirit from Toronto in January 2004[6]. Strengthened in our declaration, we headed for Rome.

The keys of the Kingdom do not reside with St Peter, Rome, or anywhere else for that matter. They belong to the people of God and are there for us to herald the new levels of authority that all of us long to see. With Europe on hold, and Canada likewise, with no government at this time, so it is our time to rise to a new level of understanding and anointing, calling through new days and a new plumb-line for the continent of which we are a part.

On Saturday another nine team members join us for the final few days. On Tuesday we will be joined by John and Yvonne Pressdee. Across the three generations that we will represent, we will call through the new day that this forty-week season of walking has marked out for us. There is no where else I would rather be!

---

[5]Twelve is often the number in scripture that symbolises complete authority; for example, twelve disciples and the twelve tribes of Israel.

[6]In 1994 there was an astonishing and significant outpouring of the Holy Spirit in Toronto, Canada. Many believers across the western world have been impacted by its effects.

Thank you once again for standing with us. It means so much.

VITERBO, December 2005
Team: Chris S, Adam, Annie, Val, Chris M, Sharon, Steve W, Tim, Andy, Ro, Gemma, Sheila, Paul, Anthony, Clare, and myself.

There have been many wonderful moments of intercession since this forty week season of prayer walking began. From the purple moors of North Yorkshire to the plains of northern France it has been incredible to ride a wave of the presence of the one with a voice like the sound of rushing waters. Whether making our way down the Rhone Valley or coming out of Marseille, the openness of the heavens never ceases to amaze me. Walking this afternoon with eighteen others down of the hills of Tuscany was one such time. It is as if the heavens are full of the intercession that has risen from Toronto, Berlin and many other key places these last twelve years. Truly, these are awesome days.[7]

We are now in Viterbo, just 80km north of Rome. Inspired by some of the team members I have been reflecting on the Apostle Paul's journey as he returned to the city of his birth. No doubt he would have known that he was almost certainly walking towards his death. Quite possibly he was reflecting on his life and his birthright as one of the tribe of Benjamin. Perhaps he would have been

[7]Europe has been a focus for prayer for the five years since the millennium, with many believers around the world targeting the most godless continent on the globe. The prayer rising from Toronto, the Berlin Congress in this very month, and this walk itself are just three examples of that.

provoked by the head of the wolf on the flags of the different legions that lined the Apien Way, for Rome undoubtedly carries a devouring spirit that always emerges when governmental anointing is corrupted. Yet the tribe of Benjamin was also the one that sat between the shoulders of the Father; safe in His identity and covering, they were able to flow out of the place of government free from the need to rule for the sake of self-interest.

We are walking for a new governmental mantle to fall upon the church; one that releases and empowers, as Paul did for Timothy, and unlike that of Saul in the Old Testament - another Benjamite, who refused to give ground to the Davidic grace that was rising.

We will arrive in St Peters Square late on Tuesday afternoon. We will then give space for John and Yvonne Presdee to lead us in the breaking of bread, for we go in the spirit of the one who went as a sheep amongst wolves, like one led to the slaughter. We then return to St. Peters Square to make our declaration on Wednesday at midday during the shortest day of the year - the time of twilight and turning. We will be focused, determined and strong, for there is no fear between the shoulders of the Father.

Thank you again for those standing with us. Your prayer has been all around us.

REFLECTIONS FROM HOME

The memory of our two-day approach to Rome will stay with me for the rest of my life. I have no idea what observers made of us storming down the country roads, laughing and fooling about amidst genuinely heartfelt prayers. On one occasion there were about a dozen of us motoring down the road, strong in prayer and walking as fast as anyone is able to go. The heady mix of laughter and comradeship was so high that, in response to an invitation to the Lord from one of the team to come with us into Rome, another retorted that he would not be able to keep up, such was our speed!

At another other extreme I will never forget walking behind another member of our group as he wept his heart out for a situation back home, tears streaming down his face over his own inadequacy and inability to change things. Such moments are priceless.

On the last morning of our journey on the outskirts of Rome we gathered for our early morning coffee rush. There, in front of some astonished Italians, I found myself hitting an unparalleled stream of rhetoric and friendly abuse of all and sundry (something quite out of character, I hasten to add). The anticipation and excitement of the many months and miles that had gone before had reached fever pitch. The mood was light and anyone looking on would have realised that adventurers were passing through, with many a tale to keep the fire going late into the night.

I was glad that some days before this we had thought about the declaration we were to make the following day, for at this moment we were dizzy with anticipation. If it had been left to now, who knows what we might have said? The words were rich and Chris did a wonderful job of crafting it. Somehow it encapsulated the hopes and longings that had fuelled us all the way from Whitby.

DECLARATION FOR ST PETERS SQUARE

We declare, Lord, that we are impressed with You, Your Kingdom, Your Ways. We refuse to be impressed with

Empire, or impressed with Rome. We declare a breaking down of every throne which exalts itself against You, Lord, a putting down of the mighty, a raising up of the meek. We are looking for a throne founded on righteousness and Justice. We bring with us days of throne breaking. We have no Caesar but Christ!

To all you Roman ways, which arch across Europe, we prophesy your pulling back. We shut you down; we speak a breaking, a winding down and a rolling up of all your lines of control. We pull you back and out of these lands and bring to bear every step and syllable of prayer against your hold and dominion. We cancel every unclean decision made in Whitby and pull a new, heavenly legislation across our continent. We declare the Wild Wind and Ways of God shall come into your midst. We call for the rising that we look to the horizon for, the breaking of boxes and a Kingdom coming into European places. We call a greater Kingdom down!

Empires break and slave nations go free! To the people of God, we declare a day of liberty, of Jubilee, we declare days of the exodus, days of running free – we say pyramids and towers can stay unfinished; we go looking for our lands of promise! Because of the mandate of the great commission to go, we who have walked the other way say that 'temple, we will no longer serve you'; we go FROM Jerusalem to Judea and to the Ends of the Earth!

On the shortest day, we proclaim a shortening of Roman days and the lengthening of New ones. Into this twilight day of daylight turning, we rebuke fear, make a choice and pray for life. We call for and bless the days when hidden decisions find a grace far wider than imagined, and where lepers put armies to flight. We call for days of siege breaking in the midst of twilight, and the fleeing away of empires which have starved our places of sight, our places of vision. Flour and Barley for a Shekel in the gates of Samaria! Sight in the places of seeing. Empire, begin to ship out! No more! New days, new risings, new anointing, more-ancient ways, stronger words, deeper senses, further sight. We pull tomorrow in through the Spirit of Prophecy within us; we call the Testimony of Christ in. Caesar, your testimony is dismissed! Lord, breathe your words into Europe.

So we loose the sounds of the trumpet, the sounds of the New Year and of slaves going free. Let the sound of breaking thrones fill heaven's gates. We call earth and heaven's hosts to bear witness to a breaking on the shortest day. We bear witness to new days coming through, of exodus, of people walking another way, of old sieges lifting and ancient promises finding space in these lands. Let old prayers find days of answer, Lord. So we place again this window of Grace into Your hands. We hand you six months of seeking for scalpel, of declarations of sword and of agreements by prophets. We place them before you as these days close and call for change across this corner of creation. Complete what You have started. We give You Glory, Lord, every step and breath is yours, as ever. We love You.

Amen

ST PETERS SQUARE, 21 December 2005

I write this from an Internet Cafe just a few metres from the Vatican. This evening I, and the team who have walked with me, will return home. We will do so having found ourselves privileged to participate in an awesome moment that, if we are given grace, may be pivotal for many of us.

Having arrived in St Peters Square yesterday afternoon and concluded the walk, we returned to the Square today to pray into some foundational issues relating to Christendom and the spirit of Empire that has dominated the history of Europe and, sadly, the history of us as the church. We went with high expectations, knowing the incredible timescale that we had been tracking with. We also knew that in Edinburgh, York, and perhaps many other places across the globe, there were others joining with us in prayer as we spoke out the declaration that we had prepared. We came away two hours later in awe of the hand of the Almighty.

There is much that I could say at this point. However, all I want to refer to is that, at this appointed twilight time of turning, on the shortest day of the year, forty weeks to the day from when I first stumbled out of the door on the way to the Tower of London, and within a few days of the twelfth anniversary of Toronto, the living God called the highest of dignitaries to witness our repentance, prayer and declarations. With the Pope arriving in the Square at exactly the same time that we arrived, and leaving at the moment we began our declaration, it was as if both we and he were there by the invitation of the Maker himself. Into that context incredible grace was given to pray deeply into the foundations of Christendom, and also the city of Rome.

So a forty week season of walking comes to an end. Not everyone who reads these reports, or indeed all those who have walked, will fully understand that we have found ourselves tracking with. You may not agree with all that we have sought to work through. However, we have simply endeavoured to be faithful to what we have seen and to honour His word amongst us.

So, if I may be so self-indulgent, I conclude by saying a thank you that by no means will do justice to all those who have participated in this incredible season.

To Stew and Beci Thomas, as two people who share our home back in Leeds, I say a huge thank you. You carry well the grace upon your nation of Wales. Without you, Stew, I would never have set out for the Tower of London forty weeks ago. Without your covering in our home, Beci, I could never have left for Rome. It is a privilege to be discovering community together and I honour you both. Come on, Wales! Provoke, ignite and set the pace for us. We need you so much.

To Martin, Linda Harding and Chris Seaton I also say a massive thank you. Your encouragement and covering has released me to follow the finger of God. Without the three of you I would never have begun this journey. To John and Yvonne Presdee, thank you is not enough. For opening the door and encouraging me on, I will always be profoundly grateful. You are all an inspiration to me and I count it an honour to be a fellow journeyman with you.

To all those who have walked with me these last forty weeks and sowed financially into the walk, I say thank you. You have enriched my life massively through the laughter, tears, inspiration and depth of prayer that you have carried. Especially to Sharon, I say thank you. The nations of Europe can be walked and prayed. These are truly new days for us all.

To Sally Ann Dyer, Pippa Gardner, Sharon, Clare and other prayer warriors who have stood in the gap for

Kathy and me, again, thank you is not enough. I honour you all, and trust that I will be as faithful in prayer for you as you have been for our household.

Lastly to my wife Kathy, I say thank you. Thank you for releasing me to follow the finger of God, even when it costs you dearly. Thank you for being prepared to risk all in the wonder of the journey and thank you for welcoming me home at each and every point.

We wait now to see what the Maker of heaven and earth might do in response to our prayers. We have walked and we have sought to watch over your word, Lord. With great reverence and respect we say that our eyes are now on you. Come, perform your Word.

REFLECTIONS FROM HOME

The afternoon after our encounter with the Pope we made our way to a nearby restaurant, about thirty of us gathering to mark and celebrate the end of the walk. In-house jokes tumbled out, as any remaining secrets of the road were gleefully displayed for everyone to pick through and find great mirth over. There is no better way for friendships to deepen and new ones to be found than to be thrown into an adventure, with the script waiting to be written. I knew for myself that many friends had been made and the imagination fired by the wonder of all that we had walked through.

Yet there was some trepidation as the trip home beckoned. Would I be able to adjust again to so-called normal life? Was this it, the end of the adventure; or were there other horizons to pursue? It is a bizarre experience to walk across a nation and then to find yourself at the school gates with other parents, or to join the queue at the local supermarket, as if walking to Rome was the most normal thing in the world.

So I was all ears when the conversation began to turn to Jerusalem. After all, in journeying from Whitby to Rome we had been tackling seventeen centuries of Christendom, seeking to roll back the straight and pre-dictable paths of the Roman ways. Surely now the obvious step was to continue all the way back through the remaining three centuries, to the very land where Jesus walked and breathed?

Excitement began to stir afresh, even before we had left for the airport to return home; though that excite-ment was laced with fear as the troubles faced by the lands that encircle the most contested city in the world began to dawn on me. Could this be possible? Could we continue, or would I soon return to life within more normal boundaries? And how would Kathy and I survive financially if I was to stay on the road? Were the chal-lenges of this fair on her, or should I now take my place on the much-neglected career ladder that I had studiously ignored for so long?

I kept these thoughts to myself as we headed for the airport and returned to the comfort and familiarity of home, content in the knowledge that I had just experi-enced some of the most wonderful months that anyone could hope to enjoy. In the company of some great friends we had walked nearly three thousand kilometres, from the eastern margins of what was once the Roman Empire, right to its heart. The earth hadn't shaken and Europe was not ablaze with the sounds and sights of the Kingdom of God. However, we knew that a way had been opened up for a new movement to begin to rise in the lands of Europe; a movement marked by the unpredictability of those early Celts and their reckless abandonment to the pathways of faith. Now was the time to sit back and enjoy the wonder of what could unravel as a few, crazy people dared to believe that their small and insignificant lives could make a difference.

The words of Neo in the cult film The Matrix (1999) rang round my head as we made our way to the airport for our final flight home: "I didn't tell you how it's going to end. I came to tell you how it's going to begin. I'm going to show you a world without rules and controls; without boundaries and borders; a world where anything is possible. Where we go from here is a choice I leave to you."

CHAPTER 13

Rome: Mother, Soldier, Servant, Queen

Chris Meredith

Chris once more picks up the tale of the city we had held in focus for the many miles we walked through the heart of France and Northern Italy. In his early twenties, he is one of those rising at this time that carries the DNA of the early Celts.

The Mother

The imperial cityscape was being slowly polished by the dawn. Its marble buildings, content to throw off the subtle starlight, began bathing their colonnades in the morning's glare instead. The Tiber flowed quietly through the city, as it had done for hundreds of years, moving steadily from the Tuscan mountains to the Tyrrhenian Sea. Regal bridges straddled the banks, some as monuments to great military victories and some simply as testaments to Rome's expansion. Here and there the low water-level left a bank accessible underneath their arching stonework, exposed by water but hidden in the shadows. It was to one such bank a mother was now desperately attempting to return.

Crouching low, her heart pounded in her chest. Her nose was full of the smells of the city, but her eyes never left the far side of the river and the shadowy nook beneath the bridge. She couldn't afford to be seen now. Creeping into the city had been hard enough, but creeping out was proving torturous. For hours the hungry mother had worked the city's shadows, moving silently from one corner to another. Sneaking down alleys and behind street vendors, she would lift unwatched food from its place, or else rifle through heaps of waste in the hope of finding something nutritious. She had not been disappointed, but getting the full bag of food back to her little ones was proving a significant test.

Making a break for it, she bounded across the bridge. Reaching the far side she turned quickly and caught her breath before scrambling down the bank to her family's hiding place below. The incline was steep and wooded. All four of her limbs had to work furiously at getting her safely down, the bag gripped between her teeth. The descent was unglamorous, but swift.

They had been told not to venture from the cover of the bridge, even if they thought they heard her return, but she was surprised not to be met by six hungry faces nonetheless. Relieved, she found them waiting almost exactly where she had left them, though any sentimentality was swallowed up with the arrival of food, which provoked considerable excitement. They snarled and whined during its distribution, which was a short-lived, unceremonious affair. They soon seemed satisfied enough, and she beamed over them as they drank from the river. They huddled into one another, yawning at the warm morning, almost ready for sleep.

"We want a story," piped up the eldest who, though tired, was obviously resisting heavy eyelids. His exhausted mother grimaced, but the idea had taken root among his siblings and she knew there was little chance of escape.

"What about the one with the twins?" asked one.

"Yeah! *They* were sleeping near the river, weren't they Mum?" The eldest, excited that his suggestion was on the cusp of approval, looked hopefully up at her with a toothy grin.

His mother conceded, and they all lay down on their bellies, eyes wide with anticipation.

"You must always bear in mind that how people choose to *remember* their beginnings tells you more about them than the beginnings themselves; and there are many stories of the beginning of Rome. But the most famous tells of with war and vicious competition, pride and premature death.

"We start with Silvia, a scared young lady in the throws of labour. Silvia's uncle was the king. He stole the throne from her father, and then forbade Silvia from marrying, fearing that she would produce an heir to challenge his tenuous reign. But despite his orders Silvia became pregnant." She leaned in closer to the intent faces, dropping her voice to a whisper. "And though no-one knew who the father was, some say it was Mars, the god of war himself!" The younglings seemed suitably impressed by this revelation.

"Silvia gave birth to twins called Romulus and Remus, and if one believes the Roman storytellers they were unusually large and unusually beautiful. When

Silvia's uncle found out about them he ordered his servants to throw both them and their mother into the Tiber." Her young audience gasped, eyeing the lapping currents of the nearby water with sudden suspicion. "But, because of the beauty of the twins, the servant couldn't go through with it. Instead, he placed the babies on the flooded river in a basket, which carried them gently downstream, and eventually came to rest on a bank much like this one. There the twins were found... by a mother-wolf."

This was one of the most exciting parts of the story. Little mouths opened further and a couple of them shuffled with enthusiasm where they sat. "She took the twins up to the centremost of seven hills, where she suckled them as her own cubs." They erupted with disgust at this suggestion, sniggering and shouting in horror at the thought of humans drinking wolf milk.

"That's disgusting!" concluded one, sticking out her tongue and screwing up her face in disapproval.

"That's as maybe, but not everyone is as normal us are they?" her mother replied, licking her daughter's face.

"They became strong the milk of a mother-hunter, growing up with invincible courage and daring, until one day they were brought back to the hills on which they had been nurtured. There the twins began to argue about where to build their great city. Romulus wanted to build it around one hill; Remus around another. With the help of some eagles Romulus won the argument – exactly how is another story - and so Romulus began to build the first walls of Rome. But Remus, the weaker of the two, insulted Romulus, mocking his walls and leaping over his foundations, accusing them of being too shallow."

"So what did he do, what did he do!?" they chorused. They knew the story well, and strained in anticipation of the bloody ending.

"He did what all good wolves do when there is a challenge to leading the pack: he butchered his brother." Her lips twitched around her sharp hunter canines at the thought of the kill, her fur standing on end. "Yes, Romulus fought Remus until he lay dead in the dust. Romulus preserved his pride and protected the honour of his own vision. Rome was born. And Romulus put the image of the eagles that had helped him on his army's banners, and set men in wolf skins at the front of his legions in remembrance of the milk that made him great. And so the wolves of Rome hunted across the whole of the world."

The tale concluded, their mother hurriedly nudged and nuzzled her exhausted little pack together. She sat and watched their tails and ears cease their movements as each one slipped into sleep. She was an urban hunter, hungry, bloodthirsty, kind only to those prepared to suckle from her. The sounds of the day grew around them, soon obscuring the gentle noise of the Tiber lapping against the nearby banks.

The Soldier

After four minutes and seventeen seconds of resistance Calidius gave in to his overwhelming natural instincts, and blinked. It was longest he had managed all day, and he congratulated himself with a wry smile. The lonely sun beat down from the cloudless Mediterranean sky and his armour and helmet, far heavier now than at the start of his shift, were scorching to the touch. Daytime guard duty was sweltering, and the relatively unimportant government building for which he was acting as sentinel was a particularly boring station, prone to the worst of the afternoon heat in a notoriously uneventful part of the district. He shifted his weight slightly and did his best to ignore the bead of sweat that was nudged into a descent between his shoulder blades.

Though the street rarely bustled, it was almost never completely empty. There was usually somebody walking, running, or pompously promenading across the white square cobbles, which Calidius had now counted and recounted several times. The vast majority wore Senatorial togas, or at least the flowing garb of the landed merchant elite. Though, Calidius noted sadly, the two invariably seemed related these days. Sometimes a slave girl might hurry past, arms full of provisions for her mistress; or a retinue of Roman priests, plying their own agendas and expounding the will of the gods to the rank and file of politicians, who might be persuaded to add weight to one side or another of an impending debate. Calidius couldn't help but wonder what went on behind all these different eyes; how many footsteps had led them to this point, and where would they would go after passing to his left or right and disappearing round the next corner?

Twice a day a small squad of troops would march in tight formation past his post on their tour through the city. Their commander's scarlet cloak fluttered around him, his baton of rank held proudly, shields covering the soldiers from neck to thigh. Calidius longed to fall in behind them, even if just to stretch his legs. Perhaps it was the thought of their route, perhaps their door-like shields, or perhaps Calidius' longing to be back with

Legions in the field; but he suddenly found himself thinking about his childhood dreams of being a son of the empire, and serving in her army.

Like most of Rome's soldiers Calidius had followed his father into the ranks. As a boy, during his father's long stints away at war, he would often wander past the temple of Janus and wish he were with him. The temple, in the Forum Holitorium, would open its doors while the Legions were battling, and close them only during times of peace; and his mind rested on the time he had spent waiting between those doorposts, which had towered over his boyish frame. Calidius wondered how many times those doors had actually shut. In fact, in the three hundred years since the temple's dedication, they had been closed on only four occasions: four moments of peace in almost as many centuries.

It was said Calidius' military line went back to the early days of the empire. His forefathers had been part of the first legions, when land ownership was a prerequisite to serving. They had been there at the overthrow of the first of the city-states. They had been there when Sicily became her first province, when Carthaginian ships had been stolen and their technology copied. They had been there when the Mediterranean had been tamed. His ancestors had fought in the great Punic wars with Carthage, when the peaceful Phoenician trading empire had been subsumed into Roman rule, and Carthage itself had been crushed and destroyed.

He recalled the pride in the empire that had risen so visibly in his grandfather when he had talked about their familial line. "Rome," he would say, "was the only city strong and wise enough to tax its vanquished foes each year in military men." He remembered with fondness his lessons on how Rome's victories had always prepared her for the next battle. "Taxing protectorates in men absorbed the losses of war and extended our numbers," his grandfather had orated – on several occasions. Calidius allowed himself another smile at being able to quote him so exactly.

What Calidius' grandfather had refused to elaborate upon were the stories about the first battles with Carthage, when the North African city-state had used war elephants as part of her cavalry. It was rumoured that the Roman army, having never seen such an animal, especially one in full war-armour, had fled at their very appearance; and the confiscation of such beasts had formed part of the final treaty agreement. Calidius didn't really believe the Roman army had ever fled before anything. His forbears had taken Egypt and confiscated her grain so Rome's own soldiers no longer had to farm for two seasons of the year. When the armies of Rome's enemies had to return to their homesteads to sow and harvest their crops, the legions could march on. Images of the battlefronts, of falling Egyptian armies, and of wolf-clad banner-bearers criss-crossing the west filled his mind.

A refreshing breath of wind brought Calidius back to the street for a second. It ran its fingers through the crimson bristles of his helmet and momentarily warred against the weight of the scorching afternoon. His eyes involuntarily fixed themselves to the hips of a merchant's wife as she glided past, staying on her until she left his tight field of vision, at which point they whipped back up once more.

Rome, he reflected, was not just a city. At its heart weren't her senators, or her walls. Nor even, he conceded, her unparalleled army. It was the drive to keep the doors to the temple of Janus open – the strength and will to keep conforming the world to herself.

The street had quietened while his thoughts were wandering. He let out an audible sigh. Time, perhaps, to begin counting the cobbles again.

The Servant

The carriage thundered on through the city in the driving rain, and the hooves of the dark, wet horses which had pulled it across much of the northern peninsula chattered incessantly on the ancient cobbled highways of the city's seven hills. Responding to each gentle movement of the bits in their foamy mouths and the ever-present whip behind them, all four horses pressed on without complaint, eyes wide and nostrils flared. Their livery jingled as they turned the final corner to join the long approach to their destination and, as the Holy See of St. Peter began to loom into view, even the animals sensed the end of a journey.

The trip across the north had not been easy, with changeable weather conditions and a relentless shortening of the days. Traversing Lucca and Sienna, the last two cities in which they had lodged, had been nightmarish in the failing light. The cardinal's crest, which he had emblazoned on the ornately carved coach doors before they had set out, had significantly eased the passage through many sets of city gates. But there was only so much a traveller could do when the light failed completely, and both servant and master were keen to end their journey, get off the road, and sit in as comfortable a chair as either could find.

The coach stopped beside the gates into St Peter's Square, and a surly guard – cloaked, hooded, and dripping wet - rapped sharply on the door. The small window in the carriage door rattled open and a hand, holding a letter, was extended tentatively, recoiling slightly as it met a barrage of cold raindrops. Snatching the letter from the young man's hand, the guard unfolded it. His eyes quickly scanned the fluid script and, holding the seal up to the light for a moment, he grunted, turned on his heels and disappeared. Seconds later came the unmistakable sound of keys turning in the other side of the lock, and the doors swung open with a reluctant groan, granting passage through the imposing columns.

Buttoning his coats about him, Benjamin waited for the carriage to come to a complete halt before opening its door and kicking its stiff steps down onto the concourse. Hurrying out into the bitter evening, he helped the Cardinal from the coach and passed him into the care of the servants and pages who were gathering about them. Benjamin had long since decided that the collective noun for a group of papal servants should be a 'flap', and they flurried around the priest with their usual clucking as he made his way inside.

As Benjamin went to the back of the coach to unload the cases, he began to take in his surroundings. He was not impressed. The obelisk in the centre of the square may have been the only original Roman example to still be standing, but ever since it had been moved there during the redesign he had never felt that it quite fitted; the sooner the golden globe at its pinnacle was removed, the better. High above them a silent circle of stone saints watched events intently. Benjamin glanced warily up at their serious faces. He could never remember which one was which, even though they were depicted with the means of their martyrdom.

He was exhausted, though elated and relieved, to have finished his journey across most of western Christendom. The rugged margins of what was left of the Christian Empire flashed through his mind as he stood at the foot of the Holy See. He was suddenly overwhelmed by the contrasts in his surroundings. It was as though the beginning and the end of his journey had folded into one another, like the meeting of the two ends of a piece of string, and the middle seemed strangely tangled in his head. As his mind tiptoed between distant northern cliff tops and the more immediate curves of Rome's marble figures, he felt as though he could have slipped from one world into the other and back again in an instant. There was something wonderfully solid about Rome; but under the granite gaze of the saints he also felt the absence of something wonderfully wild. The storm clouds growled thousands of feet above him, as if articulating some kind of answer to his questions. "Nonsense," he muttered to himself.

His master had been met by a gaggle of scribes, advisors and lesser clergy at the summit of the cathedral's sweeping steps, and was being escorted to the meeting and his waiting colleagues. Now the journey was over it was every man for himself. Benjamin would be required to seek out food in the Vatican's kitchens alone this evening, though he was privately relieved not to be eating with his grumpy old leader again.

He was not even sure what the Cardinal's meeting was about, though he had picked up enough to give him the idea that it involved the crushing of potential dissent among young clergy in various parts of the continent. Benjamin didn't understand much about his master's work, and he was no scholar, but he wasn't sure why everywhere had to conform to Rome. He understood that before the Reformation, Latin had been a more common language than English ever would be; but that was no longer the case. He understood that the known world had once revolved around these opulent corridors of power; that the church had taken over the running of the once expansive Roman Empire, and had ruled its old borders for a time; but he wasn't sure why so much energy had to be spent re-enforcing the importance of those corridors. There were so many trips in and out of the city: messengers, meetings or synods - each demanded allegiance to a Roman way. It was as though the gates were never shut.

Having safely unpacked the Cardinal's luggage and readied his room, Benjamin found himself a steaming dinner and a quiet corner of the kitchens. His thoughts had not yet left his sense of contrasts. He was a little irritated with himself; after all, he had been in service since he was a small boy. What could he possibly know about any of it? He thought about the little he had been taught regarding the great achievements of the ancient Romans; the power and technology, the literature and the art. He mused on the influence of the church; of her clergy and her doctrine. He let his mind wander across all that the soil of Rome had offered up for over a thousand years. "I am just being ridiculous," he said to himself between mouthfuls. "What would the world look like if all of that had rested in the hands of a servant instead of a ruler?"

The Queen

The interviewer sat in a high backed chair in the foyer of the hotel, legs crossed, overwhelmed by the ubiquity of marble and gilt edging. His corduroy jacket, replete with leather elbow patches, hung over the back of his seat; the glass on the table in front of him, once full of iced water, now sat empty. The chair opposite, however, remained woefully unoccupied. He ran his hand through a mop of unkempt, red hair, scratched impatiently at his stubble, cleaned his glasses on the tails of his shirt, and took another laboured look over his shoulder towards the revolving doors behind him. The interviewer had been warned she would be late.

The receptionist smiled thinly at him as she busied herself behind her needlessly expansive front desk. This only served to frustrate his finely balanced temperament a little further.

There was no mistaking her eventual arrival. The bright orange sports car roared at speed into the court-yard, braked suddenly and stopped parallel to the main doors, its V8 still growling. The number plate read simply: '8EA5T'. Getting out of the car, she stood and waited for the doorman to push the revolving doors on her behalf, before gliding into the foyer. She didn't pause, but moved straight to the empty chair and half sat, half collapsed into it. The Roman Way looked across at the interviewer, shot him a predatory smile, and crossed her legs. As she did so he caught a glimpse of the fabled 'S.P.Q.R' tattoo over her ankle.

"Ciao." Dressed entirely in white she was a picture of provocative Italian fashion. Still pouting, she moved her wide, square sunglasses onto the top of her head and, without taking her eyes from him, threw a set of room keys over her shoulder. They landed on the polished floor beside a young man loitering in the background. The interviewer had not seen him follow The Roman Way in, though he could not understand why; he tottered dangerously under the collective weight of shopping bags and shoe boxes, each proudly boasting some exclusive brand-name or another. "Room six-hundred three-score and six", she called out, her thick Italian accent commanding his unthinking obedience. The interviewer was at once repulsed and intoxicated.

He bent down to the black shoulder-bag at his feet. He retrieved a small dictaphone, which he set to record and placed on the table.

"He's new," she said, flatly.

"Really?" asked the interviewer, fumbling with his notes. "What happened to his predecessor?"

"He asked too many questions." The Roman Way was matter-of-fact.

"Shall we get on then Ms. Way?" he said brightly, though his enthusiastic tone failed to convince even himself. He cleared his throat, composed himself, and then cleared his throat again.

"There are a lot of rumours about where you're currently living, and what you're working on at the moment. Could you tell our readers what are you presently busy with, Ms. Way?"

"Well," she sighed absently, admiring a perfectly manicured nail. "I lived in London for quite a while, and did a lot of travelling from there – East India Company etcetera - but I spend most of my time in the States these days. I still do an awful lot of work in capitalist Europe though, and the Protestant church circuit is just as demanding as the Catholic one ever was." She smiled disarmingly. "A lot of businesses want my input, and I'm *heavily* involved with the retail industry." The Roman Way looked more relaxed now she was talking about herself.

"So you have your fingers in a lot of pies?"

"No. I have a lot of pies. And that's very different. Do you mind if I drink?"

The interviewer glanced at his watch; it was not yet eleven in the morning, but he realised a second too late that it hadn't been a real question. She was already waving over a passing attendant with near-painful elegance. She flicked through the heavy-bound cocktail menu for a second. "Bloody Martyr," she said and thrust it into his chest. He scurried away.

The interviewer was trying hard to allay the onset of a stammer. "And so, Roman...What would you say to your critics, those who believe you should be making room for a new Way – certainly as far as Europe is concerned? How are you responding to them?"

"Da-rl-ing," she cooed, focussing all her attention upon him for the first time. "I have always had *critics* and there have always been *questions*..." At this point the waiter placed the Bloody Martyr with gentle precision on the table in front of her. Pausing mid-sentence, she lifted the glass, extracted the cocktail stick with one hand, and poured the thick, red liquid into her mouth with the other. It disappeared in a single swig. She replaced the stick, returned the glass to the table, and removed a stray, scarlet droplet from the side of her lips with her thumb. "But critics often have a nasty habit of backing off, or strangely disappearing... when push comes to shove." She toyed playfully with the silver crucifix around her neck as she spoke. The interviewer suspected she wore it more as a symbol of torture, or of the old days, than for any other reason.

"If you are referring to one of the several incidents of sudden disappearance or death among certain individuals", said the interviewer, "I'm not allowed to write about ongoing criminal investigations."

"Haven't you heard? They are no longer ongoing." She grinned. "Some of the judicial figures had a change of heart". She leaned forwards, studying his reaction. Peering over the frames of his glasses at her, the interviewer raised a suspicious eyebrow. "You have a very fluid view of justice, Ms. Way."

"I've always seen justice as more of a commodity than a principle. And besides, there is no reason for me to move aside. I am Rome. I will always have children."

Her eyes flicked down to the dictaphone between them, its reels innocently looping behind a perspex window. They flicked up to meet the interviewers' once more. He suddenly noticed that the receptionist had vacated her front desk. Turning his back on The Roman Way to look properly, he realised there was no-one in the foyer at all. Even the doorman had left his post. "The key," she whispered, "is *communication*. Or a lack thereof..." The cocktail stick snapped effortlessly between her fingers.

The interviewer swallowed, hard.

FACT FILE: ROME

The 'royal we' was first used in official imperial circles because Romulus and Remus were said to have referred to themselves in this manner when sitting together in judgement over local disputes. It continued to be used in the eastern Empire for this very reason until the late seventh century. They also believed the designs for soldiers uniforms were given by divine inspiration to Romulus.

Brown, Peter (2003) The Rise of Western Christendom *Oxford: Blackwell Publishing, p.177*

In the last century of the Empire Latin almost entirely replaced all other dialects on the European continent, some of which had existed since prehistoric times. It was a far more prevalent language than English is today.

Brown, Peter, (2003) The Rise of Western Christendom *Oxford: Blackwell Publishing, p.232*

While trumpets were used to give signals in the Roman cavalry, the Roman infantry used Bagpipes instead!

Lloyd and Mitchinson (2006) The Book of General Ignorance *London: Faber and Faber, p.88*

So bound up was the Christian faith with the Roman Empire that it took until the 5th century for suggestions to be made that Christian mission should take place beyond the old borders of the imperial system.

Fletcher, R. (1997) The Conversion of Europe *Hammersmith, London: Fontana Press, pp. 28-33*

SECTION 2

ROME TO JERUSALEM

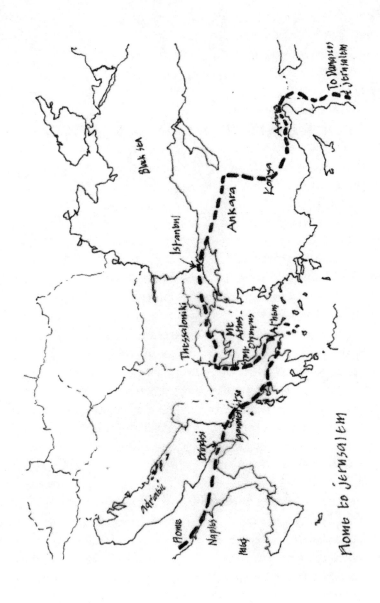

Route to Jerusalem

CHAPTER 14

Rome to Athens

REFLECTIONS FROM HOME

"WILD - not domesticated, tame or cultivated; not civilised, desolate; bleak, very enthusiastic, uncontrolled, unrestrained, unreasonable, untameable by human will, dynamic, exciting, beyond human control." (*Wild Wanderings: 21st Century Adventures with God* by Karen Lowe, published by Shedhead)

The choice to continue walking turned out to be a much harder decision than it had appeared at first. I was aware that, should I continue the journey, I could be written off as a total maverick; someone who was unable to settle back into ordinary life and someone who wanted to linger in the attention of the moment. The hard thing was that some of this could well have been true. I did not however, want to be irresponsible and, like most of us, did not want to be misunderstood.

Equally I was aware that whilst there were strong convictions regarding the walk to Rome, and the evidence of the hand of God with us was incredibly strong, it seemed now that the heavens were strangely silent; that the choice was, in fact, mine. I could choose to go or I could choose not to go. Suddenly the words of

Neo seemed too close for comfort. Though the pathway to Rome had been clearly marked out, there was no such shape for what lay beyond.

This was unnerving. It was not difficult to see reasons for going, and some of the reports that follow seem to ring with conviction. And conviction there was, for the issues provoked by such cities as Athens, Istanbul and Jerusalem stirred me greatly. However, on reflection, my footsteps were far more tentative. I gently pushed the boat out to see what might emerge failing, maybe, to understand that there is a new pattern of leadership emerging that doesn't have to have all the answers, and doesn't need to point the way all the time. Perhaps all that is truly needed is the willingness to go.

It would take me many hundreds of kilometres to resolve some of the internal debates that were now echoing round my head and it was the wise and caring context of friends that helped me along the uncertain paths that beckoned.

Preparation for the walk
out of Rome February 2006

On the 16 March 2005, Stew Thomas and I set out to the Tower of London. Exploring the mythology of Tower of London ravens we walked and prayed, calling for creation to come free from the many ways it is locked up to the rich and the powerful, the nation state and the church. Forty weeks later I entered St. Peters Square in Rome. No longer focused on ravens, our call was for the keys of St. Peter, declaring a message of freedom and liberation that we carried from the margins of Whitby in North East Yorkshire, down through seventeen hundred years of church history, all the way to Rome.

On Friday 17 March 2006 I will find myself back in St Peters Square. This time my face will be set towards Athens, the seedbed of the dualistic thinking that helped shape Christendom. It is there, under the influence of Plato, that space was given for a divide to open up between the so-called material world and the spiritual world. This in turn gave space for the clergy/laity nonsense that dominates so much of the life of the western church.

Walking through Southern Italy to the eastern port of Brindisi I will be joined by two teams of walkers, before we hit the western coastline of Greece in the second half of April. Carving out time from the pressures of earning a living and looking after body and soul, we will be putting the highest value we know on prayer. It is not the only way to pray, nor necessarily the best. However, it is our response to the continued crisis that is rising within Europe at this time, whether it is from bird flu, the developing patterns of mass migration that Europe is no longer immune from, fundamentalist Islam, or the consequences of the gross inhumanity of our history of Empire within our own continent. The demonic powers are calling for blood sacrifice. We are walking to declare a better way[8].

We walk from Rome knowing the papal authorities of ten centuries ago called for and legitimised the crusades of old, with appalling consequences for Jewish and Muslim people alike. We walk in repentance, saying 'no' to every manifestation of the crusades in

---

[8]The prophets have been saying that the years between now and 2012 are critical years for the UK and for mainland Europe. Many observers were still in shock from the riots that ripped through France during 2005, which followed on so quickly from the London bombings of 7 July 2005.

21st Century clothes and 'yes' to the wild, wonderful ways of the Holy Spirit.

We walk with the joy and freedom of those living under the laughter of heaven. We care not for the posturing of politicians within Brussels over the new European constitution, and their desire to remove all reference to the Christian foundations of our continent. Nor do we walk in fear of any perceived threat from fundamentalist Islam. No! We declare that we are the people of the margins; that the government of God is upon His shoulders, and that the days of Christendom are coming to an end.

In rejecting the God of knowledge and false wisdom we declare that we are people of the Spirit and that those who are led by the Spirit will keep in step with the Spirit. So, whilst grateful for our God-given intellect, we repent of the god of the mind, declaring that we want to learn again the unusual and unexpected ways of the one true Lord.

As we walk, twelve years have passed since the movement of the Spirit of God in Toronto, which called for the biblical lands to begin to open up again to the gospel; for signs and wonders to once more break loose across our continent; and for a Benjamin generation to rise full of the power of the Holy Spirit, flowing in signs and wonders.

Knowing that we are 'in place' and 'on time', we are calling for the nations of Europe to come fully free into their destiny and to line up with their God-given future. We declare that Europe belongs neither to Rome nor the gods of Athens, but to the living God.

So we will begin by retracing Paul's steps down the Appia Way through to the south-west coast of Italy, just above Naples. We then cross over the mountains, arriving in Brindisi on the 30 March. We return home that day, picking up the walk again on the 19 April 2006.

Thank you for those who will be with us in prayer. In 2002 I discovered that there is grace for a household to turn and for a city to turn. Now I walk with faith for nations and for a whole continent. If the Lord gives us favour then Jerusalem is in sight. For now, though, we walk for Europe, and for new beginnings to be found.

I will put reports on the internet as access allows.

ROME TO JUST NORTH OF NAPLES,
March 2006
Team: Dave, Katie, Val, Guido, Joyce and myself.

We landed in Rome just over a week ago. It seemed strange to be back in St Peters Square only three months after the end of the walk from Whitby. We did not linger long, however, turning our backs very quickly on the presumption of that place to walk across Rome and pick up the Appian Way. Our route took us past the Coliseum, a moving reminder to the blood of the martyrs who refused the path of self- preservation for the sake of the upside-down ways of the Kingdom. At long last it felt good to be walking away from Rome, having had it in my field of vision for so long last year.

Being back on the road was wonderful, though it quickly became obvious that the incredible grace that had been upon us all the way from Whitby was to be more elusive for this next stage of the walk. A twelve year season had been concluded, and we had played our small part in that journey. Now there was something new to open up.

Those of us who have journeyed long in the ways of Jesus know that there are times when the flow is strong and heavenly experiences seem at our finger tips. There are other times when life can become a dog fight! This seemed to be the case for us as a team when, working our way south, we hit a mix of poor health, appalling weather and some seriously sore feet. It seemed, in the words of a close friend of mine, that for forty weeks our clothes and shoes did not wear out. Now the forty week season is over. We are looking to cross over into our inheritance, free from the cynicism and the stranglehold of unbelief that is such a straight jacket to the western church. In the UK we have six years before the Olympics come to London. In this time, we must begin to rise into our full authority as the people of God, free from the Greek mindsets that have dominated the landscapes of Europe for so long.

It seemed wonderfully ridiculous, therefore, that a tiny bunch of sore-footed hobbits, drenched from head to foot as we wandered south, could make any difference at all. Yet that is the way of the God of all creation; using the totally unreasonable to reveal the limitations of the world of reason.

There are probably a couple of highlights to talk about during this first week of the walk. First, as ever, is the team walking and living in such close proximity; a make or break environment. Once more I have found myself amazed at the capacity for goodness and simple acts of kindness within one another. Hosted by a Canadian- Italian called Guido, we discovered yet more of the wonder of being caught up in the wealth and variety of the Body of Christ. The sense of purpose was strong, further fuelled by the many who kept in touch with us through text and email, encouraging us day-by-day.

Secondly, it was with great amusement that we found ourselves passing a series of posters depicting the Eiffel Tower on its head, and the pyramids of Egypt likewise! Small tokens like these encourage us and remind us of the upside-down Kingdom that we are looking for.

One team has left for home; I await the arrival of the second, which will help take us over the mountains of Southern Italy across to Brindisi. Today we rest. Tomorrow we go back to work.

JUST NORTH OF NAPLES TO BRINDISI,
March 2006
Team: Katie, Andy, Tim, Ro and myself

I write this from Brindisi at the end of the Appia Way, a highway that runs all the way to Rome itself and is dedicated to various cults of the dead. This week we have worked hard in prayer as we climbed up over the snow-line and down onto the eastern side of Italy. With clear blue skies and stunning scenery, there was much that was simply breathtaking. Indeed, I recall one particular section when the whole team fell silent for what must have been over an hour. Contrary to our normal style of noisy intercession and declaration, the silence spoke loudly: "God is in heaven. Let the whole earth be silent."

I recall another morning's walking when two of us stumbled across the location for the shooting of Mel Gibson's 'The Passion of the Christ.' Recalling the scenes that ran up to the crucifixion as we made our way back on route was a profound time of encountering the reality of the Biblical landscape.

This has been a rich fortnight, but it has also been tough. If the first week was characterised by a contending with the elements - the weather, sore feet and ill health - then this week has been marked by a contending for the mind, with most of the team hitting periods of significant mental examination. With Greece behind the shaping of much of the rationalistic mindset of the western world, the mental contention should not surprise us. Keeping focused in prayer for eight hours a day is a challenge when the flow is clear and grace abounds. When the flow is not clear then we cannot throw away our confidence, for if we persevere we shall be richly rewarded.

Sitting here on the harbour wall in Brindisi it is tempting for just a moment to jump on the overnight ferry to Igoumenitsa, in Western Greece. If you had told me a year ago I would walk the length of Italy and be sat looking over to both Greece and Turkey then I would have stared at you blankly. However, these are days of the Lord stretching our horizons and I remain convinced that it is our time in Europe. For this to happen space must be found within our rationalistic mindset for the breaking-in of the Almighty. There is no alternative and that is what we are walking for.

However the pull of home is strong, so we return tonight to England, before picking up the walk on 19 April. Huge thanks again for all those tracking with us in prayer.

REFLECTIONS FROM HOME

This had been a tough period. Disproportionately worried about a mark that had appeared on my face and unhealthy speculation about skin cancer, my mind was all over the place as I tried to focus on the wonder of the mountains of Southern Italy. Anxious about the state of our finances back home, I began to question whether, in fact, I had made a mistake. Perhaps we should have concluded in Rome and I should now be back taking my place in mainstream life.

In preparing myself for this section of the walk I knew that money, or the lack of it, was going to be an issue. I had determined some months ago that there would be no way through the nation of Greece if I was yet another of the ranks of the professional clergy, as I had once been, albeit a dirty and smelly one! I understood enough about the dangers of prayers that were not backed up by the integrity of the ground that I was seeking to position myself on, to realise that it was now up to Kathy and I to fund this part of the journey. Yet the reality was that we were sliding into more and more debt, contrary to the careful way in which we had always conducted our finances. Was this right? Was I being completely presumptuous in the decision to keep walking? Little did I realise that we would be over the other side of Mount Olympus in Northern Greece, another 1000 kilometres further on, before some answers began to trickle through.

IGOUMENITSA TO ATHENS April 2006
Pre walk ramblings

It is almost two years ago since I travelled out to Northern California with Martin and Sue Scott to walk the length of the North Californian coastline. Making from the Oregon border down to San Francisco was a great adventure; a time when we travelled to the edge of the western world in order to pray back into the heart of western civilisation. Sometimes it is on the edge of the edge, and in intense wilderness times, that we discover the reality of the Lord with us.

During those weeks of walking there were many times that we prayed into Athens, for the ancient city was in focus with the Olympic Games fast approaching. On Wednesday 19, I will go to Greece to walk from the western coastline of the nation back into that city. Recently there has been election after election: the Ukraine, Germany, the EU and most recently Italy. If this reminds us of anything, it is that this continent of Europe remains in the balance[9]. So we go to pray and to carry the conviction that burns within us; that nothing is beyond the redemption of the Lord.

For those of you who may be wondering, our teams are not made up of the idle and the affluent, eager for a laugh and a bit of adventure. If only that was so! Rather, there are a growing number of those who carry the emerging testimony of a new generation of believers who are not prepared to sacrifice their lives at the altar of work, career and paying the mortgage. Taking considerable risks, many are looking for an alternative way of working and living, declaring that there can still be space for adventure, wild living and also career, but free from the slow death of the mortgage trap and the fear of being without. With growing numbers experimenting with

---

[9]This was a remarkable time across Europe as nation after nation went to the polls. The Ukraine, Germany and Italy all had closely contested elections, the Ukraine needing a recount and Italy having to call in the judicial system to adjudicate. With the EU in turmoil after the Netherlands rejected the proposed treaty, it did seem as if here was a sign of a continent truly in the balance.

different models of household and community we walk looking for the ancient paths that cry out for an alternative to the domestication of life in so much of western culture. Come, free creation! People of God rise up to declare a different way of living! We refuse to be dictated to by the economic powers, announcing through our lives that there is space for the unreasonable people of faith who refuse the god of the rational.

To state the obvious, we walk with our feet and not with our minds. So we place one foot in front of the other and follow the unreasonable paths of the Holy Spirit. If we are out of our minds, then it is for Christ's sake. If our words are not eloquent and we have no microphone in our hands then that is good, for we prophesy with the testimony of our life choices, our finances, our laughter and the blisters on our feet.

We walk for all those seeking to be faithful in the place of work, and also adventurous and outrageous in these wild days that are rising. We walk for all those who would love to walk with us, but through physical affliction are unable to do so. For all those in front-line mission situations struggling for resources we walk for you, calling for the wealth of creation to be unlocked. For those experimenting with new models of communal living and new patterns of the monastic, hold through to that which you have sight of; prophetic communities have to arise that model different rhythms of work and life. For you, also, we walk.

We walk for all those who have left Rome behind but are uncertain as to the pathways ahead. We walk for the sake of the gospel in Europe and a lifting of the shroud of unbelief that is but the wisdom of this world. Finally, we walk to discover the full meaning of the words of

Jesus when he said "the work of the Father is this, to believe in the one who was sent."

For those who follow our schedule, we fly out Wednesday 19 April, arriving in Igouministra to start walking the morning of the 21st, aiming to walk back to Athens by Saturday 29. There we will be met by local believers, and together we will walk to Mars Hill, the place where the Apostle Paul encountered the Spirit of Greece. There we will conclude the walk that has taken us from the centre of one ancient and falling empire to another.

Many thanks again for all those tracking with us.

IGOUMENITSA TO CORINTH, April 2006
Team: Val, Steve H, Stew, Helen and myself

It is an awesome thing to walk with the One who walked through the gardens of creation. We have now journeyed from the islands of the north-east edge of Europe to the islands of the south-eastern corner of Greece. It is almost as if, like seeds from a pod, we have been blown along the ancient root-ways of Europe, carrying so ineffectively the cries and urgency of so many. If we have felt unqualified to do this, then maybe there is greater grace upon this current team than we deserve, with Welsh, Scottish and English walking together towards the global gateway that is the city of Athens.

Walking down along the western coastline of Greece was as wonderful an experience as anyone would expect it to be. The rugged coastline is magnificent and the views across to a multitude of islands continually take the breath away. We cannot pretend that that we carried on walking past the many little coves en route, with their attractive bars and restaurants. A few cold lagers at the end of a days walking is an amazing antidote to sore feet and tired legs.

We are now just 120km from finishing, with Corinth our next city. We conclude mid-afternoon on Saturday and will join with local believers to break bread and share food together.

If ever I needed extra conviction about the all-pervading influence of a dualistic system fuelled by a professional priesthood, then that has vanished as I have witnessed the grip of Greek Orthodoxy upon the lifeblood of a whole nation. To be here during the Greek Easter is to blow away any uncertainty as to the desperate needs of a nation that has never known revival. Whilst not doubting the gems that are inevitably there to be discovered, neither can I doubt the neutralising influence of such systems of religion. So we walk with fire in our hearts for a destruction of the deception of religion across Europe, and a release of a movement of ordinary people who have discovered that Jesus, rather than the priest or mother church, is the source of all life.

For those with an eye for the global agenda, we take note of the visit of Condalisa Rice to Athens so recently. Athena is the God of War and once more the sounds of war are being heard. So we walk for the ordinary people of this crazy world and we resist the acceleration of the schemes of the evil one. We walk for every global connection to come through from east to west and from west to east, and we call for the Chinese church to keep walking as they track back to Jerusalem.

Many thanks to those who have emailed encouragement to us. One of the team today commented that he had no right to be walking with the level of fitness and focus that he has found, taking it as an energising sign of the acceleration we are in. We have a foot in the doorway of this gateway, and we intend to keep walking through.

I will email any further thoughts or reflections on my return to England early next week.

REFLECTIONS FROM HOME

It was walking down the west side of mainland Greece that another major error of translation occurred; the sort that causes locals to laugh together for months after the visitors have gone. On a particularly pleasant morning, feeling especially well disposed towards the Greeks, an unusual level of cheeriness came upon one of my companions as we walked through one of the many villages on route. Deciding to greet everybody with her newly acquired Greek she proceeded to say "Kalamari" with great gusto, believing this was the friendliest of morning greetings. Quizzical looks did not deter and soon the whole village square was being subjected to this cheery greeting from these strange passers-by.

Only once we had left this bemused village behind did the truth dawn on my kind- hearted companion, for unbeknown to her everyone we had encountered had just been offered a succulent portion of squid! The normal greeting of "good morning" is in fact 'Kalimera'. Needless to say the rest of the team had fun at her expense for some time to come.

CORINTH TO ATHENS, April 2006
Team: Val, Steve H, Stew, Helen and myself

The final days walking took us along the coastline near to the port of Piraeus, before turning inland to our finishing point at the Acropolis in Athens. The sight of the harbours of Greece is so similar to the landscape of San Francisco and I cannot help but wonder at the incredible grace I have found these last two years, as I have tracked from one global port to another.

We came to this seat of humanism and reason with a strong message of hope, for there are clear signs of a weakening in the mindsets of unbelief and hierarchy that dominated Plato's thinking. We came to affirm the wonder of the created order in the face of a creation-denying philosophy that points us away from the Creator and elevates the place of mankind. Convinced that this is our time to recapture the vacuum that humanism has created in science, medicine and the arts, our prayers were strong and confrontational.

Welcomed into the city by a wonderful multi-cultural mix of church leaders I was so grateful for the covering and help of Mike Love from Leeds, as together with our host George Markakis, we sought to bring a conclusion to the 1200km of walking and prayer since leaving Rome

Empire and race are two sides of the same coin, for inherent to the empires of both Rome and Plato's thinking is hierarchy and domination. Incredible grace came upon Mike as he affirmed the power of multi-cultural and unity through which God has made known his wisdom to the principalities and powers. With over 10% of the population of Greece being immigrants we knelt at the feet of a band of believers from across Africa and as far east as the Philippines, calling for an end to the inherently racist spirit of empire.

This was an awesome moment, which had echoes of St Peters Square just four months previously. It was as if the Lord had hand picked the team for such a time, as we carried together three interlocking circles of grace and unity; Stew and I from one home; Mike Love and I from one city and the three nations of Wales, Scotland and England represented across the team. Together we called for alignment to come through across the thousands of miles from our starting point in Northern England, all the way through York, London, Paris, Lyon, Marseilles, Nice, Genoa, Rome and Brindisi, here to this global gateway for Europe and the western world. Taking the testimonies of our journeys of death in the pursuit of unity, we drew great strength as we proclaimed the words of the Apostle Paul that there is neither Greek nor Jew, male nor female, slave nor free.

I cannot finish this report without giving my heartfelt thanks to the wonderful guys who have walked with me since leaving Rome. With blisters on our feet and, at times, messed-up heads, we have nevertheless sought to carry a declaration of faith through to the gates. To the young and not so young prophets of Leeds: Andy, Dave, Tim, and Katie, I say thank you. To Scottish Val I say you are a living legend and a blessing to so many. To the Welsh warriors, Stew and Steve: heartfelt thanks to you both too. I also say thank you to Ro, Helen, Guido and Joyce. Each and every one of you has contributed so much.

So we return home with fuelled with images of Constantinople and Jerusalem. If the door opens to us it may be that I, or indeed someone else, picks up the baton in the autumn. We have to call the western world out of the Greek mindset dominated by humanism, back to the more Creator-focused mindset of Hebrew thinking. We must keep walking in repentance for the anti-Semitism of both Rome and Plato and we have to uphold the Chinese church as they journey back to Jerusalem.

In the meantime, I return home for my eldest daughter's wedding in a few days' time, and must face the reality of returning to China to adopt our fourth daughter. I also return to take up the responsibilities of the household and, along with everyone else in the world, earning my way in life. As Paul said to the Thessalonians, it is good to "live a quiet life, mind our own business and work with our hands."

REFLECTIONS FROM HOME

It was hugely satisfying for me to reach Athens, especially after the mental struggles of recent weeks. I was grateful for friends who helped me keep going, and it was incredible to think that we had walked from the north-western edge of Europe, through to the south-eastern corner; it was wonderful to linger round the busy port of Piraeus as we waited for the flight back home; and exciting to be going home to the wedding of my eldest daughter, Hannah. The prospect of returning to China to adopt our fourth daughter also loomed large on the horizon. Life was challenging, but also wonderfully full.

For a few days therefore I was able to leave behind the anxieties that come to those who abandon the tried and tested paths, which had focussed on the small investments we had made into property and my complete lack of any career plan. To rediscover the place of peace was like manna to my soul, as I was safe in the knowledge that the Chief who is my Shepherd declares "I shall not want."

There were no signs to mark out this section of the walk that I can relate, but I was grateful for that unusual peace that descended on me as we flew back to the UK. It was going to be five more months before we would return to pick up the walk through to Istanbul. In the meantime, I had one daughter to give away and another, on the other side of the world, was about to be given to me. How crazy is that?

Tim Hooper, one of the team looks out over the cliffs of Whitby, thoughts no doubt turned to the walk ahead.

Laughter and fun in Rome as Chris Meredith (at the forefront) and Steve Watters enjoy the moment of arrival. Though the photograph is taken in a car I promise you they walked!

St Peters Square, Rome. The moment the Pope arrives to hear, as we like to think, our declaration.

Children gather around us in St Peters Sq and in the Umayyad Mosque in Damascus. It should not surprise us that children are often the first to respond to the release of angels. Their laughter and childlike delight was a stark contrast to the religious imperialism of the setting.

The inner courts of the Blue mosque in Istanbul. Built in 1603, it is
an amazing example of Ottoman architecture.

With its six minarets and a great cascade of domes, the Blue mosque emulates the Byzantium Hagia Sophia just a few minutes' stroll to the north. These two symbols of imperialism and religion stand directly opposite one another.

Locals fishing in the Bosphorus, Istanbul.

Minarets pierce the Turkish skyline throughout the land. These temples sit on the shore of the Bosphorus

The coffee house at the eastern gate of the old city of Damascus; the place to go to listen to the storyteller; a marker moment in our journey.

From left to right Richard Haworth, who walked most of the way from Athens to Jerusalem. Kathy Garda, writer of the Adana tale, myself, Dave Herron, (Ankara) and Paul Wood (Istanbul and Damascus), relaxing in one of the many wonderful restaurants of Damascus.

The city of Damascus, thought to be the oldest city in the world.

Straight Street in Damascus, the place where the Apostle Paul was told to go to receive back his sight.

The guest house in Nazareth where we stayed. We were sat underneath the arches when a young boy came to give us all sweets.

Our welcome to Jerusalem. Another boy decides not to give us sweets but to throw some stones. We are reminded of the welcome Jerusalem gives to prophets; a good sign!

Street art on the security wall in Bethlehem.

Some of the team prepare to leave the West Bank to cross the security wall. From left to right, Mark, Chris, myself, Shelley, Steve W, Kathy, Vicki, Val, Lucy, Richard, Nigel and Dave. Steve, Lucy and Nigel were all living out in the West Bank and were crucial to helping us find our way through.

The security wall arches it way across Israel and Palestine.

Some of the team relax on the Mount of Olives at the end of the walk.

Some of the team overlooking Jerusalem. From left to right, Vicki (who hosted us in Istanbul), Kathy, myself, Richard, Paul (author of the Istanbul and Damascus chapters and the man behind the camera most of the time), Chris(author of the Jerusalem chapter), Val and Dave.

Journeys end on the Mount of Olives for myself, or is it?

CHAPTER 15

The Athenian Time Machine

Steve Hallett

Steve is an accountant, who lives in Cardiff. He is married with three, grown-up children. His love of philosophy was nurtured during his studies at university. A devotee of good food and wine, he greatly enjoys travelling, carrying a particular affection for Eastern Europe. This is a witty and insightful take on the ancient city of Athens.

For some, time travel is a fascination. For others it is a nightmare, best watched from behind the sofa. One recent author even portrayed it as a disease. I can't say it ever interested me very much, until I got to do it for myself. OK, maybe I exaggerate: I don't actually do it myself. But I do know something that does.

It all started in a bit of a mess; a damp, soggy mess, actually. It had been a great holiday, pretending I was eighteen again and island hopping off Greece – the Cyclades to be precise. With an EasyJet flight to Luton booked for the next day I had intended to find some-where decent for my last night on Greek soil, but the ferry was delayed. We docked in Pireas, the port of Athens, just after midnight. There were maybe twenty of us; in reality we were strangers, united by the fellowship of random travel. There was safety in numbers and it was dry and warm as we kipped down near the quay. Sleep soon followed. It was a pity that I didn't read the Rough Guide until afterwards: "Few visitors stay in Pireas... Sleeping rough in Platia Karaiskaki, as some exhausted travellers attempt to do, is unwise. If thieves or the police don't rouse you, street-cleaners armed with hoses certainly will – at 5am."[1]

Next came the rudest of awakenings. Soaked to the skin, heart pounding, and no idea where I was, I scrambled for cover. I instinctively checked my pockets. Wallet, passport: OK. But what about my iPod? Luckily as I retrieved my damp rucksack I found it, wedged between some kerb stones. I slipped it into my pocket and thought no more of it. There was some drying out to do, breakfast to find, and a plane to catch.

Somewhere over the Alps we ran out of clear weather. With only clouds to look down on I fancied some music. Oh no! This wasn't my iPod. Worse still, it wasn't an iPod at all. It was slim, metallic and about the right size, but there the similarities ended. There was nowhere to plug in the headphones and no obvious way of charging it. It might even be dangerous; I had noticed airport security had seemed pretty casual. Anyway, it was a bit late to do much about it now. So I didn't, until I delivered it to 'Techno' a few days later. Now, if I hadn't grown up with Techno I would certainly doubt whether he were human, but behind the robotic exterior is one very clever chap. From antique hi-fis to ailing laptops, Techno can fix anything. It was some weeks later when he rang me:

"It's incredible! It's some kind of time travel device. It's taking ages to crack the codes, but I think it's full of stories - all to do with Athens. There seem to be several million of them, every one by a different person. They each have a name and date; though don't ask me how they could use terms like BC and AD hundreds of years before they were invented. The breakthrough came when I found a kind of record of the specifications.

I've managed to decode some bits: *'Time-free story recorder... Memory size: infinite... Technology: scientifically digital, but principally imaginative... Design objective: to prove that cities and nations can change because of decisions made in the living rooms of ordinary people.'*

``Actually, Steve, the number of stories seems to match the population of Athens, now and through history. It seems everyone has a story to tell. I only wish I could decode them more quickly. Anyway, here are some extracts."

Pericles: statesman, 429 BC

They say every city needs a father. When it comes to Athens, I was the right man, in the right place, at the right time. OK, the city already had quite a history, going back to the times of gods and legends; but when I arrived... what a shambles! There were famous names a-plenty: Athena, Poseidon, Theseus and Academos. But what use are legends when your city is just a blackened shell? The times of the early legends had been followed by centuries of obscurity and some brave attempts at democracy, before everything had been devastated by the Persians. By the time I came on the scene there had been some recovery. People had moved back and started to rebuild the walls. We had won a few battles, sorted out Corinth and even managed a truce with Sparta. But

Athens itself was no more than a shadow of its old self; an orphan city, longing for love and attention. It needed a restoration of pride; a return of its special status; and a reinstatement of the "wow" factor. I was determined to make it a beautiful place, to set the scene for a golden age; and so I appointed Ippodamos, probably the greatest architect in the world. The Parthenon, the new street grid in Piraeus – that man was way ahead of his time.

Another part of the package was military might, needed to secure a strong empire. Good alliances (well, good for us anyway) were just as important. I'm proud to say that what I started as the Delian League soon became the Athenian Empire. It made sense to consolidate against the Persians and avenge the invasion of our land. One hundred and fifty cities joined in the alliance, united against a common foe. At first the whole alliance contributed financially, but as time went on we Athenians provided soldiers and sailors rather than cash; lack of jobs for those returning to the city meant no shortage of manpower. It just so happened that I was the league treasurer, which was pretty handy. The money from the other cities rebuilt Athens, multiplied our navy and took unemployment off our streets. It kick-started new projects that extended our boundaries and increased our dominance. Some have called it the biggest embezzlement in history. I call it good investment; the way a capital city ought to behave.

Needless to say, Athens was soon the envy of the world. Corn from Carthage, cheese from Sicily, pork from Tuscany, metal goods, carpets, cushions; we had them all. I managed to sort out a deal to finance academics and politicians, and the best minds of our time flocked to the city. I'm sorry to harp on so much, but I need to dwell on positive achievements. Positive thinking has always served me well. Right now, I need it more than ever.

We are three years into a terrible war. It is not for nothing that the Spartans have a reputation as warriors. Wars are fine if you are away from home. You may take casualties, but it's all for the empire and there's not too much to lose. This is different. Our enemies are within a few miles and we lack the strength to turn them back. Not long ago, the navy had won some big battles and diversionary tactics might have worked. But then it came – the plague. One third of the population are dead. The grand temples are full of corpses. Those left alive are struck down with grief, shock and deep despair. I myself am ill and near death. I have gone back over all my great achievements. Who knows what history will make of my efforts? For me, I just see the cycle repeating itself; a great city returning once more to chaos. Perhaps you do reap what you sow; the city that oppresses will be oppressed.

I just wanted to see Athens flourish. What was it all for?

Plato: philosopher, 347 BC

Hi. Plato here! If anyone can change the world by what he says in his living room, it's me. I'm quite a thinker; some would say a bit of a clever dick. I like to get behind the world we see to another realm where things are *just right*. It may be a bit abstract, but I certainly prefer it to the real world. How am I so smart? Well I guess it started with Socrates. I was his star student. We had such a close relationship that some even wondered if we might be lovers. For the record though, our relationship was purely platonic.

Athens seemed a pretty good place to live – great buildings, lots of great philosophers – but in some ways it wasn't all that great. There were some bad characters about and our homes were pretty squalid. It was no wonder we spent so much time at the Academy and the Gym. The government wasn't that marvellous either. They condemned Socrates to death, just because he was too close to the previous rulers. He could easily have escaped death, but for him order in society and obedience to the state were all important. For him not to have taken the poison would have been inconsistent. He lived according to reason and according to reason he died.

With time on my hands I thought and thought; there just had to be a better place than this. I travelled to Egypt, and studied geometry and mathematics. I tried to write down all Socrates had taught me. I can't say I ever found a better place to live, but I certainly thought of one. In fact, I have thought about that place so much that it has become more important than the grimy, sordid world of everyday. It's a place where anything that is good exists in perfection. In our world, we see a bit of love, a bit of truth, a bit of equality; but where do these things exist in perfect form? In a perfect world, of course! We don't live there... but let's say our souls do, before we are born and after we die. Then, like the gods, we can be immortals. I guess to honest, it was only an idea, but it seemed a pretty reasonable one.

My ideal world is a place where answers are exact, like in science and mathematics. Only through reason can it be grasped, but once you understand, you become someone special. It's not really a place for ordinary people. It's a place for intellectual heroes; the philosopher kings, who I say should rule the earth. People never succeed without leadership and direction. Our ancient religions had oracles and priests; my vision is of a secular world, governed by reason alone. And who better to implement that government than the true intellectuals - a class apart? Everyone should obey and look up to them!

I must get back to my books, but let me just share one more thing. I'm usually far too rational to pay attention to the oracle. The supernatural doesn't really fit my box - it's far too gritty. But one prophet guy I know did come out with some interesting things. He said that my books would still be read in thousands of years' time. He said that my way of thinking would affect governments and religions throughout the rest of history. It would affect the ordinary people throughout the known world and beyond for centuries to come. They would live as if my ideal world really existed, without realising what they were doing; and it would do nothing to really improve their lives.

Now that made me do some real thinking, with my heart as well as my head. I think I need to own up now before it's too late: it was only an idea!

Paul: apostle, 51 AD

It is not just those who belong to a place that influence its history. Those who pass through also have a part to play. I am Jewish by birth and was only in Athens for a very short time; but that is why you find me with a contribution here. The message I bring doesn't always sit too easily with human reason, but I do like to follow an argument. When in Athens (and all that) it seemed only natural to head for the student quarter. I didn't even get as far as the University. The place was awash with philosophers, intellectuals, debaters and academics.

Surprisingly, given their reputation for philosophy and learning, they were actually quite superstitious; even religious. Temples, altars, you name it; every deity, every cult, every denomination all seemed to have a slot. There was even an altar to the "Unknown God". Maybe this was just some kind of insurance policy, but it suited me well. I had wondered if I would get a hearing. Now I could get into preach mode straightaway. After all, I had met this unknown god for myself.

Those who travel with me will agree that when I preach, things happen: miracles, riots, imprisonment, floggings, earthquakes; and now and again quite a few conversions. But in Athens it was different. They listened politely. One or two made a personal response, but most of them did absolutely nothing - except to invite me back. That had never happened to me before. What a waste of time! My message requires action. If it doesn't turn the world upside down (often enough it's my own world) I might as well keep my mouth shut. Some friends have said that I missed it in Athens, and that my words were not up to much. I disagree; as I often said in Corinth, my words are *never* up to much. I think it's the Athenians that have the problem. There's too much talking and listening; too much mind-candy and not enough action. For them, it's *all* in the mind. They've invented a separate world of ideas, disconnected from the reality we all live in. They even seem to think this strange place of the mind, the soul (the whatever) is more important than the real world.

My message could not be more different. Jesus was (and is) both completely human and completely God at the same time. He was born in a dirty stable, grew up in a humble family, and worked for his dad as a carpenter.

He did physical miracles, calling for action not just words. He was executed as a criminal, not because he deserved it, but because we did. He came back to life and lots of people saw him, including me. At least, I certainly heard him. I was knocked off my donkey and went blind for days afterwards. Then he began to fill me with his Spirit. That was pretty physical too; strange languages, extreme drunkenness, you name it! Then he sent me on these incredible journeys, with a message for the whole world.

Now, I haven't kissed my brains goodbye. The way we think is important. It moulds how we live. But these must be a connection between thought and action, between heaven and earth. That is how our Hebrew worldview differs from the Greek one. For us, thought and action, heaven and earth, go hand in hand. My highest aim is not to find myself "up there" somewhere, but to see what God wants to happen right down here. Ever since that flash of light on the road to Damascus, I know that God's revelation comes first. Once I met Jesus all the broken bits of my life and my thinking began to make sense.

As for your separate world of thoughts, ideas and so-called spirituality, you can keep it. Woe betide us if we ever get it mixed up with the way we live as followers of Jesus. If I can't feel the dirt between my toes I want nothing of it.

Corinth beckons. I had better move on.

Spiro: retired carpenter, 2007 AD

If history was just a place for kings and generals, I would have no story to tell. I'm just an old man, but my whole life has been spent in Athens. Maybe I have done a little to help make the city. What is more certain is that the city has moulded me. I have lived through seventy-odd years of turbulent history with joy and with tears; sometimes, I think, mostly tears. Don't kid yourself that Athens has always been great. When my father arrived in 1919 its proud history counted for nothing.

Yes, I said arrived: although I'm as Greek as the next Athenian, my family are from way East; Konya, in Turkey, to be exact. Two of my sons have also moved countries. Aristos has a restaurant in London; Georges is in New South Wales. But they have chosen their new lives. My father had no such choice. He was Armenian. He never talked about it much, but they say he was lucky to escape with his life. These days they call it ethnic cleansing. Two years earlier his mother and her two young sons had been forced to march to Smyrna. He rarely talked about his father. Needless to say, I never knew my grandparents. My uncle once told me that when the Turks entered Smyrna in September 1919 they sought out the Armenians, torched their houses, and herded them down to the quay. Rescue was not swift, but by October they and about 180 000 others were in Athens.

That is why I am here. I was never a great scholar, but one thing I always remember from school is that in the 1920s the population of Athens more than tripled. It was our family and others just like us. The other thing I picked up from history lessons was that Athens was the place where democracy was first invented. It therefore seemed odd that the Greek government was rarely elected. Kings came and went, and generals seized power. Those who dared protest could be shot or imprisoned. My earliest memories (I guess they would be from around 1940) are of soldiers on the street.

There was a strange mixture of excitement, hardship and fear. First we saw Italian bombers, then British, then German. We never knew which side to take. I'm only glad I was too young to fight. I later found out that my uncle was part of the resistance. Until his death he was bitter about those who collaborated with the Germans. The other thing that stands out from my early years is the hunger. Bean soup was often all we had. We didn't see meat or cheese for months on end. News was scarce, but I later learned that many thousands of people starved to death. One date I do remember from the war is 12 October 1944. The allies were approaching, the resistance was growing in strength, and on that day the Germans pulled out of Athens. I was eleven years old, and happy to be alive.

I would love to say that we lived in peace ever after. In fact it was to be thirty years, the best part of my life, before Athens really became a place of peace again. British occupation; American occupation; constant civil war; rigged elections; military coups; student protests; tanks on the streets – we had it all. I didn't do too badly out of it myself. The military brought lots of building work; getting into the trade was a good move. I finished up running my own workshop. I had always fancied making furniture.

And then there's Amelia. We met in 1959. We've been very happy. Two of my sons didn't hang around long, but they do get back here sometimes. My other son lectures in the Polytechnic, the same one that was bulldozed by tanks in 1973. My daughter lives quite close. She's a lawyer. I guess that if things had turned out differently I might have been a bit of an intellectual myself. Maybe it's what Athens does to you, this city of philosophers.

Actually, if I'm honest, a few things worry me. I do have questions. How is it that a place can be so brainy but make such a hash of its history? Why have I seen the birthplace of democracy seized by generals and fought over by opposing armies? What happened to the simple faith of our Armenian fathers? Why in Greece is it the priests who always have all the answers?

Perhaps what worries me most is that my kids seem to have everything so tidily worked out. A lawyer and a philosopher: OK, but why do they have to have an answer to everything? You should hear them talk. It's so abstract. The arguments sound great, but deep down they're not really sorted. I sometimes wish they would just pick up a mallet and a chisel, and do something solid.

Yes, maybe you do get like the city you live in. It moulds your thinking. The track record of Athens isn't that great, though, is it? Wouldn't it be better if we could do the moulding of the city, not the other way round? Where do we start?

FACT FILE: ATHENS

Ancient Athens was:

Inhabited since the early part of the fifth millennium BC. Possibly the oldest continuously inhabited city in Europe.[2]

The legendary home of Theseus, participant in the 'Argonauts' expedition and early social reformer.[3]

Given its first laws by Drakon (624 BC), from which we derive the word 'draconian' – his laws were very harsh.[4]

The site of first known attempt at democracy in world history under Solon (594 BC).[5]

Devastated by the Persians (c. 500 BC).[6]

An intellectual centre where Socrates, Plato and Aristotle founded modern Philosophy (404 – 335 BC).[7]

Following the conquests of Alexander the Great (356 – 323 BC) Greek (effectively Athenian) philosophy and culture spread throughout the 'known' world. Athens became the world's foremost university. Its importance as a centre of learning and culture was affirmed by the Romans throughout the period of their empire.[8]

Modern Athens:

1916 – 1920 - Massive influx of Armenian refugees forcibly deported from Turkey doubles the city's population.[9]

1941 – 1944 - Athens occupied by the Nazis. Some 300 000 die of starvation and related diseases.[10:]

1944 – 1949 - Virtual civil war under British/American occupation.[11]

1950 – 1967 - Democratic government under heavy American influence.[12]

1967 – 1974 - Military seize control. Increasing protests, leading through to a student demonstration in 1973; tanks on the streets leave 20 dead.[13]

1974 – Junta replaced by elected government.[14]

1981 – Joined European Economic Community.[15]

2004 – Hosting of Olympic Games in a multi-racial, multi-cultural city of over four million people.[16]

References

[1], [16] Ellingham, Mark et al (2004) *The Rough Guide to Greece*, Tenth Edition, Rough Guides Ltd.

[3] – [6] www.sikyon.com/Athens/ahist, accessed 13 January 2008.

[2], [7] – [15] www.anagnosis.gr, accessed 13 January 2008.

CHAPTER 16

Athens to Thessalonica:
Autumn 2006

Steve Lowton

REFLECTIONS FROM HOME

The summer of 2006 was one of the most memorable of my life; the time when Kathy and I travelled out to China to adopt our fourth daughter, Jin Zhou. This was the fruit of what seemed like a crazy decision made seven years before to have what to all intent and purposes was a second family. Going to China in 2002 to bring home our first adopted daughter was a definite life-marker for us; to be travelling again was a source of untold joy. The unspeakable magic of knowing that your own life is about to be joined to that of another, somewhere on the other side of the world, is an incredible experience. Without a doubt our future is now intricately tied to this vast nation. When we were at last given a name and a face for our new daughter, just weeks before we travelled, it did not surprise me that even in the choice of names that the Wanzai Social Institute had made, there was a coming together of journey that had the finger of God upon it. Stay with me as I try to explain.

For so long the church in the western world has been an irrelevance. Occasionally it breaks out with wonderful reforming acts of abolition and salvation, but in the main returns to a way of living meaningless to most of society; dualistic in every way and exactly the opposite of the Hebraic tradition that flowed into the early church. This was a tradition with an instinctive understanding of community and the interlocking nature of the material and spiritual world. Greece is the seedbed of this separation and elevation of rationalistic thinking, something alien to almost every culture except that of the west. That is why we had to go through Athens on our way to Jerusalem, even if it was several hundred kilometres out of our way; to call in prayer for a Hebraic worldview to find root amidst the idolatry of the mind that dominates our culture.

Into this huge gap in the creative plan came a walk shaped out of the insignificant lives of a bunch of cultural lepers. Into this gap came also one tiny life from a culture on the other side of the world where there are no such distinctions; a culture carrying a completely different world view, and a culture within which sits the fastest growing church across the globe - one that has seen incredible evidence of the supernatural realm.

Jin Zhou means "Beautiful Universe", as expansive and inclusive a name as anyone could wish for; no separation of parallel worlds here. Suddenly, as with Chun Zhen and the "new beginnings" spoken of by her name in 2002, symmetry emerged between our own journey as a family to China, and the positioning of the walk itself. It seemed to us that implanted in the name given to her just weeks after being separated from her birth mother were the seeds of all that we were journeying for as we trudged those long miles through the heart of Greece; a view of the universe that refuses to be compartmentalised and refuses the dominion of the mind over every other God-given faculty. Once more the echoes of decisions made in the living room seemed to be reverberating far beyond anything we could have imagined.

Over the coming weeks we made our way north, out of Athens and up over Mount Olympus, home to the Greek deities and gods. During thus time it became obvious that little life of Jin Zhou was coming under some serious pressure. This is something we observed upon entering into Rome, where we had news of several children facing life-threatening conditions. Imperialism always comes to threaten the life of the next generation, as we see in the vindictive rage of Herod that was aimed at new-borns around the time of Jesus; or, indeed, the rage of Pharaoh that was aimed at the generation of Moses.

This now seemed to be the case with Zhou, as a period of many months followed when her health was under serious contention. For me the uncertainties and pressures surrounding our finances were suddenly multiplied, as her little life became caught up in our journey. Added to this was the knowledge that soon after her marriage Hannah, my eldest daughter, succumbed to chronic fatigue. With further health complications for Laura, my second eldest, the pressure upon us was intense.

It was to be nearly 3000kms and over twelve months later before these conditions were fully lifted. Was this just a series of coincidences, or had I asked too much of

204

my family? Was the gap just too big for a few nobodies to place themselves in? The weaving together of story lines is wonderful when it is all good; it is not so wonderful when the contending kicks in.

Looking back, I suspect my nerve would have failed me without the clear signs that were to unfold as we descended the shoulder of Mount Olympus, as you will read of in the account to follow. The backdrop of life at home, though, was always in my mind. Without a doubt, this was an uncomfortable time.

ATHENS TO MOUNT OLYMPUS,
September 2006
Team: Dave, Richard, Chris and myself

We arrived in Athens and, unusually for us, allowed ourselves a couple of days before getting out on the road. Heading into the down town area in search of food we very quickly picked up whispers of heaven, enjoying a meal in an Israeli-owned restaurant with a Palestinian cook. A few minutes later we found ourselves just 200m up the road at a pro-Palestinian demonstration, immediately before proceeding to a pro-Israel conference we were, with mixed feelings, about to attend.

This whole scenario seemed to be a snapshot of all that lay ahead of us beyond the nations of Greece, Turkey and Syria, as some of the enormous tensions surrounding the lands of Israel/Palestine were displayed before our very eyes. As wanderers needing sign posts to get our bearings, and with thousands of kilometres ahead, we drew strength from these coincidences.

In glorious sunshine we headed north out of Athens, quickly climbing into the barren hills that characterise this beautiful nation. Some big miles lay ahead of us, and with Chris and me quickly succumbing to injuries serious enough to take us out of much of the walking, it was down to Richard and Dave to keep us on schedule.

For me this was a time of considerable introspection, as I reflected upon both pressures at home and the enormity of all that we were walking for. Our intercession was strong and focused, but I also carried questions as to whether the door was really open for us to go further. It was, therefore, nothing less than momentous for me when, coming down off the northern slopes of Mount Olympus, it began to dawn on me that once more the living God had marked out the timing of the walk with two further forty-day markers. With sweat streaming off my forehead I noted that it would be exactly forty days of actual walking that would take the teams from Rome, through Athens, to Istanbul. In addition, it would be exactly forty days of both walking and rest back home between stepping off the plane in Athens and the day we fly out of Istanbul in a few weeks time. This revelation was manna to my soul and fuelled my walking considerably. Once more I had the word of the Lord confirming that this is not some reckless excuse for a bit of fun, but something that carried the evidence of the hand of the living God upon it.

We are tracking from the gateway of Christendom in Rome, to what would be perceived by most Europeans as the gateway into Islam; Istanbul. In other words we have an overlay to all that is unfolding in Israel/ Palestine at this time with, some would say, Christendom and aspects of Christian Zionism rising to one side and Islam to the other. A gross over-simplification, I know, but one I believe has some weight to it.

We are walking between two gates that, it could be said, are a metaphor for all that is rising in the Middle East; declaring that there is space between the gates; that we will not be steam rolled into a premature Armageddon; and that we will call through everything the Lord has for us at this time.

We also walked with a growing understanding that the grace of reconciliation can only flow from those free from issues of empire and ownership. What is so wonderful to me is that on this team there are huge differences of theology on some key issues. However, we are still able to walk free of ownership that quenches relationship and our joining in Jesus.

So huge thanks again for standing with us. We so appreciate you all.

STORMS OVER MOUNT OLYMPUS, THE PARTHENON, AND NORTHERN GREECE, September 2006

We arrived back from Athens early this morning Wednesday 11 October around 3am, having driven down the length of Greece yesterday. Given the torrential rain we had walked through we were not surprised to hear that Northern Greece had been declared an Emergency Area by the Greek authorities following severe flooding. From the moment we crossed over the watershed of Mount Olympus the weather began to change, leading to four days of downpour before we left Athens on Tuesday evening. Indeed the walk came to a premature end when we found the road we were walking on closed, due to the collapse of a sizable road bridge.

This Wednesday morning, the 11 October, we arrived back in Leeds. On arrival, we found that The Times carried a full colour picture of lightning flashing across the sky behind the Acropolis and the Parthenon; an image more associated with Greece than any other, as the supposed cradle of western culture. The Acropolis was where our walk into Athens ended in April, and where we met to pray before walking north just two weeks ago.

The cradle of western culture is being shaken and it would seem the heavens are taking notice of our steps!

As I have walked across Europe there have now been four times when severe weather patterns seemed to mark out our journey, as if the groan of creation was giving voice, and the heavens responding in turn. At no point, so far, has there been loss of life. When we left Whitby in August last year, and Rome in March of this year, we had little idea of the untraceable paths of heaven that we were seeking to walk with. Yet here we find ourselves in autumn 2006, positioned between the gates of Christendom (Rome) and the gates of Islam (Istanbul), surrounded by a major disturbance in the crucible of civilisation that is Greece.

Standing in this place we refused to be squeezed by all that would steam roller us down demonic paths, calling afresh for blood across Europe and beyond. Rather, we declare that there is space in the gates for something new to open up; that there can be a shift in the mindset and spiritual atmosphere over Europe that brings through the breaking of the dawn and the wild ways of the Holy Spirit.

I now carry two photos with me that I value beyond all others. One is of the sun setting through the Coliseum in Rome, setting over the Roman ways and all that we walked for leading up to the 21 December 2005. I can now add a photo of lightening over the Parthenon, declaring to me that there is space for a major shift in all that is squeezing Europe at this time.

I conclude with a few comments about prayer walking, for the wonderful thing about the process we give ourselves to is that our declarations have not been cheap. We do not fly in to cast a few prayers about, and then beat a hasty retreat. No! Rather we sow our lives into the purposes of the Lord, matching our words with every mile walked. Behind the sweat and blisters line up a whole range of other choices, as to how our time, finances and families are positioned to enable us to flow with the spirit of the Maker.

The next team fly out on Saturday 21 October, to pick up the baton and take the walk through to the border with Turkey. I will not be on this team as I need to be at home. My friend Andy will lead it, with four others joining him: Val, Andrea, Debbie and Steve. I know they would be grateful for your prayer as they prepare.

REFLECTIONS FROM HOME

We later heard that five people had died in the floods that hit Northern Greece. I was greatly sobered by this. Had we in some way contributed to their deaths? Had the gods of Greece indeed been stirred, and this was their vengeance? On the other hand, if this was indeed the groan of creation, then surely it was better that the sons of the Kingdom were there to hear it and join in the earth-shuddering cries, rather than things just being left to run their terrible course. Could it be that if we understood issues of the land more, teams could go before natural disasters break to stand in the gap and pray, somehow softening the travail we had witnessed?

Again, I drew strength from the ways in which the Lord had marked out our paths. The forty day seasons, far from being some number game to keep me from losing my marbles on the long hours out on the road, were in fact life-giving signs that helped to keep my feet from stumbling. I was grateful for that, and my sleep was peaceful as a result.

CHAPTER 17

Mount Athos

Steve Lowton

Just to the south of Thessalonica lie the great monaster-
ies of Greek Orthodoxy and the Byzantium era. Indeed,
the monasteries of Mount Athos stand at the apex of
Greek Orthodoxy. To journey on without capturing the
sights and sounds of the monastic ways of a bygone era
would not have done justice to our journey. This short
story seeks to capture some of the atmosphere and
tensions that surrounds these great institutions.

Father Alexandros sat alone at the foot of the cliffs.
To the west, the winter sun slipped behind the few clouds
that gathered. Above him towered the bleak, black pyra-
mid of Mount Athos. It cast shadows across the ash-
coloured monastery, which rang with the gentle sound of
kitchens at work. Soon the bell would toll, signalling the
evening meal. For now, however, the Father seemed glad
of his own company and was in no rush to climb the
steep steps carved into the side of the cliff-face above.

The wispy beard that ran down the front of his black
robes quickly told anybody who cared to look that the
monk was not young. He had seen many days draw to an

end from the boulder on which he now sat. A scholar and teacher in the Monastery of Lviron the Abbot had now given him a freedom during the day denied to the dwindling number of novices who passed through the ageing teacher's classes. So long as he attended morning and evening prayers then there need be no more back-breaking work in the gardens, or gutting of fish in the kitchens. He had time; time to contemplate on the forty years he had spent almost entirely within the confines of the monastery that rose above him that November day.

His usual calm reflections, though, had been disturbed these last few weeks. He was not able to pinpoint why, but he knew that the violent storms of late September had marked a change in his mood. Lasting for four long days, he had never known such ferocious winds; the seas were stirred into a tempestuous display of foaming anger that terrified even the sea-hardened boatmen who kept the monastery in supplies.

From these very boatmen he had heard news of the damage suffered by the mainland; the landslides over Mount Olympus, the loss of life, and even the lightening strikes in Athens that lit up the Parthenon in such an awesome display of majestic power.

But why the feeling of unease?

Nagging questions had begun to encircle his carefully bordered mind. Behind him were decades of training, deliberately designed to keep the conscience from exploring paths that opened up the unanswerable. Even if his mind did wander this place of retreat, next to the tranquil sea, was normally so calming to his soul.

The rhythms of his life had been disturbed.

The sound of the bell shook him from his melancholy reflections. Wrapping his robes around him, he began the steady climb up the many steps that led back to the monastery. Grateful for the knowledge that the meal would be had in silence he slipped in quietly, if somewhat out of breath, thinking to allow the disturbing feelings that surrounded him to find cover in the uniformity of monastic life.

But to the surprise of the other monks, he continued through the great hall as if subject to a sudden and uncharacteristic change of mind. He made his way to the library, for which only he and the Abbot had keys. He shut the large wooden door firmly behind him, as if hoping that the gesture might somehow cause the thoughts that had pursued him in the weeks gone by to recede.

Looking round the room he took in the familiar smell of rotting velum, drawing comfort from the shadows that danced across the room as he settled the lantern down on the desk in front of him. This library of memories and documented aspirations had been a constant source of inspiration over the many years of study that had gone before. Drawing breath, he paused, glad of the privacy the space afforded him; no one but the Abbot himself would dare disturb him here.

To his right were the beautifully illustrated scrolls documenting a myriad of Councils. Next to them lay theological papers, charting the history of Orthodoxy since the terrible and cataclysmic schism with Catholicism that had ripped open in 1054, many centuries after the poison had first entered the system. Covered in dust, to him they were a reminder of how disenchanted he had become by the Machiavellian politics of his own religious institution.

Picking up a couple of leather bound books he placed them carefully to one side. The interest of Alexandros in the Desert Fathers, who had sought escape from the claustrophobia of imperialist ambition, was known to most of the men in the monastery. Little, though, was known of his interest in those other wild people of the Way that dwelt on the margins of the North-west Europe. He paused for a few moments, pondering once again why such extreme people of the faith seemed most happy on the edges of civilisation. After many years of reflection he had some answers, but he knew they were lacking substance.

His attention turned to the map of the world that was laid upon his desk. Letting his gaze rest on the Middle East and the ancient Bishoprics of Jerusalem, Antioch and Constantinople, he tried to ignore the pain in his soul, as reminders jumped out at him of the devastating decline the church had suffered in the last one hundred years. In Istanbul the last descendants of Byzantium were leaving what was once the capital of Christendom. As for the east of Turkey, the Syrian Orthodox Church was virtually extinct and in the Lebanon the Maronites had all but completely abandoned that most beautiful of countries.[10] Indeed, he acknowledged, many of the monasteries that once rang to the sound of life now lay empty. His own home was a rare exception. The gardens were long over-grown and where there might still be a few ageing monks left, they carried the forlorn look of those who had long since lost hope in that to which they had given themselves. No longer were there candlelit processions to darken the winter nights or the great councils to stimulate debate and pride, for all that was left were memories and the sounds of the prayer call from the nearby mosque.

---

[10]Dalrymple (1997) From the Holy Mountain Flamingo.

Moving to the far side of the map, his manner lightened as he looked upon the western seaboard of the United States. It might not have been so, but it seemed as if a smile just began to turn the corners of his mouth up as he settled back into his favourite chair. During those few minutes of contemplation it was as if he was somehow transported back to those shores and the wonderful months of walking that had taken him down the coastline of Northern California from the Oregon border, tracing the pathways of Russian Orthodoxy all the way through to San Francisco. Smiling broadly now, he remembered the clear, blue-skied days during which he walked through the redwood forests, dipping down off the hills into the beautiful vineyards just north of that great city. There, in that incredible place of San Francisco the pilgrimage came to an end, for a pilgrimage is what it had become.

It was only the third time since entering the monastery forty years ago that he had left its confines. The first was for the death of his Mother; the second for a reason only the Abbot knew of. On this last occasion, just over two years ago, it was to walk and to pray somewhere far away where he could leave his robes behind. Indeed that is what he did, until a chance encounter just a few days before returning home.

Almost as if he had suddenly caught sight of something, he drew a small key from the inside pocket of his robe, and unlocked a hidden draw just beneath his desk. Carefully, he brought out a set of rosary beads. Placing them on the desk he reached further into the draw and gently eased a small photograph out of the recesses. Picking it up, he moved the lamp nearer as he let his fingers glide over the beads on the table.

The photograph was dated 29 May 2004. It showed him warmly shaking the hand of another man of the cloth, though one most obviously not of the Orthodox ways, given the garments of Rome that he wore. The tenderness of the moment was readily apparent.

To the rear of the two men could just be made out a sign on the front of the Catholic Mission. It said 'Sonoma Mission House', then underneath in small letters, 'The most northerly mission house in California.'

He sighed as he cast is mind back to those few days, and the wonder of a chance meeting that had opened up in a most beautiful way. Quietly he savoured the memory of Father O'leary, on finding him looking round the mission, inviting him back to his home, and them both talking long into the night. Chuckling, he savoured again the taste of whiskey as they shared a small glass together. Then the moment of genuine apology, as the two acknowledged the tragedy of all that had separated their churches for centuries. Even now a tear came to the corner of his eye. There were many tears late that night in Sonoma.

He lingered longer in that far western corner of the globe. He enjoyed the memory of the breakfast shared the following day, and the incredulity they both felt when they realised that the year of 2004 was one of the few years in the calendar when the Orthodox date for Easter and the Catholic date for Easter coincided. "Not only that," Alexandros had said, almost shouting out loud as he did so, "But Easter also lines up with the Passover Festival." A stunned reverence fell on them, as they allowed their minds to explore an astonishing backdrop to their chance encounter.

Returning to the map in front of him he allowed his finger to trace the outline of the coastline as he tracked the movement of Catholicism, spreading as it did up the coastline from Mexico. He let it to run across the northern most point of Alaska, subconsciously tracing the paths of Russian Orthodoxy down all the way to San Francisco. There he allowed his finger to linger, almost as if he was rehearsing in his own mind the meeting point of these great bastions of the faith, thousands of miles away on the other side of the world.

A connecting point had been found in a chance encounter with a Priest of Catholicism. The gap had momentarily been bridged between Rome and Constantinople, Catholicism and Orthodoxy. It was the very reason he had asked to stay on Mount Athos these many years gone, praying year after year that this unbridgeable divide might one day close again.

Carefully he placed the beads and the photograph back in the draw, turning the key very precisely, knowing the huge misunderstandings that would unfold should they ever be discovered. Idly he picked up the embossed invitation that lay on his desk. There in wonderful calligraphy was the invitation that had caused envy across the whole of the monastery:

'The Patriarch Bartholomew invites Father Alexandros to attend the Divine Liturgy led by Pope Benedict XV1 at the Church of St George, Istanbul, 28 November 2006.'

How can this be? Could it be that these two meetings, half a world apart, were somehow linked? Of course, his rational mind said it was impossible. But this was indeed why he had entered the monastic order those many years ago, so full of youthful endeavour and high ideals; to see a coming together of these two great institutions and a closing of the great gulf between them. For so long it had seemed as far away as ever.

Deep down he marvelled at the beautiful way in which his insignificant life had been crafted into some greater plan.

Turning to blow out the lamp it seemed as if suddenly his mind was made up. The indecision of the last few weeks was gone. Opening the door, he made his way back through the empty hall and out into the moonlit courtyard. The cobbled stones were smooth and hardly made a noise under the muffled footsteps of his sandaled feet. Looking up into the starlit sky he felt sad that his days in the monastery were about to come to an end; but he was glad that the decision had been made.

Opening the door of his cell he allowed himself a couple of minutes to compose his thoughts. Sitting at the small desk that rested against the white-washed walls, he pulled a piece of paper out from the draw. Picking up a pen he began to write:

'Dear Abbot,

After long reflection and prayer, I have decided that it is time for me to leave the monastery and find a fresh pathway elsewhere. I write, therefore, to ask your permission to make this final exit through the gates of these walls just after my visit to Istanbul in a few days time. I have a journey to make that cannot be confined to the monastery; a journey that will take me south to the lands of Egypt, and north to the edges of the western Isles of Scotland. I humbly ask your blessing that I may, in these lands, find fresh direction for the new course my life must now take.

Peace be with you,

Alexandros'

Putting down the pen he sighed, with the sigh of a man who knew the return of the inner peace that he put such a high price on. Looking up at the white washed walls he noticed the frame hanging at the head of his bed. There, in wonderfully illustrated letters, was the document that marked his ordination those many years ago. For a moment it held his gaze. Had he looked closer he would have seen the date of that ceremony performed those many years ago: 28 November 1966.

Standing up, he moved across to the window that looked out on the moonlit sea. It had been a big day and he was glad it was over.

Somehow, sitting there in his cell, the room seemed to fill with the presence of something else, or was it someone else. He knew that in recent weeks he had been set a demanding test; perhaps more demanding than anything since he entered the monastery forty years ago. "Maybe there's life in the old bones yet," he thought to himself, as he lay down on the bed to sleep.

CHAPTER 18

Thessaloniki to Istanbul

Steve Lowton

**THESSALONIKI TO THE TURKISH
BORDER October 2006
Team: Andy, Val, Andrea, Debs and Steve H**

Yesterday a team arrived home after taking our journey
out of Greece and into Turkey, crossing the political
boundary that marks the end of Europe and the beginning of Asia. The geographical boundary will not be
crossed until we bridge the Bosporus Straits, but already
we in transition for all that lies before us. On Tuesday 31
October the third and final team for this leg fly out to
take the walk into the huge gateway city of Istanbul. In
the meantime, this is the report for last week, written by
Andy Crump, the leader of the team.

Andy writes:

By now we should not be surprised that so often what we
consider to be a fairly random week's walking, with a
random group of people, turns out to have the Maker's
fingerprint and design all over it; and so it was with this
section.

The team dynamic was very different from last time, as we included a female majority, with people from across the UK, including two Celts, Welsh and Scots. The wisdom of heaven on this soon becoming apparent.

Walking away from Thessaloniki we saw the physical damage from the earlier floods, including ruptured land, roads and bridges with rubbish and debris deposited in towns and fields, as if the whole place had been shaken, with all the hidden debris becoming exposed. It was in to this rupturing of the land that we found a grace to speak words of healing, with songs of the Father's love for the nation of Greece and the bad choices of the nation.

In the places of idolatry and Greek myth, so evident as you walk, we were able to proclaim the wonderful story of Jesus and His great exploits; it is the greatest story, with the best hero. The squeeze is on, however; many on the team were battling throat and chest infections, with no ability to sing or shout. BUT our God is a fire and he is shaking all: "for God is not an indifferent bystander. He's actively cleaning house, torching all that needs to burn and He won't quit until it's all cleansed. God himself is Fire."

In this region there is a tangled web of bad history between the Greeks and Turks, with much bloodshed, war and occupation. Our host was not able to enter Turkey because of his family name; death threats were given to his father as he studied in Istanbul in the 1950s. We can only thank God that He is able to unravel all of the mess and bring healing to the land. We rest in the knowledge that He is God and we are not.

Nearing the border region looking towards Turkey and Istanbul, where the Celtic anointing was so needed, God gave us a sweet sign. Whilst walking I was

approached by a Greek man of 81 years, who asked if
we were walking from the UK. He had lived in Scotland and England, fought in the war alongside the
French and Italians, and then lived in Jerusalem for
four years. His name was Constantine!

On the day we crossed into Turkey, we soaked in
God's presence before walking. Seeking His face and
fragrance the Fathers heart and travail was heavy upon
us, particularly the females amongst us, as they carried
the burdens of heaven for the women suppressed by
empire, Christendom and Islam, bound by man and religion. It's with humility and peace that we are able to
overcome, so we laughed and sang our way through this
day, coming in the opposite spirit to the contesting we
encountered as we passed through customs in to Turkey.

Six, rich days of wonderful prayer, fun and joy (after
all, we were dubbed, 'the holiday team') came to an end,
some 10km within Turkey, having just happened to stop
outside a large grain storehouse, with 'Celtic' written on
the side. We broke bread, celebrating the Father's love
for this land and people, with our feet amongst the grain
and seed, scattered all over the road.

Hey, wonderful days.

TURKISH BORDER TO ISTANBUL,
November 2006
Team: Paul, Richard, Dave, Chris and myself

I write this from Istanbul, having just given myself to
what is probably my last day of walking this year. I
return to the UK tomorrow with yet another team who
have given themselves totally to all that we are walking
for. I also return knowing that two forty- day seasons

have run their course. I am alert to the moving of the hand of the hidden One. I also return overwhelmed by the privilege of having participated in a walk across the breadth of a continent, and my deepest respect goes to every single person who has walked with us, stood with us in prayer, encouraged us, laughed at us and journeyed with us as we have tracked with the ancient pathways.

To bring insight to these few days of walking I have asked Paul Wood to make some comments on our journey through Istanbul.

Paul writes:

Whether it is still the 'City of the World's Desire' or not, Istanbul was a major focus for these few days, sitting where Europe ends and Asia begins, where East meets West and on the major sea route from Russia down to the Mediterranean. As we approached we felt the tremendous squeeze on the city between Eastern and Western powers, if a city of some 18 million inhabitants that spreads for 80km could be called 'squeezed'.

Here is the funnelling of the spirits of war and capitalism into the Middle East and the spirit of Islam into Europe, with the nation of Turkey not knowing who to align with. The cost of misalignment has been high in the past. So our call to the city was not to align with any empire, but to align itself as a gateway with heaven. As empires are shaken there is danger that, with rival empires preferring to live with each other than be crushed by the Kingdom that comes down from heaven, Istanbul could stand for many unholy alliances.

To illustrate this, at the heart of the old city stand the Haghia Sophia, once the cathedral of the Eastern Roman empire, and the Blue Mosque, mimicking one another's massive squat domes fringed with sharp towers. How little difference there is between religions aligned with imperialism.

We passed through the broken-down Topkapi gate in a blizzard and took refuge in a cafe while we waited for our hosts to meet us. 'Otherside' by the Red Hot Chilli Peppers was playing and the words struck us with prophetic impact: "Once you know you can never go back / I've got to take it on the other side".

Carrying with us the squeeze of unresolved situations at home, we knew that there was to be such significance in not stopping here in this city but pushing through, taking what we carry to the 'otherside', the opening out into the unknown beyond of Asia.

Steve writes:

So we pushed through with strong declarations. We were 120km into Asia before we finally came off the walk for the winter. With snow on the hills we marked the point at which teams will return in the spring, to journey through a land drenched with the blood of martyrs. Through four nations and many wonderful cities we have began to taste again the wild ways of the early Celts. From the purple moors of Whitby and North Yorkshire we have seen the sun set over the Coliseum in Rome and lightening strike over the Parthenon in Athens, and we have heard the prayer call of the Mosques of Istanbul as they herald in the dawn of each day.

We walked out of Europe knowing that everything has its time and place to shift. Mountains do indeed move at the command of the Ancient of Days. We now turn our faces to Asia and to walking through Turkey to the borders of Syria. We wait for instruction on whether we then go through Damascus or Beirut. In the meantime, if you would like to be considered for one of the teams then I will be putting details out very soon.

To Dave, Val, Guido, Joyce, Katie, Tim, Paul, Andy, Rowena, Stew, Steve, Helen, Richard, Chris, Andrea and Debbie I want to say thank you for making my life richer for your companionship whilst on the road. Since leaving Rome we have prayed many prayers and walked many kilometres. You are heroes to me and I am grateful to for you all. Finally I want to thank and honour Kathy, my wife. Through these forty days since leaving Athens you have nursed our newly adopted daughter, Jin Zhou, in long sleepless nights and some anxious days. Thank you for holding through in the synergy and tension that connects this walk to home.

Our intercession is our life and on the breaking of this fortieth day I declare space for Jin Zhou and for every household squeezed at this time. So through thousands of kilometres walked our declaration remains strong; there is space between the gates of Europe.

REFLECTIONS FROM HOME

Our progress into Istanbul was as dramatic a time of walking as I have ever known. Istanbul is a place full of history and to walk in under the shadow of the city walls an amazing experience. Furthermore, it's not that often anyone gets to walk from one continent into another.

To return to the UK knowing that we had walked across the breadth of Europe was incredible. Somehow teams had come together for every step of the way; a mobile prayer movement was beginning to emerge.

We took note of the planned visit of the Pope to Istanbul, scheduled for the 28 November, just a few days after our departure. Having walked during 2004 in the most western point of the world that is California, where Russian Orthodoxy met Catholicism, it seemed another of those strange "coincidences" to be here in Istanbul just prior to the new Pope coming to meet the Patriarch of Greek Orthodoxy, a sister to its Russian counterpart. In California we had followed the movement of Orthodoxy all the way from the Oregon border until it encountered in San Francisco the spread of Catholicism up from the borders with Mexico. Furthermore, with Orthodox and Catholic dates for Easter coinciding that year, as did the date for the Passover Festival, here we were again sandwiched between a coming together of east and west, even as both San Francisco and Istanbul sit at points where east meets west. Strange affairs indeed and a subject I continue to meditate upon.

On the plane home I was convinced that there was a shift for us as a family also, on the issues of health that threatened us also in our small business. Faith was high and the heady mix of all that we had walked through and into, a potent driving force. Ever so slowly however, I began to realise that the moment of turning that I had been looking for was not to be. This was as tough as it could get for Kathy and me; after all surely the Lord owed us on this? We had risked so much in this walk across a continent. Surely he understood that? With credit card bills pressing in and Zhou's health no better I felt as low as I could go. Indeed a growing sense of shame began to ensnare me, as I tortured myself with accusations of irresponsibility at the way in which Kathy had been left to cope with so much. Seemingly I had misread the signs. Despite the strength of declaration on the road it seemed Zhou's guts were as bad as ever and that, in fact, there was no space at all for her life to prosper, whatever we had declared between these global gates.

Over the coming weeks I spent many a morning watching the early morning rush hour traffic wend its way into the city of Leeds, looking as I did out of the front window of my home. Had I completely missed it? Was I indeed on some wild goose chase and should I now return to normal life? Was it just a load of nonsense that the little people of life could in fact influence the affairs of our world? Bruised and hurting I looked for comfort, but the self-questioning remained.

CHAPTER 19

Istanbul: Under Byzantium's Crescent Moon

Paul Wood

Paul is a great friend and one who, having lived in Egypt for eight years, understands well the ways of the Middle East. Currently living in the south of England he is married and has two teenage children. In between the addiction to adventure and nurturing his love of Africa and the Muslim world, Paul gives himself to painting and decorating as a way of earning a living. Here he describes something of the incredible history of Istanbul.

The Gateway
"Carry the pressure right through the gates," the Celtic saints urged us. "We found God in adversity; you can too. Why would he be anywhere else?"

They might well say that, for the city we were heading for knew more than any other what it is to be under pressure from all sides. So we set our faces to the icy wind and dragged our aching limbs and unanswered prayers the last few miles towards Istanbul.

The 'City of the World's Desire' it was called. Who could live with that kind of attention? A global gateway opening up the lands of the East to the West and the lands of the West to the East, the Northern lands to the South and the Southern lands to the North. But more than that it seems, a gateway between heaven and earth; where heavenly ambitions reached down to earth, and earthly ambitions rose to the heavens.

Amidst swirling snow we passed through the gateway and when we paused on the inside we heard the ghosts of embattled gatekeepers calling down to us from the walls.

"Take it on the other side," they said. "You gotta take it on the other side!"

No lingering here then, so after a brief rest we plodded on deeper into the city; closer to the end of Europe. We had no idea of the history we were walking into, or the enormity of the shattered dreams that lay around our feet.

Byzas of Megara

A man stood on a hilltop in the last of the evening sunshine and gazed out over the landscape that spread out around him. He had landed a few weeks previously on the beach below, after navigating his way across the great sweep of sea that he could now see stretching away to the southern horizon. He was a Greek, lean, strong and in the prime of life. He had come all the way from Megara with family and followers in search of new adventures and a new life, following the paths of the gods. Back there, there was no room for men like him: men with ambition. Many were leaving in search of new lands. So he had been to Delphi to consult the Pythia, the oracle through whom Apollo spoke. That encounter had changed his life.

"Opposite the blind; opposite the blind," he muttered to himself, recalling the words that had come from the mouth of the entranced old peasant woman.

To the east he saw the channel known as 'Cows Ford' or Bosphorous, which separated the hill on which he was standing from the distant shore of Asia. There were Greek settlers, like him, already living over there. They called it Chalcedon. He could just make out the last few fishing boats heading home for the night. To the north he could see there was a wide river flowing out into the Bosphorous. The hill he was standing on was surrounded by natural harbours and abundant fishing; it was protected by water on three sides and so only needed to be defended on one side. It was a gift of the gods, a natural fortress. He puzzled over why the settlers on the other side had overlooked this hill and chosen to settle in Chalcedon, on the edge of the great unknown continent. They must have been blind.

Then it suddenly came to him: yes, they were the blind ones and this was the place that Apollo had directed him to.

The ground under his feet heard, and trembled imperceptibly. The deities that had long rested on that hill drew around close to mark his words. He turned and walked back down the hillside towards the small encampment by the shore, where his family and the others who had travelled with him had built their temporary homes.

Byzas was a typical Greek. He came from a land where gods and men mingled freely, and where a man might become a god through great achievements. Strength, heroism, doing what no-one else had done; that was what made a man great, and he felt like a great man that evening.

The smell of fish cooking on the fire greeted him as he walked into camp. His brothers had been successful too, it seemed. That evening as they sat round and ate, Byzas was restless and distant.

"What's on your mind, Byzas?" his brother asked.

He seemed not to have heard. He was rapt in visions of the city that would make his name great. There had been other revelations given to him at Delphi. It was to this very shore, many years ago, that a beautiful woman named Io had fled. She was the daughter of a river-god, mistress of Zeus, and had come disguised as a white heifer. She had swum the strait to the other side to escape Hera, the jealous wife of Zeus. That's how the place got its name. Io had been carrying the child of Zeus, and that child was his own mother.

He came to and looked up, realising the others were watching him expectantly.

"Tomorrow we must move," he said. "I've been up the hill today and I know now it's the place that Apollo directed me to."

Byzas was filled with the confidence of a hero that evening. The gods were with him. Now he knew he was a son of the gods himself.

"We're Greeks aren't we? The gods have chosen us; the mantle has fallen on our shoulders. They're just Barbarians. They can either leave, or be our carriers. People will soon come and join us and our city will be great; maybe one day greater even than Athens."

A crescent moon of extraordinary brightness was appearing in the darkening sky. Byzas looked up at it and a shiver ran down his spine. The destiny of his city was surely marked out in the heavens.

So, by stages they moved onto the hill and began to build their city, and the hill became the first hill of Byzantium. The year was 675 BC.

As Byzas had foreseen, Byzantium became a great city and stood for a thousand years. The crescent moon became her symbol and her position at the gateway of continents made her the desire of all who aspired to world domination. But there were secrets of her potential that remained hidden, waiting for the extraordinary vision that would unlock them.

One day such a visionary came through her gates. He exalted her above all rivals, named her after himself and left her as his legacy. Under a new name – Constantinople - the city revealed her full nature. She became capital, not only of a political empire, but of a religious one. The light of Constantinople's crescent moon shone for a thousand years, as Byzantium's had done before her, with the simple addition of the Virgin's solitary star.

On the hill where Byzas had first stood, a great church was built. It was the epicentre of the Christian Empire, through which it was imagined the whole world would be enlightened. It was known as St Sophia, the Holy Wisdom.

Constantine XI Dragases

On the evening of the 28 May 1453, Vespers was in already in progress in the great church of St Sophia when Constantine XI, the last Byzantine emperor, walked through the great doors, accompanied by his knights. That night everyone in the city who was not able to fight, rich and poor, Latin and Greek, had laid aside their differences and gathered under the great dome for a mass that, for most of them, would be their last.

The giant Theodosian walls that had stood for a thousand years were all that separated the Christian city from the vast Muslim army now arrayed against it. For forty-eight days the Sultan's artillery had kept up a relentless bombardment. Though the defenders laboured tirelessly day and night to shore up the damage, food in the city was now running out, and they were leaving their posts for ever longer periods to forage for themselves and their families. The Ottoman fleet, ascendant over the Byzantines for the first time in history, ensured that no relief ship or fishing vessel got through. Just seven thousand men able to bear arms stood on the walls to face the young Sultan Mehmet's army of a hundred thousand. That day Constantine had refused both his own opportunity to flee and the terms of surrender offered by Mehmet. Tomorrow, Mehmet had told them, he would storm the city.

In St Sophia that evening Constantine, turning to each of his companions, asked forgiveness for any wrongs he might have done them. Then, humbling himself before the priests, both Orthodox and Catholic, he begged forgiveness for his sins.

Later that night he returned to the church alone. It was deserted and darkened, but for a few candles that flickered precariously in the darkness. He collapsed on the floor and wept, beside himself with exhaustion. He had hardly slept in weeks. His sobs echoed and faded, lost in the vastness, and his tears fell on the cold marble slabs.

There had been terrible omens. Three days earlier the priests had been carrying the icon of the Virgin around the city, beseeching her for deliverance, when she had slipped and fallen. They had struggled vainly to raise her from the ground. No sooner had they got her up and moving again than a thunderstorm had burst over the city and torrential rain flooded the streets, causing the procession to be finally abandoned. At dawn the next day a thick and eerie fog shrouded the city like a corpse. When it lifted the great church was lit by a strange red glow that seemed to rise slowly from its base to the top of its dome, then lift off it. Those who saw it dared not speak of what it seemed to imply. Was there yet a prayer that could save the holy city, or had the presence of God departed from this, the first and last bastion of Christian empire?

There was silence.

Eventually Constantine's sobs subsided, and his exhausted mind and body dragged him to the brink of sleep. In that borderland of consciousness the footsteps of the generations that had trod the floor on which he lay grew louder and clearer. Voices echoed in the darkness, and ghostly figures appeared in visions.

He saw the gates of a city enveloped in dark clouds, crumbling and falling, and from them came an emperor, carrying a great cross and leading a long procession. The procession crossed many lands and came to a new city, which they entered. The emperor took a quill and into a stone pillar carved the words 'The New Rome'. Then he sat down on a throne on a hill at the centre of the city and said, "I myself was the instrument God chose." All the people bowed down before him and the cross. As he sat on the hill a church was built around him and a crescent moon descended onto the top of it.

Constantine recognised that this was his ancestor, Constantine the Great, son of a Helena like himself. Was the builder of Constantinople returning now to save his city?

"Constantine, where are you?" he shouted. "Is this how your dream ends?" But the Great Emperor on his throne had faded from view.

Then he saw another figure: a bishop, standing by the high altar. He was gesticulating wildly, angrily. Fireballs came from his mouth, falling on the palace and the statues of gods and goddesses, which caught fire and began to burn. He knew this person. It was John Chrysostom.

But before John could answer an angry Empress appeared, surrounded by soldiers, and they drove the fiery cleric out of the church. As John crossed the threshold there was an earthquake and the church itself caught fire behind him.

Amongst the burned ruins of the church, another emperor appeared. He rebuilt the church with ten times the glory it had previously displayed. Precious jewels were brought from the whole world to adorn it. Then the emperor stood under the great dome, looked up to heaven and declared: "Oh Solomon, I have outdone you!"

"Justinian!" Constantine cried, "Will your temple stand in this hour, or will it be torn down?"

But, like the others, Justinian too disappeared and he was left alone.

He woke and sat up with a start, breathless and reeling from what he had seen. He was suddenly alert to past, present and future, to heaven and earth, in a way he had never experienced before. Gradually, his heart stopped racing and he knew exactly what was required of him. He felt small and utterly crushed; yet if this was to be his Gethsemane then there was a prayer - a legacy - which, even if unanswerable in his last, short hours, could still be thrust into the ground for the sake of generations to come. A prayer began to pour from the depths of his soul:

"My God, why have you turned your face away from us? Who am I that the fate of these people, this city, should now rest on my shoulders? But if this is to be our last hour, Lord, let me fight for my people with courage and, if I must, die alongside them with honour. Remember me, Lord; remember that I have not abandoned them. Oh God, have mercy on us.

"And as for this city, this dream of a light that would shine upon the world has slipped through our fingers like sand. She is the city that the entire world desires, yet she crushes those who embrace her. Christianity is a faith this city has not understood. Now her sins have heaped up to the heavens and judgement breaks over us like the waves of the sea. Though her light be extinguished and we be cast into darkness, let it not be forever. But when the time of judgement is finished, bring gatekeepers to watch over her who are faithful and true. Let her light one day shine bright and pure, and let what is seen in her illuminate the world. For this was her destiny."

And with his palms he ground his words into the marble floor, mixed with tears and sweat. And the ground beneath him drew them in and sighed deeply.

There was silence.

He felt a hidden strength flow into his heart and limbs and, with renewed courage, Constantine rose and walked out into the night. He mounted his horse and rode briskly to the palace, where he said farewell to his mother and the servants. Then he went out to ride the length of the walls one last time. As he went he called out to his men, exhorting them to acquit themselves as the true heroes of Greece and Rome always had. Around midnight he went to his chosen position on the walls. None of them had long to wait.

Mehmet II

Outside the walls, the Turkish soldiers had been sheltering from the torrential rain that had poured down a few nights before. In the morning they had all seen the thick fog over the city. Mehmet had been told of the strange glow that had lit up the great church and he was concerned. He was well aware that his Father's old advisers were set against attacking Constantinople. Maybe there were surprises lurking inside that ancient city, with its strange religion. What did these signs mean? He sent orders for the astrologers to attend him at once.

They came prepared with their interpretation:

Their counsel spurred him into action. There were rumours that a relief army might arrive for Constantinople from the West. They had waited long enough; the city had to be taken without delay. One day for preparations, one day for prayer, and then the attack would begin on Tuesday 29 May.

At 1.30 on the morning of the 29th, just an hour and a half after Constantine had taken his position on the walls, Mehmet ordered the assault to begin. Turkish trumpets, drums and war-cries mingled with the pealing of church bells over the city as wave after wave of infantry, siege towers and ladders were flung against the walls. For a few hours the resistance stood firm; but before dawn the walls were breached and the Turks poured through the gaps. The last emperor of Byzantium threw off his royal garments and flung himself valiantly into the incoming tide. He died as he had resolved; alongside his friends. His body was never found.

For many, St Sophia was the last sanctuary that morning. Matins was disrupted as the Turkish soldiers burst through the door. The people were cut down in the aisles, or where they knelt or stood, but the priests resolutely continued their ministry to the last. As the Turks reached the threshold of the high altar, it is said the last priest gathered up the chalice, plate and remaining sacraments in his arms, stepped through the wall and disappeared. It is believed he still waits patiently inside for the tide of history to swing again. When the city once again becomes Christian he will re-emerge and continue administering the sacraments where he left off.

By sunrise the cries of battle had abated and the bells of the city had fallen silent. Mehmet walked back to his tent and sat down. Apart from dispatching a rider with news of the victory, there was little to be done now until his army had had their customary three days of plunder. He could see the crescent moon of the Ottoman flag now fluttering above the walls. Had not his ancestor Othman, father of the Ottomans, dreamed of a crescent moon stretching across the whole world, from east to west? Dreams were coming to pass that day, even as old dreams were dying.

Late in the afternoon of the same day he called an abrupt end to the looting, mounted his mule and in royal regalia made his entry into the city. It would be fitting to end Istanbul's first day by giving thanks to God. He rode down the main thoroughfare directly to St Sophia. He wept to see the destruction that he had wreaked on a city of such incomparable beauty. At the door of the Church he dismounted and knelt on the ground. At the age of twenty-one, with all the brashness of youth, he had done what his predecessors had advised against and thought was impossible. He had conquered the great imperial city of Christendom that had resisted all-comers for a thousand years. He had raised the crescent moon of Othman's dynasty over the city of the crescent moon. He had ushered the Ottomans into the one city that could put an Islamic empire at the centre of the world's stage. It was destiny. It was God's will.

He reached out and took a handful of dust from the ground at the foot of the steps and sprinkled it onto his own head. The hill beneath him groaned inaudibly under the weight of sacrifice that had been poured out upon it; and the crescent moon gazed down on the carnage and smiled on her new king.

Rising, he entered the church. He dismissed the looters who were still there amongst the mutilated bodies and pools of blood, hacking away the last remaining items of value, and summoned a muezzin to call the evening prayers. St Sophia, within the space of twenty-four hours, had heard the last prayers of the last emperor of Byzantium and the first prayers of the first Sultan of Istanbul. Constantinople had shed her aged skin, just as Byzantium had done before her, for Constantine the Great. A radiant new Istanbul emerged, rejuvenated for a new era, a new religion, and a new empire.

Mustafa Kemal

In the late summer of 1938, a most unusual guest walked into a Greek taverna in a small fishing village on the edge of the Bosphorus. He was Turkey's most celebrated son, Mustafa Kemal, known and loved as Atatürk, the Father of the Turks. Strangely, he had come unaccompanied by his usual bodyguards. He knew he did not have much longer to live, so there was little point now in worrying about personal security.

The tanned, wrinkled faces of the old fishermen, glowing with pride at his presence, reminded him of the faces of the Macedonian troops that he had commanded back in April 1909. They had been at his side when he had been thrust into the limelight of revolutionary politics. Back then, they had arrived in Istanbul by train and in three days they put down a rebellion of Muslim fundamentalists who had risen up in protest against modernisation.

In those days the powers of Europe and Russia had been gathering like vultures around the death throes of the stricken Ottoman Empire. Action was needed, and fast, if the Turks were to salvage a nation from the wreckage of empires that would result from the gathering storm. The counter-revolutionaries, who had demanded a return to traditional Islamic law, were tried and sentenced in the St Sophia.

This popular and courageous general had laid his hand upon the destiny of the Turkish nation as one would lay ones hand to the scruff of a dog's neck. Undaunted by the scavenging powers that surrounded them he had dragged them, writhing, into the modern world.

For a few hours he drank and danced with the local fishermen, and they remembered the tumultuous years that had marked their short lives.

Twenty years previously he had fought for his life on the Gallipoli Peninsula and had led Turkey's defenders to a costly, but unimagined, victory over the British and Anzacs. He had been injured, fought on, and become a hero, but in the long run the Turks could not hold out. The next year the Ottoman army was pushed out of

Damascus by the British and out of Beirut by the French. The Ottoman Empire crumbled, the British army marched into Istanbul on 13 November 1918, and the war was over. For the Islamic Empire the unthinkable had happened. After 500 years their capital had fallen into Infidel hands. But worse was to come.

Mustafa Kemal fled from Istanbul to the security of the Anatolian highlands, where he drew together a resistance movement. As the great powers retreated to lick their wounds after the bloodiest conflict the world had ever seen, only Greece, the ancient enemy, was left to try and steal the scraps of the old Empire. Kemal rallied the fledgling Turkish nation to defend itself, which it did with gusto, snatching Thrace from the Greeks before the final boundary lines of World War I were drawn up.

Kemal's work had only just begun, though. On 1 November 1922, as the first president of the Grand National Assembly of the new Turkish nation, he separated the political and religious powers; the sultanate and the caliphate. A few days later Vahideddin, his rival from the old order, the last sultan of the Ottoman Empire, fled from Istanbul in fear of his life. The next year the British troops boarded their warships and sailed away from Istanbul, leaving it again in the hands of the Turks. But the city that had given its heart to two world religious empires, could not be trusted to play a part in the future he saw for his people. He abandoned it as a capital a few days later, moved his base to Ankara and began his ruthless and visionary transformation of the Turkish nation.

On 3 March 1924 he abolished the caliphate and Abdul Mecit, the last religious leader of an Islamic Empire, left Istanbul for Paris, to live out the remaining twenty years of his life in exile. The only future Kemal saw was with the modernising, secular powers of the West. The conservative, backward-looking, religious powers of the East had to be dealt a death-blow. He went on to abolish every last vestige of institutional religion. He outlawed traditional clothing, religious practices and polygamy. He did away with Islamic Shariah law, the Muslim lunar calendar, and the Arabic script that could never be disentangled from the Quran. He replaced them all with their European counterparts. He closed the religious schools, and even went as far as making every person take a second name, western-style.

At last he had annulled the 1600-year marriage of religion and state that Constantine the Great had instituted. But the crescent moon that had shone down on Byzas that first night, and that had flown over the city under Byzantines and Ottomans, remained unmoved on the flagpoles of the new Turkish nation. The gods of the first hill were more tenacious than anyone knew.

That night at the Taverna, Atatürk returned to the very origins of the city with which he had wrestled for Turkey's destiny; a few Greek fishermen who lived their lives on the edge of the Bosphorous in a way not much changed since Byza had first led their ancestors there. They were the ones who had long ago followed the footsteps of their gods to discover a place upon which the whole world turned, and who probably understood it better than anyone.

After a few hours, anxious security staff burst in at the taverna. They were surprised, but relieved, to discover the president safe and in good spirits. They escorted him back to the Dolmabahçe Palace, where he retired to bed. Atatürk was dying of liver disease. He never appeared publicly again and died a few months later. All Turkey mourned for him.

The End of Europe

At dusk on a cold November day in 2006, my companions and I emerged from the crowded streets of Istanbul and found ourselves in the Sultanahmet Park that separates the city's two greatest icons. The massive, squat domes of St Sophia Church and the Blue Mosque, each fringed with needle-sharp minarets thrusting upwards into the grey winter sky, stood just a few hundred metres apart. They seemed to glare at one another across the neat pavements, lawns and fountains. Virtually identical in shape, size and ambition, they reminded us of the unearthly divisions and pressures that have marked the city throughout its life, and of how little difference there is between religions when they are married to state power. We felt like insignificant specs in that vast space, compressed between these two great monuments to imperial religion.

We were standing on a hill that has shuddered under the claims of empire builders and been saturated time and again with blood spilled for divine causes. The city under the crescent moon imbued her leaders with expansive vision, but always, in the end, staggered and fell under the unbearable weight of the heaven she tried to live up to.

That evening we wondered if perhaps now, free from the imperial burden she has carried for two millennia, Istanbul would have room to breathe; space to reorient herself. Was it time for deep, long-forgotten cries to be answered, for brave souls to come and stand in the gates; gatekeepers who will turn their backs on power and, in diminutive weakness, set their shoulders to the pressing in of north, south, east and west. Then perhaps, against all odds, this city at the centre of the world will rise to the divine connection that something deep in her foundations has always pointed to. And, declining alignment with any earthly empire, will align herself with heaven for the sake of the whole world.

For a few moments we huddled together against the vast sweep of history and the icy winter wind and took a few photographs. Then we responded the only way we knew how. We looked through the gates and set our faces to the great unknown that lay beyond, and hurried on the last few steps to the edge of the Bosphorous; the very end of the end of Europe.

FACT FILE: ISTANBUL

Crescent Moon Symbolism

The crescent moon was used as a symbol of a goddess in Sumerian culture as early as 2100 BC.

In 670 BC, the citizens of Byzantium made the crescent moon their state symbol after an important victory. Byzantium was the first governing state to use the crescent moon as its national symbol. It was the symbol of Artemis/Diana, goddess of the hunt.

In 330 AD, Constantine rededicated the city to the Virgin Mary, whose star symbol was added to the crescent.

In 1299, conquering what is now Turkey, Sultan Osman had a vision of a crescent moon stretching over the world; it thus became the symbol of the Ottoman dynasty.

The crescent symbol came into general use by Muslims after their capture of the city of Constantinople in 1453.

Some Muslims today object the use of the crescent moon as the international symbol of Islam because of its pagan origins.

(Moon and Star Symbolism, www.wikipedia.org, accessed January 2008)

The End of the Sunni Caliphate

In a videotaped pronouncement in 2001 Osama bin Laden made mention of the humiliation and disgrace that Islam has suffered for more than eighty years. He was referring to the overthrow of the Ottoman Empire; the partition of Muslim territories amongst infidel nations; the occupation of its capital, Istanbul, by the British; and the abolition of the Islamic caliphate by Atatürk. The caliph, or commander of the faithful, is the spiritual and political head of Sunni Islam and, until 1922, the caliphate had continued unbroken since the prophet Muhammad.

"It remained a potent symbol of Muslim unity, even identity; its disappearance under the double assault of foreign imperialists and domestic modernists, was felt throughout the Muslim world...Many Muslims are still painfully conscious of this void, and it is said that Usama bin Laden himself had - or has - aspirations to the caliphate."

(p xvii, Lewis, Bernard (2003) *The Crisis of Islam: Holy War and Unholy Terror* Phoenix)

Istanbul Today

Istanbul's population was 10 million in 2001, of which 99.5% in Muslim. Since 1900 the Christian population of Turkey (Armenian, Assyrian and Greek) has declined from 22% to less than 0.5% due to massacres and emigration.

(pp663-634, Johnston, Patrick and Mandryk, Jason (2001) *Operation World* Paternoster Press)

International Espionage

During World War II, Istanbul became one of the world's major espionage centres. Agents of all the world's powers still use it a base to observe each other and trade in information.

People Trafficking

"Turkey is a major destination and transit country for women and children trafficked primarily for the purpose of commercial sexual exploitation."

The women are shipped across the Black Sea into Istanbul, mainly from Ukraine, Russia and Moldova. Profits from this trade are estimated at   3.6 billion annually.

www.gvnet.com/humantrafficking/turkey
www.ungift.org
www.countertrafficking.org
All accessed January 2008.

CHAPTER 20

Turkey to Syria:
March 2007

Steve Lowton

REFLECTIONS FROM HOME

Kathy and I talked on and off all through those winter
months as to whether the walk should continue. Neither
of us were quitters by nature, but that in itself can be a
weakness. Putting the walk on hold was a genuine
option, but we did not want to live our lives out of the
fear of consequences. There had been a slight improvement for Zhou's health, but Hannah was still very ill.
Financially we had restructured our debt and sold at cost
price part of a deal we were involved with. That meant
we could keep out on the road a few more months. Without a doubt, though, the clincher was the rise in encouragement and support that came from valued friends
across the city of Leeds. The knowledge that there would
be people meeting in our basement lounge each and
every day I was away, to pray for the home and for us
also, was massive. What was also a huge factor was the
team I had with me. Richard and Dave had walked with

me all the way up through from Athens and were to stay out on the road with me all the way to Jerusalem. Along with a good friend, also called Steve, I was as confident as I had always been of the team that was shaping up. We decided to go for it; so it was with genuine excitement that I prepared to get back out to hit the road that faced into all the mystery that is the Middle East.

We had decided that to go via Ankara, the capital city of Turkey even though it was some extra 200 km out of our way. To understand Turkey Istanbul is not enough, for it is Ankara that controls its destiny, or so it thinks.

PREPARATIONS FOR TURKEY
March 2007

It is with great excitement that I will be getting back out on the walk through into the heart of Turkey this Monday, 19 March. With the Near East in sight, and just over the horizon Syria, Israel, Palestine and Jerusalem, fresh energy comes to a journey that began two years ago when I started to orientate my focus into mainland Europe and beyond.

For me there is nothing quite like the freedom that comes with long-distance walking. Whether it's the sun, wind and rain in your face, the buzz and energy of team life out on the road, the sight and taste of new landscapes and cultures, or the opportunity to leave behind the responsibilities and clutter of every day life, everything comes together to make a huge impact in the life of almost everyone who has connected in on one of the walks. Gratitude rises in our hearts with every day that passes; for good health, families who release us and a Master who always has new horizons for those of the forward movement of the people of God. With no need of "reality TV" to bring excitement to our lives, it is so therapeutic to leave behind the sterilised environment of the west and to turn our faces east, adding our voices to the many others calling through the new wine of the Kingdom.

The winter months for Kathy and I have been genuinely testing, as we have felt the pressure of being positioned quite literally between the east and western gates of Istanbul. At the same time they have been months of huge discovery as I have devoured every book I could lay my hands on regarding the Middle East and the fault- lines of imperialism that run so deep, from Turkey through to Afghanistan. Whether it be the devastation reeked by the Crusades, or the appalling consequences of the post- World War I carve-up of land that the 1920 Treaty of Versailles facilitated, we pick up our journey acutely aware that once more the legacy of European imperialism has been, and continues to be so damaging. You only need to look at the history of the Lebanon, Israel and Palestine, Iraq and Syria to find distressing evidence of this.

The next few days will take the walk up over the hills that lie to the east of Istanbul, and onto the central plateau that the capital of Turkey, Ankara, sits on. Across Europe Turkey is much in the news at the moment, as to whether it will align itself with the west and become a member of the EU. Given its strategic significance there is much at stake here. Yet this will not be our prayer. Rather, we will be seeking to call Turkey through into its on identity, neither aligned with east or west but able to rise up into a gateway anointing, a peace-making nation in the pathways of war.

Thousands of men, women and children have been slaughtered across the breadth of this land in the Armenian genocide that ripped through the heart of what is now modern-day Turkey, just after the conclusion of World War I. Even here it seems that history would declare the Crusades as the seedbed from which sprang hatred and murderous intent towards the Armenians. So we go to walk the land and to pray that the nations would begin to yield up the fruit of their Creator; that the legacy of this nation would rise again, a legacy that once echoed not to the terror of genocide, but to the sounds of the Kingdom as revival swept across Asia from Ephesus.

We do not pretend that our contribution is anything but small and incredibly inadequate. However, it is our contribution and we know that before the chambers of heaven it really does count. Prophetic action always carries with it an incredible sense of destiny and it is that which we sense as we leave the UK on Monday.

ISTANBUL TO ANKARA AND SOUTH TOWARDS KONYA March 2007
Team: Steve H, Dave, Richard and myself

Walking out of the coastal lands surrounding Istanbul up onto the Ayatolan Plateau provided three wonderful days of walking marked out by blue skies, incredible scenery and as strong a sense of purpose as I have carried for some time. The four of us on team worked hard as we gave ourselves to prayer for this gateway nation of Turkey and the capital city of Ankara.

Without a doubt had we decided to go the most direct route to the Syrian border then we would have failed to understand this nation as fully as we needed to, for in Ankara you discover the steel fist of the military and a centre of control as strong as I have seen anywhere in the world. Evidence of the Masonic under-girds so much of this twentieth century nation, and the adoration of the 1920's founder of Turkey, Ataturk, is akin to worship. To be fair, if you are neither Armenian or Kurdish then the gratitude to the army is very real for a nation who's national identity has passed between the western and Greek Byzantine Empire, and the Selcuk (Mongolian) / Ottoman Empire of the east. If you add in the plundering of the Crusades and the post-World War I attempted carve up, the level of fear and searching for identity becomes totally understandable.

Yet beneath this strong iron facade there is a church that is slowly growing in confidence, for where there were just a handful of believers in Ankara twenty years ago there are now several hundred. From amongst these we were hosted in the city by a wonderful Korean couple; two of the fourteen thousand missionaries the Korean Church has currently out across the world. It seemed fitting to me that we should connect with the first evidence of the church in the east that is journeying west, just the other side of the global east/west gateway that is Istanbul. They are a gateway couple with connections into lands further east. There is an order in all things.

On leaving Ankara we turned our faces south towards the centre of Islam in Turkey; the city of Konya. The next team, led by Paul Woods, will walk into this city. However, what I am growing to understand as I cast my mind back to the nations we have walked through, is that each nation has its fault-lines. I found myself remembering the day twenty months ago when we walked through the navy area of Greenwich in London, on our way to the coast and into France. Against the backdrop of cannons being fired to celebrate the 200th anniversary of Nelson's death a young friend from Leeds helped me to understand how the navy was our insurance policy, protecting the wealth of the nation during the days of the slave trade. Surely the time is coming when this ungodly foundation will be judged by the Ancient of Days? Likewise walking through France at the time of the riots it was as if some of the fault lines of that nation were being underlined, giving perhaps a chance for redress before the need for accounting comes. And so in Italy and Greece I could go on.

Here in Turkey it seems that the walk has been positioned along the fault-line these two cities of Ankara and Konya represent. Never have I walked upon a road as marked out by signs of the occult as this one. As Istanbul is a global fault line, the north/south road from Ankara to Konya is the simmering fault line of Turkey itself. Somehow these two cities encapsulate the tensions between the aspiring modern state looking west to the EU and the suppressed residue of fundamental Islam for which Konya is a motif.

So, after 450km of walking, wonderful moments of connection with the global church, and great times of laughter (normally at the expense of one or other of the members of the team), we return to the UK in just two days time. To all those who have prayed for us and for our families and households back home, I say a huge thank you. We can only go as far here in Turkey as there is a deepening of the corporate flow of life back home.

The next team leave for Turkey to pick up the walk in just over a fortnights time. Paul will send out a report, as will I when we return in May to lead the final team through Turkey to the Syrian border.

REFLECTIONS FROM HOME

It was during this leg that I began to wonder whether in fact this journey was going to go beyond Jerusalem. This had probably been lodged somewhere in my sub-consciousness for some time. Now, with the connection with the Koreans and the church in the east that was journeying west these idle thoughts took on further shape. Obviously our own connection with China fuelled this inclination and now was the time when I began to speak it out to a few trusted friends. I was also aware however that there is something very seductive and evocative about the eastern lands. The dangers ahead were and are very obvious to see; hence the real need to make sure that I was not being drawn into some romantic dream world that could end very badly. Having just adopted two daughters I was not quite ready for martyrdom. Kathy would be hugely cross with me!

The next team to go was only the second team since leaving Whitby that I had stepped out of. I was so grateful to Paul Wood for his initiative here, giving me space to share in the responsibilities of home. It was Paul who had chartered our route through Turkey, ignoring my blinkered approach to such important matters and gently steering us through Ankara and then onto Konya itself. It was also Paul that was being placed alongside me now, with all his experience of the Muslim world and the several years that he lived in Cairo.

Driving back form Ankara at the end of this first team of 2007 afforded us the most incredible views of the eastern mountains of this huge land. Magnificently rugged they stood starkly before us, shrouded in snow and the mystery of the nations of Iran, Iraq, Kurdistan and Armenia beyond them. We were aware that high in those hills sheltered the Kurdish Liberation Movement, terrorists to some, heroes and freedom fighters to another. We were also aware that we were beginning to get into some parts of the journey that could offer up some tricky situations to say the least. That great care was needed was underlined by a near fatal high speed accident on the motorway as we drove to get our flight home.

CHAPTER 21

Ankara

'The Last Fez'

Dave Herron

Dave is one of the few athletes amongst us. Lean and mean he eats up the miles. He is a natural long distance walker. Carrying a real love for people this is his interpretation of some of the issues surrounding Ankara, and the nation of Turkey. He is married, with three grown up children.

High on the hilltop, swaggering in its lofty grandeur even amidst Ankara's ranks of high rise buildings, the Ataturk memorial casts its cold eye over the city. From Ancient Egypt or Rome to Nazi Berlin or Communist Russia, the need for totalitarianism to build its symbols strong and high endlessly repeats itself.

Ataturk's memorial is both story and statement. The story, displayed in the memorial's museum, is told in the ordered detail of the great man's life. First, in fading photographs and documents, his youth in the death throes of the once glorious Ottoman Empire. Next his rise to prominence in a military career that saw him confront the invading sons of another Empire on the beaches and cliffs of Gallipoli and then expel the Greek insurgents eager to capitalise on the demise of their fading neighbour. Then, in the aftermath of the Great War, his firm grasping of the reigns of the New Turkey. And, in the final chapter, his establishing of the modern, secular state in a courageous, relentless – even ruthless - wave of reforms to mould the face of a nation.

And the statement? This emerges from the story. Yet, if the memorial's museum tells the story, then the story is incomplete. For a nation's face may well be modified in a generation – but not its heart, its true identity. There beneath the surface lie the contradictions, the fault lines – fault lines of geography, religion and culture which are deep seated and have creaked and groaned for decades, even centuries. These are not so easily eradicated.

And so the memorial, with its vast square and ranks of pillars, its strutting guards and lofty position, makes the man a symbol - a symbol repeated in the obligatory statue in every town and village; a symbol which embod-ies the statement. And that statement is that the fault lines will hold, the cracks will not be allowed to surface, the edifice will not be marred. The creation which is modern Turkey will remain firm and the military tradi-tion which both spawned and was shaped by the great man will, in his memory, devote itself and its might to preserving what its greatest son created.

As Husnu sat warming himself in the early after-noon sunshine at the side of the first set of marble steps past the vast memorial gateway, he remembered the awe he had felt as a seven year old, some twelve years previously, when he first visited this place. The memorial was awesome enough. But he would always remember the feeling of pride, mixed with a strange kind of terrifying responsibility, which rose within him when his father pointed to the enlarged photograph on the museum wall. It was a photograph of officers, Ataturk in their midst, surveying the scene of a great and bloody victory.

'There, Husnu,' he had said, pointing gravely to the side of the central figure. His voice was hushed enough to convey respect for the surroundings, yet loud enough to ensure the attention of the surrounding onlookers. 'There. Your great grandfather, Faruk. He knew him from officer training. They were very great friends.'

Now, with the sound of traffic rising from the bustling city, Husnu's thoughts turned again to the telephone call that had drawn him here at this appointed time. Just a few words from Alma, daughter of his father's cousin; polite, a little tense, expressing a wish to meet with him, emphasising the need for 'discretion' and stating the time and the place.

What could be drawing her to the capital? Katsamonu, the ancestral home nestling in the centre of the Black Sea plains, was 250 km to the north. Only a handful of times could Husnu even recall meeting Alma. A couple of weddings, some family business, a sickness, all in Ankara where his side of the family had made their home for three generations. And then once, just eighteen months or so ago, at the funeral of his cousin Ergin in Katsamonu itself, the only time he had ever been there. The military tradition has a powerful call and even his father could not fail to answer, although, even on such a sober occasion, there had been friction. They were a divided family. The tension had been palpable at every meeting and occasionally, as after the funeral, words had been exchanged.

Husnu's father had never spoken of the rift but once, some four or five years before, in response to his probing, his mother had given the briefest of explanations. Had she known everything then what follows is the more detailed tale she would have told.

Husnu's great grandfather Faruk was the youngest of two brothers. Faruk, outgoing and adventurous, had chosen a military career and had quickly been thrown in to the path of great battles, military honours and, of course, Kemal, the Father of all the Turks. As a child it had been a special treat for Husnu to be handed the array of medals, polished and glinting despite their years, which still had place of honour amongst Father and Grandfather's awards in Father's study.

Abdullah, on the other hand, was a dour and bullish man, totally lacking the sophistication and dash of his younger sibling. Devout at the mosque, mistrustful of change, he was happy to warm himself at the embers of the dying Ottoman flame and saw no virtue in the upstarts who would, he said 'hack every flower of the true Turkey to the ground and replace them with stinking foreign weeds'.

The flashpoint came in the spring of 1926, whilst Faruk was home on leave. Only months earlier, as part of the raft of modernising reforms which would see, amongst others, Arabic script replaced by a Latin version, the capital moved from Constantinople (soon to be renamed Istanbul) to far away Ankara, the banning of polygamy, and the introduction of western style surnames... Ataturk banned the Fez!

The Fez, that most traditional of headgear for the last one hundred years, was, for Ataturk, a relic of the old ways, a symbol of decline and stagnation, a challenge to the new order. In those early years he still remembered the sting when serving his country as an overseas delegate and, taking the opportunity to shape his ideas in the pages of French revolutionary literature, had been ridiculed by an insensitive Frenchman for his traditional choice of headgear. And so, in late August 1925, the wearing of the Fez became a punishable offence and, despite outbreaks of rioting and a number of arrests, the scramble to import homburgs and fedoras, bowlers and flatcaps gathered pace.

But Abdullah was not to be moved. Through the autumn and winter, as 1925 turned to 1926, in the backwater that was Katsamonu, he continued to wear his Fez. Three times he was arrested and fined. On more than one occasion he was involved in prolonged scuffles with several young men of Ataturk's persuasion. Always he would draw admiring glances from townsmen self-consciously sporting legitimate headgear bearing labels of German, Italian, British or French origin. By the beginning of spring, against all odds, Abdullah continued to wear what had become known locally, whether in jest or fact, as the last Fez in all of Turkey.

And then Faruk arrived home.

From the outset the two brothers engaged in earnest, heated discussion long into the night. Faruk occasionally banged the table and spoke of the shame on the family. Abdullah, surly and gruff, held forth in dour tones with references to honour and tradition and even family betrayal. As Abdullah attempted to leave the compound the next morning in his normal headgear, the outcome was a full blooded fist fight in the courtyard. As neighbours and passers by flocked to the spectacle attracted by the din, as cockerel and hens scattered in a whirl of feathers and sound, the women of the household had shrieked and implored intervention.

Husnu's mother had been able to give only the sketchiest outline of these events, but little more, save that Faruk had gone from strength to strength in the military and Civil Service, settling and beginning his family in burgeoning Ankara. Abdullah, meanwhile, had ploughed a lonely furrow in the old town, scarcely venturing from its confines and choosing to walk its streets bareheaded.

And so the rift in the family continued to this day. Husnu's own Grandfather and Father flourishing in Ankara, both serving in the military and then in public office in their later years. The Katsamonu clan stayed close to the soil and the old town, their sons employed over the generations on the family farm and, more recently, in small scale manufacturing. And the interaction between the sons and daughters of the two brothers, across three generations, centred only on a smattering of occasions - weddings and funerals, legacies and sickness – and always the pain of fracture pervaded the atmosphere.

His eyes scanned the throng entering the memorial for any sight of her. There were the families of simple country folk, all ruddy complexions and broken teeth; the parties of schoolchildren, wide eyed and babbling; the young sophisticates with the latest cell phones and itineraries to fulfil. As he stared, a familiar lostness gripped Husnu's soul like an aching wound.

What was the provocation this time? The last time he had felt this way, some two or three days before, it was down to his father's anger at discovering his choice of this term's dissertation: 'The Glory of the Ottomans – their achievements and their legacy'. The days of rages and ranting, on both sides, were now passed. Disapproval, as Father had finally accepted his son's attainment of manhood, was now manifested more subtly – yet equally effectively. It was as if, like the military strategist that he was, Father had finally realised that all his frontal attacks could never achieve the conquest. 'No, Husnu was not interested in the military; no, he would not take sponsorship from father's guild; yes, he would be taking a liberal Arts degree... and listening to the music he enjoyed!'

As a child he had immersed himself, or perhaps been immersed, in the stream that ran through Father and Grandfather all the way back to Faruk, a pillar of modern Turkey, friend of the great Kemal, founder of the state and Father of all the Turks. He remembered the feeling of security and strength as he nestled in father's lap, enclosed by strong arms and military grey, listening to knowing, confident assertions amongst nodding colleagues:

'We offer them only the firm, strong hand of a father, but let them continue to refuse it and they shall feel the fist!'

It would not be long, he reflected ruefully, before this father's son learned that lesson.

It was as if his soul had been, even continued to be, strewn with landmines, sown in his relationship with his father. A memory, a comment, a certain atmosphere: there were numerous catalysts that could trigger the pain, and he would feel an aching bitterness of heart, a woundedness in his core. Here, in this place, surrounded by the very atmosphere that three generations of fathers had imbibed until they were intoxicated, it should be no surprise that the familiar anguish rose again.

Was there a cure? Could there be an escape?

Only yesterday he had been reminded of two possibilities within minutes of each other. He had gone with Orhan, a fellow student, to the glittering new Anka Mall, all Starbucks and Gucci; a place where the bright young things of Ankara would go to flirt with Europe, the West and each other. As they drank their cappuccinos Orhan spoke, eyes sparkling, of scholarships to Europe, even the USA. He had it planned. He and Husnu together – in Berlin or Paris, New York or LA - living the dream, taking life with both hands.

Then, a tap on the shoulder. The second possibility.

'Tayyip!'

Tayyip. The son of an old neighbour. A boyhood comrade in great adventures and youthful dreams. A military family with shared values. Tayyip, friendly yet furtive, an arm around his shoulder, drawing him aside. Then, in hushed, earnest tones, a spelling out of the vision and the hope for fulfilment of all their dreams. A vision for the preservation of Turkey against the foreigner and the fundamentalist, the missionary and the imam. A vision of a strong, pure Turkey, clean and powerful, with its true identity intact and unassailable. Surely, knowing his family background as he did, this was the opportunity Husnu had been waiting for: The True Sons of Turkey. A grassroots movement of purity and power! One telephone call, Tayyip as sponsor, and Husnu need never look back.

As he had listened, first to Orhan, warming afresh to the innocence and enthusiasm of his friend, and then to

Tayyip, gripped by cold fascination at the crystal clarity of his sight, he recognised, sickeningly, that his own innocence was tarnished and his own vision blurred. He knew that, whatever life journeys he might make, the scarring and bruising of his soul would be a constant companion.

Husnu glanced at his watch. Twenty past one. He smiled as he reflected on her quiet, confident assertion that she would be there precisely on the hour – the innocence of the rural dweller unfamiliar with the vagaries of city crowds and traffic. Only a couple of hours ago, as he had stepped out from the apartment, the confusing spell cast by a city expanding by the day, as it had for the last eighty years, was underlined to him. A group of westerners, poring over a map of the suburbs which was out of date before the ink was dry, were trying to find a route to the heart of the city. Taking note of their evident exhaustion, especially the two who appeared to have been walking as the others drove ahead, he had decided to forgo the errands he had in mind and squeeze in to the car to guide them to their destination and perhaps improve his English en route. He had enquired as to why they had strayed from the main autoroute and the city exits, Ankara being, despite its maze of ever-expanding suburbs, essentially a grid city, which was easily navigable on the main thoroughfares.

Their answer, or answers, were intriguing yet elusive. They appeared to be on some sort of pilgrimage. They spoke of walking and praying and connecting with a father and his son as part of a worldwide family. Jerusalem seemed to be their goal. There was something of both Orhan's enthusiasm and Tayyip's clarity about their talk, although he could not pretend to truly understand most of what was said. He was with them for almost thirty minutes. Yet their gentleness, their immediate embracing of him as a friend and the almost raucous fun bubbling through their relationships would leave a lasting impression upon him. Certainly they were like no devotees he had ever seen.

The minutes ticked by and still she did not come. As he gazed out over the city something else these pilgrims had said came to mind. They had referred to his home, this city, as being resistant, hard to get into: a hard nosed place. An interesting idea, that a place, even a city, might have a personality and a will. How strange that this concept should not be totally original to him since, only yesterday, during research on the internet, he had stumbled on an article which used imagery in a similar way and about exactly the same subject. It was part of a political commentary in a western journal and referred to Ankara as being like some bloated toad, squatting on the high ground with piercing eye, ever vigilant. Sometimes it gazed north and east to the poorer peasant lands where the Islamists waited for opportunity; or beyond, to the border areas where her might was daily challenged by the mountain men of the KKP, to the restlessness of neighbouring Iran, the chaos of Iraq and the stolid façade that masked the danger that lurked in Syria. Most of all she cast her gaze on the elder daughter, Istanbul, vast and vibrant, flirtatious and home to a hundred dangerous moods which, were any one to gain the ascendancy, could bring the painstakingly constructed creation that is modern Turkey to ruin.

This was his city. The city of his father and his fathers. Whatever Orhan or Tayyip might say, he knew that you could run in this direction or that direction, but you cannot run from yourself, or from the Father and Fathers in you that made you. Perhaps the only way was as the westerners had said: some kind of death; some kind of coming to life again.

And then she was there.

Slightly flustered; something mumbled about the train and then the traffic. Husnu was surprised by the surge of protectiveness and attraction that rose within him, sensations which soon gave place, after they had exchanged the customary greetings, to curiosity.

Alma was clearly on a mission and a schedule. Seated on the grass at the side of the square, in sombre yet purposeful tones, she spoke of her father's illness. Six months the doctor had said, a year at the most. Of course there was a medical reason – no-one actually dies of brokenness, do they? The recent years had been a time of bitterness and tears for the family in Katsamonu. Alma's older brother, Ergin, had been served his military papers three years ago and, within nine months, was on the Iraqi border 'subduing the Kurds'. Within less than a year of posting he has been involved in a KKP ambush, and was gone. The funeral had been the occasion of Husnu's only visit to Katsamonu and the last time he had seen Alma.

The news that had never filtered through to Ankara was of Alma's twin brother, Necmettin. A real son of his father, he had always been faithful to the Mosque and, more recently, to a Mudrassah in one of the nearby villages. Suddenly, along with two other neighbourhood youths, only five or six months ago – he was gone. Alma spoke in terse, clipped tones of a note, full of rhetoric, left in the hallway. The boys had gone

to the east, to the front against the infidels and imperialists, to bring glory to the family in the name of
Allah. After Ergin's death Alma had seen her father
shrink; now, he withered. The strong determined
man she had known had become a wisp. Only last
week, two of the adventurers had returned. But not
Necmettin.

They sat for a while in silence in the mid-afternoon
sun, the pain of the father so ably, wordlessly communicated through the daughter.

'He remembers you,' she finally said. 'From the
funeral when you all came back. He remembers the
discussion and the way that you stood up to your father.
He remembers and sent me to give you this.'

She placed into his hands a bag. In the bag was a box.

'There is no-one else now,' she said, softly. 'No more
sons. He says that you must take care of this and pass it
forward.'

A few more words, then she was gone.

An hour later, back in his room high above the city
streets, Husnu picked up the box. He opened it for the
third or fourth time and, once more, gazed at the Fez -
Abdullah's Fez.

The last Fez.

Then he placed it next to the array of medals, taken
quietly from the display shelf in Father's study; Faruk's
medals, glistening in the light of the setting sun.

The Muezzin's call to prayer began to echo over the
city as the first, flickering lights of the Anka Mall pierced
the twilight. And as he stood in the early evening gloom
the familiar pain of the Fatherless rose again in his heart.
He smiled, this son of so many Fathers, and felt himself
to be truly a son of Turkey.

FACT FILE: ANKARA AND TURKEY

Islam in Turkey

By the end of the seventh century, conversion to Islam had begun among the Turkish-speaking tribes, who were migrating westward from Central Asia. The initial wave of Turkish migrants converted to Sunni Islam and became champions of Islamic orthodoxy. As warriors of the Islamic faith, or *gazis*, they colonized and settled Anatolia in the name of Islam, especially following the defeat of the Byzantines at the Battle of Manzikert (1071).

(www.geographic.org, accessed February 2008)

The Great War

By the early 20th century, Turkey had been largely expelled from its European territories, and a number of 'successor states' (Bulgaria, Rumania, Serbia and Greece) had arisen to replace it. Turkey was regarded as the 'sick man of Europe' and desperately sought an alliance with a major European power to improve its political position. However, because of its declining status and its ambiguous position (a predominantly Islamic state straddling both east and west), most European powers were reluctant to form an alliance with Turkey until Germany befriended it.

At the outbreak of World War I, Turkey had already been humiliated in the First Balkan War (1912-13) and had lost territory. Casualties by 1918: 300 000 dead, 400 000 wounded.

(www.channel4.com, accessed February 2008)

Gallipoli

About 480 000 Allied troops took part in the Gallipoli campaign. The British had 205 000 casualties (43 000 killed). There were more than 33 600 ANZAC losses (over one-third killed) and 47 000 French casualties (5000 killed). Turkish casualties are estimated at 250 000 (65 000 killed).

(www.spartacus.schoolnet.co.uk, accessed February 2008)

Ataturk

Mustafa Kemal established himself as a successful and extremely capable military commander while serving as a division commander in the Battle of Gallipoli. He later fought with distinction on the eastern Anatolian and Palestinian fronts, making a name for himself during World War I. Following the defeat of the Ottoman Empire at the hands of the Allies, and the subsequent plans for its partition, Mustafa Kemal led the Turkish national movement in what would become the Turkish War of Independence. Having established a provisional government in Ankara, he defeated the forces sent by the Entente powers. His successful military campaigns led to the liberation of the country and to the establishment of the State of Turkey.

(www.wikipedia.org, accessed February 2008)

Christians in Turkey

"Tilmann Geske, a shy and hardworking man, lived almost 10 of his 46 years in Turkey. He and two Turkish Christians were found dead last Wednesday, bound hand and foot and with their throats slit, at a publishing house that distributes Bibles. Five young men were detained and charged with murder; they allegedly said they killed to protect Islam. The victims in last week's attack were members of a tiny Christian population in Malatya numbering less than 20. In Turkey, Christians and other non-Muslims make up less than 1 percent of the population, but nonetheless are objects of suspicion, main actors in many conspiracy theories and occasionally the targets of violence."

(www.iht.com, accessed February 2008)
Recent Elections, 28 August 2007
"Turkey's armed forces gave warning yesterday that concerted efforts by "pcentres of evil" could undermine the secular republic, a day before the expected election of a former Islamist as president. The Turkish military, which regards itself as the guardian of Kemal Ataturk's legacy and has dislodged four governments since 1960, threatened to intervene."

(www.telegraph.co.uk, accessed February 2008)

CHAPTER 22

Konya to the Syrian Border

Steve Lowton

KONYA TO TARSUS, April 2007
Team: Alan, Andy, Paul, Val, Martin, Vicki and David

Paul Wood writes:

Enormous thanks to those who prayed for us and our families at home. We felt your prayers like the wind at our backs. Thanks also to the team whose friendship made all those featureless miles of dry plains seem like a stroll in the park: Alan for refusing to let painful feet get him down, Val for battling at times through what Islam does to women, Andy for uninhibited joy and Martin, from Germany, who was undoubtedly awakening a strategic connection between Turkey and his native land. Thanks also to those who have committed years of their lives to Turkey, who walked with us awhile, opened doors, fed us and helped us on our way.

Following on from others before us who have walked through power centres of empires and refused to be impressed, we journeyed across the high Anatolian plateau, home to ancient settlements and civilizations knowing it was our mission not to be overawed by ancient idolatrous stumbling blocks, gods and goddesses, the queen who would be called heavenly or the shroud of Islam drawn over the gentle kindness and hospitality of the Turkish people. At the centre of Konya, the Iconium of New Testament days, a city where whirling dervishes spin to connect heaven and earth, we shared bread and wine with others whom had been planted in the city, and turned a prophetic key for the turning of Turkey. As we walked out the next day some of us danced where the dervishes dance and others prayed for a number of people with eye-defects in the streets. Let there be a double portion of sight for a city whose symbol is a double-headed eagle.

It was awesome to know we were walking paths where apostolic feet first carried the gospel, where bold preaching was confirmed by signs and wonders and great numbers believed. This is where new churches shook the foundations of idolatrous cities. Leaving icy winds and snow behind us we descended through the Cilician Gates to Tarsus, held up by explosions as a new road was being blasted through the mountainside, ending in balmy Mediterranean sunshine and the sweet smell of orange orchards.

On our return to Istanbul the front pages of Turkish newspapers reported the murders in Malatya of two Turkish believers, Necati Aydin and another young man, and Tilmann Geske, a German missionary. Sometime in the two days after we left Konya they were abducted and killed by Turkish Islamic Nationalists defending the honour of their religion and nation from the offence of following Jesus. They had been threatened before but they had counted the cost and pressed on. Somehow the

One who watched over us and gave us laughter and set our feet dancing along the roads we travelled was also watching over those who shared his sufferings. Jesus is too big for me. They overcame and we caught onto the coat-tails of their faith to believe that Turkey will turn to its heavenly purpose.

The last word I leave to Andy: "Flying back home at 30 000 feet, my belly warmed by a glass of red wine, I reflect on the richness of the last ten days' journey; the beauty of the Turkish people and their nation, the stifling grip of religion in their lives, mountainside explosions mirroring the Holy Spirit bombs left detonated and the foolishness of dancing the hokey-kokey at the concluding point of the final days walking, helping to express the freedom of our wonderful Father in the face of all that ensnares."

TARSUS THROUGH ADANA TO THE SYRIAN BORDERMAY 2007
Team: Kathy, Helen, Dave, Richard and myself

I have just returned from the final leg of the walk through Turkey; a place that has touched my heart like no other nation has done. Emotionally and physically exhausted by the experience it has been an unspeakable joy to position ourselves alongside the church in this land.

This was a team that faced challenges no other team has yet faced as we found ourselves the victims of a road-side robbery and, as a consequence, a schedule that demanded much from us all. Yet through it all the Chief Shepherd was totally amazing in his work and we returned home not only on time but with the walk through to the Syrian border complete.

Inevitably there is so much I could say. However, I leave space for Kathy Garda to write. Kathy, one of the team, can trace her own roots back to the land through which we walked.

She writes:

"As we walked into Adana, I was lifted by the fact that my grandfather lived here in his family home of many generations. In 1915, they were forced to leave and marched south towards Syria to certain death. They sewed money or jewels into their clothes and managed to bribe their way to Damascus and escaped.

"Before leaving this city we felt it necessary to visit the river running through Adana, as many perished in the rivers. It was full of bodies during the genocide. We felt to initiate something here of God's heart for this nation, to open this old wound so that it could be healed, for repentance and forgiveness to flow. The blood of the martyrs remains in the ground until justice and righteousness cracks open what has been buried, and releases healing in the land. The Armenian Christians were massacred and each one into the arms of Jesus, he took their pain and they reside with Him; they are the remembered, they are the found and they are the redeemed. Their very blood that lies in that land resonates with the song of the Lamb. As He has forgiven them, they sing forgiveness over their enemies and sing the song of the redeemed on the very ground their blood was shed.

"We prayed for an incision in the land to commence, for our heavenly Surgeon's knife to operate with a deep enough cut to open the flesh of the land, to allow the blood of the martyrs to surface and for their song to be released above ground. This moment of declaration was flooded with grace and we were surrounded with peace as we did what we had been led us to do.

"Three hours out of Adana on the highway, we were robbed. We lost 4 out of 5 passports and all sources of money except one credit card. With our proof of identity gone, our possessions and money taken, we stood in the place of the violated and the dispossessed to some small degree and what we had stood for in prayer that morning touched our lives in a very real way. After being shunted from one military commander to another with the confusion of bureaucracy and agendas, we sat at the feet of the military might of Turkey with a degree of powerlessness and insecurity and again, in a very small way, identified with those whose very lives had been in the hands of those in power.

"What the enemy meant for harm, the Lord meant for good. The consequences of this attack meant we drove 300 miles to Ankara and the nearest British Embassy to obtain new passports. This travel across the land consisted of four journeys of 300 miles between Adana and Ankara, from the point of declared incision to open the land, into the heart of the nation and its military might. So we prayed for the 'unzipping' of the land and the release of the song of the Lamb as we zipped up and down this highway for the sake of our identity (papers). On the final journey on this highway, again we called for the epidermis of the land to be severed deep enough and as a sign of something opening, there came many, many tears as a final heart cry for release.

"Turkey is beginning a new chapter, the military control will no longer satisfy her heart, the longest love story in history comes to call at her door and the romance begins. The visitations, the gifts, the attention, the calling, the wooing, the drawing of Jesus belongs to the next chapter of this nation."

Steve writes:

Before turning my focus to the next leg of the walk through Syria in the autumn, I want to pause to say a huge thank you to everyone who has journeyed with us through this incredible land of Turkey. To Dave, Chris, Paul, Richard, Kath, Val, Steve, Alan, Helen, Martin and Andy you have all been awesome companions and mighty prayer warriors. To everyone who has prayed for us, however fleetingly, a massive thank you. Lastly to those of the church in Turkey who we had the honour of meeting; our lives are much the richer for you. Thank you for your incredible hospitality, generosity and stead-fastness for Jesus' sake.

I have no doubt that I will be back to this land. Lying as it does at the apex of two continents, we have found ourselves walking and praying at a critical point in its history. Indeed as we returned to the UK and bought our first newspaper, a four page feature article in the Sunday Observer was titled "A fight for the soul of the new Turkey". What an honour, to be partners with the living God for the sake of the nations.

Massive thanks to everyone who is partnering with us.

REFLECTIONS FROM HOME

It had amazed me that we had come this far along the roads of Europe and Turkey without a major incident, like the robbery on the road these last days. That it could have been a lot worse is without a doubt, for the guys who confronted Kathy and Helen almost certainly were armed. If I had time to think I would have kicked myself for weeks at the foolishness of how I had structured that day, and how vulnerable the women and the whole team had been left. As it were all of us pulled together in an incredible way. Again the strength forged by weeks out on the road came to a fore, as we steeled ourselves for the challenge of getting through the situation.

Arriving at the Syrian border some days later was a wonderful moment of achievement for us all. It was a testimony to their own strength of character that both Kathy and Helen determined to get back out walking the road, despite what they had gone through. It was also so sweet to arrive at the border just as a Turkish Grandfather did, along with his son and grandson. As we rested and quietly prayed he wandered over to us with a rose for each of us. With little language in common we thanked him and noted the tenderness of the moment, a three generational blessing from a grandfather of this nation, as we prepared to leave Turkey behind us. The presence of the Hidden One was very rich.

Back home the pressure was beginning to lift with some return starting to come through in the business, and Zhou's health showing signs of improvement. Hannah also seemed to be making some progress. It was as if the further beyond Istanbul we got, the less we felt the squeeze that we had been in. Kathy and I drew encouragement and were hugely glad that grace and had been found to keep walking

CHAPTER 23

The Sword Maker of Adana

Kathy Garda

Kathy is married to Malc, lives on the south coast of England and has three sons. She joined the walk half way through Turkey and continued on to Jerusalem. Drawing from the storyline of her own life she is uniquely placed to tell something of the troubled and hidden history of the Armenian Genocide. In so doing she brought an intricate new thread to the tale that was unfolding around us; one that we would have been largely oblivious to without her.

Turkey, 1915. In the town of Adana, Nazaret fell into a fitful sleep amid the dread that sat on him like a lead weight. His Turkish friend had given him a warning, with the same hushed tones and kind eyes as when they had first met. Back then it had been to do with his surname, 'Kelenjian'. A name that meant 'Sword Maker' may be seen as too aggressive and so it was agreed as a silent term of employment that 'Terzian' would be safer - a 'Tailor'. It had a harmless enough ring to it and would not cause this Armenian to raise suspicion amongst the Turkish workers at the local bank.

Adana was a flourishing agricultural town in southern Mediterranean Turkey. Nazaret's family had been
there for centuries as Christians living among Muslim
neighbours. They owned land and a family restaurant
business; however, during the violent massacres of six
years ago they had left everything to save themselves.
They had returned to their home uneasily, unable to stay
away or uproot, but fully aware of the thousands of
Armenian bodies that had been poured into the Seyhan
River or buried in mass graves around them.

Now his Turkish friend came to him again and shook
the 'Sword Maker' turned 'Tailor' to the core with his
words. Trouble was on its way and this time they would
not be able to return; they must be ready to leave with
everything they could carry. Yet everything in Nazaret
yearned for his land, for all that his ancestors had built,
for every tradition that surrounded their existence and
made this place home. He and his wife worked into the
night sewing gold into clothing to take with them, trying
to steady the needle with shaking hands of disbelief.
Maybe 'Tailor' was the right name after all.

So as Nazaret finally slept he began to dream. He was
standing in one of his barns in front of his faithful
donkey, a patient and trusting creature. There was a
familiar smell of damp hay and the stillness before the
routine of the day. He looked behind his mule into the
dark recesses of the barn, where something was lurking
in the half-light. As he peered forward, there suddenly
stood before him a hideous bat-like creature with a bull's
head and huge talons. To his horror it opened its mouth,
threw back its head and let out a high pitch screeching
sound. It grew louder and louder until it was unbearable,
as if its tormented craving intensified with every screech.

Screaming wildly, the creature was filled with an insatiable lust for blood. It lunged out of the darkness, attacking the innocent, unaware donkey. In one swoop the creature devoured the mule's neck and it folded to the ground, all life extinguished. Simultaneously, the most surprising of things happened. Nazaret had not noticed that to the side a Lion was watching this horror. As the mule fell its blood was released with such immediate force that it shot sideways and hit the Lion full in the face. The Lion winced and retracted His head, but remained rooted to the spot as if He was there deliberately to catch the lifeblood of the donkey. In the middle of this nightmare Nazaret could not take his eyes off the Lion. Somehow His presence meant everything. He had known what was coming and He was there to take the full force of the bloodshed. A warm sensation began to radiate through Nazaret. Wave after wave flooded his body and all fear was drained out of him.

He was wrenched from the dream by his young son Avedis tearfully crawling into his bed. The little ones know when something is wrong, though he had tried so hard to hide it. Left with an impression of the huge mane of the Lion, a liquid warmth inside and the memory of a harrowing dream, he held Avedis in his arms, hoping that he would always be able to protect him and keep him safe.

As something insidious in the dark called for blood, Nazaret's countrymen lay oblivious in their beds, unprepared for the death and suffering that was imminent. A call from the pit of a hellish heart was unfurling, big enough to engulf a nation.

On the south coast of England, it was 1983 and a wet, blustery night. Through a blur of tequila shots, a present somehow managed to reach Isobel at the right place at the right time. It was from her mother. Half-pleased and half-disgruntled she opened it to find a book; not the sort of glamorous gift she expected for this momentous occasion of arrival.

She was sitting in a dark corner of a friend's party. They were both coming of age; both eighteen; both celebrating. She was grateful for being invited to share in the festivities, despite the loneliness that gnawed at her insides.

The book's title was *The Armenians*. She groaned. Inside the mother's inscription read 'this is part of who you are'. Why labour this point of identity when there was such brokenness between them? Everything felt so dislocated in Isobel's own existence. To even think about this painful ancestral history was more than she could bear. Maybe belonging to a broken nation begets a broken existence. Maybe the breaking continues until an antidote is administered. She could see that mending had to begin somewhere, but felt powerless to change and had no answers.

Isobel lay the book down with a sigh. The death of a nation; hundreds of thousands slaughtered with no regard, even for pregnant women; little ones thrown against rocks; senseless killing, brutal and inhumane. She had been told the potted history so that no one would forget the atrocities. Isobel's gothic garb seemed a fitting shroud for such dark truths. To hear them was enough, but to read them was too much, too real. So for the next two decades the book remained firmly closed. The contents were indigestible and to be avoided. The memories of this sad time were locked away, preserved beneath a veneer of dust.

One evening near Christmas, the children were in bed, fairy lights glistened through the house and everything had that 'frosty-outside' and 'cosy-inside' feel. She was on the inside, safe and warm; there were no dark corners and no gnawing loneliness. Somewhere in her life, the mending had begun. She slipped her hand inside the hand of her Maker and began to hold on. The tighter the grip, the greater the effect of the antidote running through the veins of her being, mending broken patterns and broken dreams that were destined to break her future.

That evening, an invitation arrived out of the blue; an opportunity to walk through the country of Turkey. The mention of the name made Isobel shudder; and as she did so some of the dust, which had waited patiently on the book for so long, stirred slightly, as if something had wafted past. She studied the proposed route and gasped as she read about the focus for the third walk, mouthing aloud the words in disbelief: 'The Genocide of the Armenians'. Without breathing she glanced at the bookcase and back to the invite; more dust was shifting. Her heart began thumping her rib cage as if this uncomfortable moment had grown fists and was pounding at the boundaries of her world. It beckoned for an unfolding of her Armenian heritage, a sequel to the revelation of her English heritage a year previously.

During that time she had found the English family she never knew; tracing her family tree she discovered that there was a part of her that was not Armenian, but was "forever England". This would be a logical sequence of events, she mused. It was as though her little life was gradually making sense of itself, and she inwardly braced herself for the next leg of the journey.

She was persuaded to go to Turkey because of her Armenian blood; yet that blood contained an ingrained repellent to that nation, and she had feared she was incapable of dealing with the horror of 'why'; but the dust sighed with relief as the forty-one year old finally opened the book and began to read the historical record of what took place almost a century ago.

1915 was the date of what has become known as the first holocaust. One and a half million people were wiped out in two years to solve the 'Armenian problem' - the ancient indigenous peoples that had lived peacefully as Christians amongst Muslims for centuries. With an imploding bureaucracy, the shrinking Ottoman Empire came under military dictatorship with a pan-Turk ideology. As East and West slavered for a piece of the pie, the First World War provided the perfect cover to begin a systematic ethnic cleansing, planned and executed to the highest degree.

She read eyewitness accounts of horrific treatment of humans by humans, testifying as if they had stared into the jaws of hell and would never be able to recover from the sight. Isobel checked the author again; it was an English professor who had sought to accurately document the genocide. She read late into the night, as if starvation from this information had in turn created an appetite to know and understand. The words carved the nightmare images that her mind had always feared. Yet somehow facing them made the truth less of a spectre. It was not about her any more; it was about these people, a murdered and almost eradicated nation now a blood clot on the side of the globe. The words *'This is part of who you are*' were coming home to roost; so she contacted her mother. Pouring over maps, she made her repeat the family stories until she comprehended their context.

'Where are you walking from?' her mother had asked.

'Adana, near the Mediterranean,' Isobel replied. 'We'll follow the coast round to Antioch and finish at the Syrian border.' Her mother's face had been one of disbelief as she fumbled with the maps, pointing at them with growing excitement. Grandfather had lived in Adana and his family had been there for generations. Incredibly, they still had the title deeds to the land they had owned stashed in the garage.

They all knew the family history. A Turkish official had saved their lives by giving a warning to Nazaret Terzian; with two days preparation, his family had sewn gold into their clothing and buried the rest of their wealth with an old relative, neither to be found again. All of their property and business was lost overnight, as the family was forced to join the people trains being marched to the Syrian Desert.

Isobel's journey would follow the same walk they had made, as they bribed their way to Damascus to somehow survive the massacres. Each night they would file past Turkish soldiers, who would demand gold and play god with who they allowed to buy their way to the coast; the alternative being to continue their way to the death camps in the desert. This was aided by the removal of a hand if anyone hesitated to pay, so that the Armenians quickly learned to give them their valuables. She would be following them, remembering them and walking for them.

She would return to the land where the brokenness of her people began. Holding on to her Maker, from whose hand the antidote poured, she prayed that as her feet touched the ground her mended existence would walk for recovery and healing.

Two months before Isobel was due to go, she had a daydream. She was standing in a river picking up two large stones from the riverbed and as she held them she knew that one represented 'rightness' and the other 'justice'. She smashed them together, as if the sound announced these two entities joining forces; and with that, a double-edged sword formed in her hands.

The river disappeared and she was standing on a green landscape, the sword still in her hands. She stabbed with the blade, making an incision into the ground, and carved a line back and forth through the land until she was slicing it open. Having finished, she peered into the opening to see a gurgling pool of blood rising and spilling from the cut she had created.

A warm breeze fanned Isobel's face as she stared at this phenomenon. Suddenly, she heard the sounds of singing getting nearer and louder. It swirled up from the opened ground and she could clearly hear words of forgiveness and mercy. The song wrapped around Isobel's ears as if the singers walked right by her, tall, majestic, full of heavenly beauty and grace. For a passing moment a Lion's face peered into her own with piercing eyes and then, as if drawn to the singing, He vanished.

With this she fell out of the daydream, scrambling for a pen to record the words of the song before it faded from her mind. Isobel was convinced this daydream was to do with Turkey and wondered what significance it might play whilst she was there.

A few weeks before the trip there was an incident that painfully echoed her dream. News came of two Turks and a German, who were murdered for their Christian faith, leaving loved ones without a husband or father. She read with tears as the widowed mother of four children expressed her forgiveness to the murderers. It was the song; the same song Isobel had heard in her dream was coming from the mouth of a bereaved Turkish woman.

So it was that the great granddaughter of Nazaret returned to his hometown, walking with other prayerful travellers into the sprawling city of Adana. She was the only reminder to the city that the legacy of Nazaret was lying here, somewhere, like gold thread waiting to be picked up and weaved into her own story. For Isobel this thread was life. She stood in that place, feet firmly planted, and offered up thanks to the life giver, almost a century on from the day her family were forced from their home, alongside so many others that would perish on their journey.

Hadrian's Great Stone Bridge of Adana still spans the Seyhan River; the oldest 'used' bridge in the world. This Roman construction was vital to the ancient trade routes from the east, and after crossing over the travellers paused to pray. As Isobel stood by the old bridge, her dream came rushing back to her, as if it had lagged behind until now and had only just caught up. Suddenly it became clear that it was about this river, the Seyhan, once clogged with bodies and now running freely, as if it had never witnessed such an atrocity. The light over the river was effervescent as Isobel stood and spoke about her dream; the air seemed to shimmer in the morning sun, as though angels danced on the surface. The peace of the moment engulfed her as she placed her feet in the water, slipped her hand into the hand of her creator and asked Him to make the dream real. Knowing she did not comprehend the fullness of what she was asking, He kept a tight hold. The next twenty-four hours would take her over rough terrain.

As the travellers walked on from Adana, Isobel looked back. The sun had gone behind the clouds, leaving a grey, gruesome hue on the landscape. An irritation began to ruffle the group, as if something unpleasant was on its way, but had not yet arrived. Arrive it did, three hours after crossing the Seyhan that morning. The group was the sudden victim of a roadside robbery, which deprived them of all forms of identity, money and valuables.

As the well-dressed Turkish man approached the car, Isobel watched, immobilised with uncertainty, as this wolf in sheep's clothing came to take advantage of their vulnerability. All became slow motion as it dawned on her that they were not safe and they could not stop this predator.

Suddenly Isobel was with those that had been this way before; with her family on the road, easy pickings for any malevolent scavenger. She could have been dressed like them, as they stood by the side of the road with their horse and cart, her family belongings piled high, while a soldier took whatever he pleased.

With no passport and no money, she found herself back in Adana, as the travellers sought police assistance. They were placed in the hands of the military and found themselves in a bureaucratic swamp, being passed from official to official. As she sat in one commandant's office, drinking yet another glass of tea, she shrank into her low chair, dwarfed by one of the many imposing desks they had encountered. She watched the officer on his raised seat and fear crawled across her. The feeling of powerlessness invaded her senses again. His face was perfectly chiselled, with beautiful eyes that any woman would long for, but his coldness froze the air around him and Isobel could imagine this young man a hundred years ago, making decisions about whether she lived or died.

A descendant of Nazaret the "Sword-Maker", with no knowledge of his suffering, she had stood in the Seyhan and given words to a dream. Now Isobel sat in his city with no identity, no money and subject to the might of the Turkish military, as if those words and dreams had given way to a deeper empathy with her ancestor. To walk through this city was to walk with those that had lost everything and just for a while, in some small way, she walked with them; the dispossessed, the vulnerable and the powerless.

The travellers were shocked at the turn of events and, having extricated themselves from the military's laborious maze of officialdom, drove through the night towards the military capital of Ankara, three hundred miles off course from their planned route. New identity papers must be sought. Adana had stopped them in their tracks and now they had to traverse the country, heading for the centre and the heart of the nation.

Isobel was in a daze, and jumped every time she recalled her own inability to stop the thief. As the car ploughed into the night her mind saw awful things, as if it was locked in front of a terrible film. Dragons feasted on fleeing people, grey bodies washed up on riverbanks and children were mown down by an invisible force; the film did not pause until they arrived, exhausted, in Ankara, at four in the morning.

After two hours of sleep and much form filling, they stood on the little patch of ground that, for them, was England. They arrived at the British embassy to regain their proof of identity and right of passage home. In three days their passports would be reinstated.

In the home of some Korean friends they found an oasis of calm, where they could gather their thoughts before they made their next move. Isobel simply sat as tired tears washed her face. The flashing images would not go away and she felt besieged. The travellers sat together and prayerfully spoke to their Maker, disarmed of confidence and direction. In her despair, she silently called out to the Maker, too. A hot air began to touch her head and face; the hair was stroked off her forehead, and she could hear Him talking, explaining. 'You cannot stand for something and not touch it. It's okay. It is a small price to pay, and you have only brushed their suffering'.

In an instant all Isobel's fear dissipated and the dark reverie was dispelled, as she suddenly understood the connection between the events of the previous day. Her discomfort meant she was tracking with the Maker's plan; it was part of something far bigger than being robbed and losing money. She was awed by this new perspective and her whole demeanour changed.

She stared at the map, which was open on the table. Gradually, Isobel began to see a different purpose in their diversion. If they returned to Adana, they would return to the place where their detour had begun, where the incision was made only the morning before. Could it be that their journey between Adana and Ankara was the cut in the dream, the slicing open that liberates mercy and forgiveness to walk across this land? Could it be that they would be making this journey between the two cities not only for the sake of their own identity papers, but also for the sake of Turkey's identity?

Deciding to make their way back to Adana, the travellers they knew they were on course. Isobel imagined the sword of justice and rightness like a blade hacking through an epidermis as they drove. This time there were no awful death scenes in her head, but rather a heavy peace that smelt like honey and poured into her being. They seemed to fly south and soon picked up the trail along the coast around the Mediterranean towards the Syrian border. Isobel walked conscious that she was amongst those who had gone before; their presence was symbolised by the poppies covering the sides of the road, as if the bright red flowers represented each life lost and where it fell. Some were in clumps and some on their own. Families, brothers, sisters; these red head stones had no inscription to read. Her job was to remember them as she passed their unmarked graves and whisper that they were not forgotten. The Maker padded beside her on velvet paws, breathing His warm breath on her, lest she felt the chill of the death she walked through.

When the time came for the journey once more from Adana back to Ankara, it felt an age away from the turmoil of three days before; what had begun as a diversion had actually put the travellers on course. They felt they were in the right place and on time as they sped back in land, slicing through to the heart of the nation.

With a sigh of relief and new passports in hand they hastened to leave to complete their walk and fly home. It was not long before they found themselves brought to a halt by fifty lorries lined up on the road like a herd of elephants, nose to tail. Isobel sat in the car, simultaneously colliding with an internal roadblock. It had begun as an uncomfortable insecurity and now it was evolving into a foreboding fear that what she had dared to initiate might not be complete. It had been easy in the dream, in the river, and since the Maker had revealed His map. But the last journey between these two cities felt like a critical test for Isobel. The moment seemed to pivot on her. How deep would she go and how much would she give of herself to ensure the final cut was deep enough?

The pressure intensified and it felt like she was sliding into a dark place where old familiar walls went up around her; a mechanical shut-down and shut-out. The isolation of the Armenian comes from a deep wound. It has the power to turn a friend into a foe and grip a reasoning mind with irrational fear. It had the power to leave her feeling alone, despite sitting in a car full of people, and swallow her into a subterranean place. Alone in what felt crucial, involuntary tears spurted from her eyes for hours. She could not stop them or understand them, but they flowed like the river she had stood in. In this deep, dark place Isobel poured out her soul, soaking it with her desperation, with the knowledge of her own weaknesses and inadequacies. She begged her Maker to intervene in the depths of this nation. The mending has to start in the core and at the root; so that is where she went. What the 'Sword Maker' cuts deep to rend, 'The Tailor' sews tears to mend; and both were imperative on the last journey back to Adana.

That night Isobel seeped tears as she slept and when she awoke they continued to spill out from an unknown source. She was aware that, in some way, she was joining a lament that had lasted for decades. Only when she tugged at her Maker did she slowly lift out of this place, like a deep-sea diver ready to return to the surface.

Gradually the lament subsided as the sunlight poured into her room, drawing her into its warmth and the promise of a new day. She had a sense that she was reaching the finishing line. She was completing the course that Adana had set her on and had managed to clear every hurdle in her way.

She searched for the medal her mother had given her before the trip. It belonged to Avedis, a top hurdle racer in his youth. It was gone; it would be left in Adana with a thief, who had no idea of what he had set in motion. Isobel smiled. If the medal were lying in the dust somewhere in Adana, she would leave it behind as a sign to that city that the 'Kelenjian/ Terzian' trophy was here to stay.

Now every thread that connected her to Adana was firmly woven into her heart and Isobel had no doubt that it was Nazaret's legacy that had been her passport.

Nazaret and his family had used their gold to remain on the coastal road and arrived in Damascus as refugees with just two other families. They had been amazed every time a soldier had taken a bribe and sent them the right way when they could have tricked them with ease. Other refugees were pouring into Damascus and with the War there was barely a living to be made. Daily, Nazaret wheeled a barrow through the narrow market streets of the souqs, selling meagre provisions, and anything else he could lay his hands on. This old city seemed to welcome trading strangers to find a home, or at least a place to rest for a while before moving on.

However, there was little food and Avedis, Nazaret's eldest, was constantly hungry. He and his friend would attempt to find supplies, making secret excursions into the British army post. One of these would prove fatal. The boys were caught in cross-fire and found themselves unable to move from their hiding place. Bullets ricocheted all around them as the fighting intensified. With no way of escape, a bullet skimmed the top of Avedis' knee and buried itself in his friend, instantly taking his life. Somehow, Avedis survived, remaining motionless beside his fallen companion for many hours until it was safe to creep home. Nazaret held Avedis in his arms until he slept. It was a miracle they had survived thus far, but Nazaret still felt plagued by the need to protect his family and to keep them safe.

After six years of living in Damascus they were still not safe. As the Turks retreated from the battlefront they arrived in Damascus, ransacking the city as they swept through. They found the Armenian quarter and began rounding up the men from every household to take them as slaves back to Turkey. Once again Nazaret was spared as the soldiers came running through his house; he jumped on to the roof of his Syrian neighbours, who kept him for six days until the coast was clear. Many men were taken and never seen again.

Nazaret knew now that it was time to move on and find his family a safe home and a place of rest. As they sailed to the island of Cyprus, Nazaret watched the coastline of his homeland with an aching heart. He felt torn and severed. The furthest he would go would be the island; his home was always in sight. He would never give up hope that one day he would return.

It would take three generations for him to do so. His body was buried, but his heart's desire survived. And so it was that his great granddaughter, Isobel, went back to Adana and discovered his legacy waiting for her. She hoped that his heart finally found its way home as she picked up his gold thread, his sword, and continued his story with her own.

Fact File: Adana and the Armenian Genocide

1909

Massacres in the city of Adana (Cilicia); around 30,000 Armenians slaughtered.

1914

Before the beginning of World War I, more than two million Armenians lived in the Ottoman Empire.

1915 – 1922

1.5 million Armenians perished by violence or hardships. In Bitlis, 15 000 Armenians perished in a single day.

Of one convoy of 18 000 Armenians from Sivas and Kharput, only 150 survivors reached Aleppo, Syria.

Out of 86 000 Armenians living in Eastern Cilicia it is estimated that only 12 000 survived in exile.

Out of 30 000 Armenians residing in Sivas, only 15 000 survived by 1922.

By 1922:

Half a million Armenians were refugees in foreign lands. 50 000 remained in Istanbul in deplorable conditions

Mustafa Kemal Atatürk expelled all the remaining Armenians in Anatolia and the Armenian population virtually disappeared.

Sources:

Bedoukian, Kerop (1978) The Urchin, London, UK:
John Murray
Kerr, Stanley. E. (1973) The Lions of Marash, Albany,
USA: State University of New York Press
Lang, David Marshall (1981) The Armenians, A
People in Exile, London, UK: George Allen & Unwin
Ltd
Nogales, Rafael de (1926) Four years Beneath the
Crescent, London, UK: Sterndale Classics
www.armenian-genocide.org, accessed February 2008
www.armeniapedia.org, accessed February 2008
www.ourararat.com, accessed February 2008

CHAPTER 24

The Road to Damascus:
October 2007

Steve Lowton

REFLECTIONS FROM HOME

Preparing for Syria was completely exciting! This is the stuff of school boy dreams, to be going to such far off lands to walk and pray. That summer I was focused on some big walks in the UK and was seeing significant numbers connecting with us, sometimes with over forty on the road together. In between, however, my mind drifted to the thought of what was in store for us in Syria. The encounter on the roads of Turkey had pricked any residue bubble of fear that lingered. We had come through that unscathed and had no reason to think anything different of the unknowns that lay before us. As it was, and as I expected, Syria turned out to be as safe as if we were walking in France or Italy. There are times to heed the warning of fears that lurk, and there are times to push through them. The prospect before us therefore was completely enticing.

THE DAMASCUS ROAD

Team Kathy, Dave, Richard, Paul and myself

Returning to Leeds yesterday was like returning from a visit to Narnia, such has been the richness of all that we have tasted in the wonderful country of Syria. Whether its the smell of shisha pipes in the coffee shop at the eastern gate of the old city walls of Damascus, the taste of sweet pastries or the aroma of spices in the souq of Damascus, the imagination is fired in a multitude of moments. The sight of the hills of Lebanon or the Bedouin Shepherds by the road side, the many and varied salads and the wonderful fruit drinks that are served on every street corner all come together to bombard the senses in an unforgettable way. The gentle welcome of the Syrians and their incredible gift of hospitality made all talk of an 'axis of evil' seem very remote, not withstanding a courtesy visit to the local army barracks when we strayed too near the Lebanese border.

Picking up the walk within sight of the green hills of the Turkish there is so much I could say regarding our journey south to Damascus. I could focus on the heart stopping road sign that we walked under, saying Iraq to the left, Lebanon to the right and Jordan straight on! What possibilities there are for the ordinary people of God to connect with these hidden and scarred lands? I could linger on the power lines we tracked that marked out the current dictatorship of President Assad, or the terrible massacre of thousands of citizens of the city of Hama during the 1980s, when an Islamic uprising threatened to get out of hand. The hard veneer of the military, as with Turkey, hides a soft and sensitive underbelly to this Arabic speaking nation.

However, for the sake of brevity I want to focus on our time in Damascus, for the level of sight that was given was way beyond anything I had expected; our mandate was as clear as with any city I have journeyed through since leaving Whitby over two years ago.

Damascus; the place where Islam first emerged from its Arabic birthplace 1500 miles to the south to draw on the power of Empire in the late seventh century, knowing an unparalleled period of expansion as this city of stories rose to stand as the Rome of Islam. Religion and empire became in that century dreadfully yoked even as it is to this day. Damascus, the place where 1500 years earlier, a young servant girl found the courage to speak to her leprous master of the prophet in her homeland and the healing that might be found just over the hills now called the Golan Heights. Damascus, the place to which a confused Aramean army returned, having gone looking for that same prophet, only to party all night and return empty handed. Damascus, no doubt the place where an even stranger prophet wandered through, dirty loincloth in hand as he went in search of the river Euphrates, under some strange instruction as to what he should do when he found that great river. Yes, and Damascus, the place where the symbol of imperial Judaism came in search of the people of the Way, only to find his own life turned dramatically upside down, the persecutor becoming the preacher. So a new wineskin burst forth from the straight jacket of Judaism, rippling west from this historic city along the pathways of the Apostle Paul.

Given the context of our journey as we have tracked the appalling abuse of imperialism through city after city and nation after nation, the two-fold mandate that was given to us was clear and pivotal. One of us would look south and east, the other west as we acknowledged the turning point that Damascus is and was. First, however, we had to sow some grit from the road into the place where Islam came in search of the protection and provision of the State. I say grit deliberately, for what prayer can make up for the thousands of miles walked, the hard decisions taken in the risk and adventure of the journey or the money sown in and choices made by those who have released us to travel and those who have walked with us? Walking the land is such a safe way to pray for it is there that we bottom these issues of protection and provision[11] and it is there that we truly connect with the land. Hearts are softened to people much maligned and grace is given.

We prayed our simple prayers therefore, that separation and disruption would start to come to this unholy alliance and that the Maker would undo the patterning of all that was set in motion in Rome when Constantine settled for the straight and predictable lines of empire instead of the wild and unpredictable ways of the Holy Spirit. Sitting on the floor in the Unmayyed Mosque, the third most sacred site of Islam, we allowed some of the sweat and grit, the tears and joys to soften this hard but oh-so-tender region of the world. Looking up from our prayers a few minutes later my mind returned quickly to St Peters Square, when some young children came straight over us with delight in the eyes (as happened in Rome) and maybe, just maybe, some angelic given

---

[11]Issues of who is our provider and who is our protector have been carried every since leaving Whitby. If we are to discover the wild ways of the Holy Spirit, knowing his protection and provision, then it is the place of adventure and risk that we find a starting point.

insight as to the liberation that had just been loosed in their land.

The second aspect of our mandate was to pray into the opening of the well of Straight Street[12]. That this is a well that carries grace to shatter imperial mindsets and open locked up hearts was confirmed to me by two dreams that came the night before we went to pray. Under the clear guidance of Kathy, a seasoned drinker of the wells that are opening up in Wales at this time, we sat down by the side of this most awesome of locations and drank deeply of the Holy Spirit; feasting on him in the open air of Straight Street. As the day before our thoughts had been to the south and to the east and the well worn paths of Islam, so this time our thoughts were to the westward journeys of Paul, even to that time in 2004 when I joined with Martin Scott to walk the western margins of the western world that is California. We travelled there to call up a fresh Jesus movement over all that lay to the east of us, even as we had travelled here to call up a fresh movement to journey west. Somehow I felt three years on a conclusion had been found to that journey, a journey that took me from Western California to the heart of Christendom and then on to this pivotal city of Damascus. That something has been loosed to surge down the miles we have walked I have no doubt. The might of Rome or the subtleties of Athens will not squeeze out the life that is already coming through. Our thoughts as a team, drifted to the place not too far away now, where Abraham dug another well, naming it

---

[12]Straight Street is where Saul went to after his experience on the road to Damascus. Blinded, he waited until a man called Ananias arrived to pray for him and see his sight restored. He was then renamed Paul.

"Rehoboth, for at last the Lord has made room for us and we shall be fruitful in the land."

I cannot finish this report without mentioning the troubles in Turkey at this time[13]. I watch with interest as we look to see what contribution our journey has made, amongst that of many others, to the denials of the past and the Armenian genocide. I also cannot finish without mentioning the fact that I would have had very little to write about in this report were it not for the sharp sightedness of Paul Wood and the strong gifting he carries of city mapping and the Islamic world, You are a man sown into the land, Paul, and as a team we honour your sure sightedness and tender heart Equally Kathy Garda and the grace she is carrying to be a conduit of the life of the Spirit of God into the brittleness of new landscapes. You are a grace-package to many Kathy; thank you big time for having the courage to join our journey. We can truly walk through the Middle Eastern lands as men and women together. As for Richard and Dave, I honour you both as two awesome work-horses of the road, who have tracked with me all the time since leaving Athens. I count it a huge privilege to be on the road with you both. Thank you for giving, as you have undoubtedly given.

We will be back out to Israel and the West Bank in early March 2008. The team is already full, but for those who are stirred by these reports more opportunity to walk these lands must surely come. Already my sights are on Cairo, and who knows, perhaps the Arabian Peninsula beyond.

---

[13]Whilst we were out walking in Syria the Senate in the United States were proposing a vote on whether the Armenian massacres were genocide or not. This caused great offence in Turkey and was destabilising to international relations. Eventually the issue was sidestepped.

Finally, to all who prayed for us and journeyed with us back home, huge thanks. We are learning together the limitless opportunities for adventure when the covering of the saints are upon us. Without you all we would not have made it this far.

REFLECTIONS FROM HOME

It is a bizarre thing to come home from such a time as this to then stand with the other mums and dads in the school playground. One moment I am in some world where we are seeking to connect with issues spanning many centuries, the next I am stood around seeking to engage the odd parent or two in conversations about the weather or the next children's party to hit the never-ending circuit of fun that Zhen seems to be on. That is my life and I cannot begin to explain it.

To add further to the mystery of the pathways I had walked these years gone by it began to dawn on me that another season of forty was concluding: forty months since walking in California to concluding in Damascus. You may well be tired of this preoccupation with counting days, weeks and months. If so, I really do not blame you. However, we walked in the trend-setting place that is California to call for a shift in the mindset that dominates our western world. Forty months on I walked into Damascus, the place where Saul's imperialistic clothing was shed and the counter- cultural message of the gospel found fresh pathways to the west. Once more faith was strengthened to believe that there is space for new wine to be drawn up into the sterility of so much of western life.

Returning home it really did seem as if we had brought some angels from Damascus with us. Within days Zhou appeared completely different and it truly seemed as if her life could now really begin to flourish. Hannah, too, had concluded her own journey back to full health[14]. The squeeze that we had been caught up in was suddenly a thing of the past, for at last the Lord had made room for us. God is so very good.

We were now within a stone's throw of Jerusalem. Another stage of this adventure was about to conclude; though already sight was opening up of Cairo and the possibilities of the Arabian Peninsula beyond. It is indeed a dangerous thing to step out of your own front door. You really don't know quite where it might end up!

---

[14]Hannah was wonderfully healed in September of 2007 when I along with around 40 others walked into Cardiff in pursuit of the wild fire anointing of that revival land. Whilst doing hardly any walking Hannah had hooked up with us, believing there was something there for her. There was indeed!

CHAPTER 25

The Storyteller of Damascus

Paul Wood

It was in the wonderful, creative city of Damascus that I began get a vision for a new story- telling venture, for surely stories have fuelled the imagination for generations. Here Paul picks up the story of what is said to be the oldest city in the world. Let your imagination take flight as he stirs the waters of this most beguiling of places.

It was nearing the end of the fasting month of Ramadan and the daily ritual of pre-dawn prayers and late night feasting had taken its toll on the inhabitants of the ancient city of Damascus. That afternoon, the watchmen at the gates of the city were drowsy, and reluctant to stir themselves for the five travellers who were approaching the gate. At this time of day all that mattered were the cool glasses of tamarind and apricot juice and the seasonal delicacies that, from where they sat, they could smell being prepared. They were easing away the last long hour before dusk, when the mournful cry would ring out from the minarets of the city, releasing them from their fasting. This magical moment stood at the heart of their beliefs, the perfect synchronisation of all the faithful renewing their covenant with Allah. It was a moment so vital that even those unfortunate enough to be caught out, still hurrying home, would pause to share dates with others on the road.

So just a few routine inquiries were all that was needed; nothing that would drain the last reserves of mental energy. Something unusual about those travellers' occupations, though, was worth a flicker of interest. They were obviously not business people, or the usual type of pilgrim, or holidaymakers with money to spend. It seemed they had nothing in common; so what had brought them together?

The travellers never found such questions easy to answer. They claimed it was a pilgrimage of sorts. They had fallen in together somewhere back on the long road down from the remote northern parts. They were all following pathways back to the ancient roots of their faith, hoping to shed the crusty accretions of time and rediscover the ways of the original folk, rough and simple, to whom their Way had first been entrusted. They even had secret hopes that they might chance upon the footsteps of the Great Shepherd King, who had arisen in the margins, but come to stand so central to everything they believed.

The watchman's eyes glazed over. This was no time for work; for making trouble.

"Ramadan is generous!" said one.

"Allah is the most generous!" responded another.

The travellers looked harmless enough, so they were waved in.

The thing that really united those five travellers remained unseen by the gatekeepers that evening, because it was tucked away in their hearts. They called it the 'Tales from the Margins'. It was a collection of stories. Some were their own; others had been entrusted to them by friends; others just overheard. But all concerned unknown, unimportant people. The tales told of unlikely encounters with the empire of heaven; the travellers believed this was advancing by means of stories, bearing in, like them, from the margins of life to shake the hearts of the world's empires. So they had set out to drag these 'Tales' with their footsteps across the miles.

Once inside they found the city pleased to receive them and willing to help them find their way. They were directed to lodgings in a quiet quarter, and as the fast was broken that evening they were welcomed to share the food of any whose table they happened to pass. Since most were poor they politely declined, and went to eat in the old Christian quarter.

Many of the restaurants there were set in the courtyards of traditional houses with a fountain at the centre and tables arrayed around it. It was in such settings that the travellers found nourishment and safety to talk over their experiences and feelings. Here was where the questions, the hopes and longings, the struggles and trials were laid out in one another's presence. Rational thought and imagination were tempered with the wisdom of scripture and humour. There was much laughter and a few tears. Around the table they became priests and sense-makers to each other's journeys.

The fountain that eavesdropped their conversation that evening reminded them of the many different springs they had drunk from along the way. It seemed to be drawing them in deeper, telling them that there were wells to be sought after in the city, places of connection that held the secret essence of life in the mysterious place.

Quite by chance they had heard that there was in the city a *hakawati* - a traditional storyteller. Apparently, he was the latest in a long line of storytellers who had, for generations, entertained audiences in a certain coffee-house every night. It sounded like a place that would understand people like themselves, with stories to tell; so after dinner, they went in search of him.

The heart of the old city was dominated by a temple of immense proportions. It sat atop a history that reached deep into the earth below and under minarets that towered to the heavens. Around it spread a maze of narrow, crooked streets and alleys that ended abruptly at its monstrous stone walls. It was in one such street, at the foot of some stone steps that led up to the east gate of the temple that they found the coffeehouse where the story-teller worked.

The outer courtyard was impossibly crowded. Patrons nestled shoulder-to-shoulder along benches and in tight circles around spindly legged, wrought-iron tables, upon which teapots and glasses perched precariously. Most had a tall nargileh pipe between their knees, bubbling water in the base, glowing coals at the top and sweet apple tobacco smoke billowing around their heads.

The travellers squeezed through to the inner room where, quite by chance, a table had just been vacated. At nine o'clock the storyteller appeared. He climbed to his raised seat, sat down and, as his ancestors had always done, laid a ceremonial sword across his knees. He adjusted the tarboosh on his head and from the folds of his cloak pulled a black leather-bound book. He opened it and began to read a tale of old Damascus:

"It has always been the case," he began, "that anyone who desired to take his message to the ends of the earth came through this city. But this city also had to be mastered, because she could cast a spell on those who came, and they would linger and take their ease until some new conqueror suddenly burst through the gates to seize her as their prize. Our Prophet, peace be upon him, declined to enter because he said he wished to enter paradise only once, at death."

He continued to tell of how Damascus had been swept up in the relentless expansion of the Islamic faith after the prophet's death. But theirs was a faith born in the austere modesty of the desert and suspicious of the effect that the long idolatrous history of these ancient cities might have on the believers. So the precinct of the old Jupiter temple was left to the Christians, and they set up their own simple places of worship elsewhere.

However, as time went by the numbers of Muslims increased. One day the sixth Umayyad Caliph, Khalid ibn-Al-Walid, cast an envious eye on the space enjoyed by the Christians. His movement had pushed back the old orders of Jerusalem and Rome. It was time for him to put down a marker befitting the ascendancy of his new empire, to show that the believers were heirs and successors of both Judaism and Christianity.

It had been a delicate matter persuading the Christians to relinquish the temple, but once that final hurdle had been removed nothing stood in his way. He would make of the temple a mosque, the proportions of which had never been seen, nor ever would be again, and with a glory mirroring the paradise that awaited the faithful.

The storyteller was speaking in Arabic and the travellers could only catch the odd word and imagine the story he was telling. The heat of the room began to make them feel sleepy. Lest their inattentiveness should cause offence, they rose as discreetly as they could to move to seats in the courtyard where the air was cooler. They satisfied themselves that they had at least seen and heard the Storyteller of Damascus. They had tasted an ancient tradition - but not yet the drinks they had ordered. Perhaps the service would be better outside.

The storyteller paused briefly for them as they moved to the door, then continued.

He related how the workforce, being mainly Christian, had been reluctant to pull down the church, so the Caliph had taken an axe to it himself. Later on they had come across a cave underneath the floor, in which was a large box; and within that box, a casket. The Caliph had been summoned and brought by candlelight into the cave. He had opened the box and the casket, and inside found the severed head of John the Baptist. The Caliph respectfully reburied the head underneath his new mosque and there it remains to this day.

The storyteller finished his story with the account of how the last Umayyad Caliphs, heirs of the Damascus temple of paradise, had frittered away their energies in the love of poetry and art, wine and women. Then the Abbasids had arisen and snatched the crown of empire away to Baghdad.

Meanwhile, outside in the courtyard, people shuffled along, rearranged their pipes and made room for the travellers as best they could. Their drinks arrived and they fell into conversation with some locals. Small engraved glasses containing thimble-fulls of the bitterest of bitter coffee were passed around, and the travellers settled back to pass the evening amidst the solemn puffing of nargileh pipes and the rich, heavy aroma of history.

Daytimes in Damascus were long and little happened. Ramadan compounded the natural inclination of the city to sleepiness and the travellers found it hard to avoid drifting under its spell. They read, slept, or ordered tea and waited endlessly for it to arrive. Mindful of all they hoped to accomplish, at times they became frustrated with their confinement, but Damascus would not be rushed into disclosing herself. It was only at night that life emerged. Beginning after dusk, it would reach a crescendo of vibrancy around midnight; and at three in the morning there was little sign of weariness, and no consideration given to anyone trying to sleep.

On the second evening they went in search of souvenirs and found themselves in the long, covered market street of Souq-Al-Hamidiyya. The shutters of shops were being raised to reveal brightly lit displays of every kind of exotic merchandise. There was glittering gold and antique silver, brass and pewter, carpets, pashmina, silks and cottons, carved camel-bone and jewellery of unknown and mysterious origin. Dusty, stuffed animals and fusty religious texts, instruments of music and instruments of war, black veils and titillating underwear could all be purchased. Everything and anything competed side-by-side for the shoppers' senses; the exotic and the austere, the old and the new, the genuine and the fake.

As they were browsing their progress was suddenly interrupted by a mass of young men, surging out from the western gate of the temple after prayers. The flood of religious fervour briefly brushed aside the clamour of the market and seemed to sweep open windows into an invisible realm both beyond and within. The travellers found themselves, for an instant, staring into the soul of the city. There was a rush of footmen and, with a clatter of hooves on cobbles, a woman appeared, mounted on a great horse. With supernatural stature and power she gazed down on the scene for a moment, then, just as quickly, disappeared.

It was a momentary vision around which the mystery of the city began to crystallize. As the market drifted gradually back into place around them, understanding dawned. They had seen Great Mother Damascus, a queen courted in her day by kings and princes of many nationalities. She was 'Mother' because under her benevolent and tolerant rule there were few who could not find a home of some sort. She only rode at night; and though often royally clothed, she was unpredictable and sometimes wore so little that men were awe-struck and speechless. In this she embodied the sensuality, as well as the royal dignity, of the city.

For a while they meandered on in silence, but eventually their attention was drawn to a small shop displaying unusual jewellery, so they went to take a closer look. A young man sitting behind the counter rose eagerly to greet them. He was Armenian. His grandfather, they discovered, had moved to Damascus from Turkey, just two years before the massacres. He had been one of the fortunate ones. He had made a home here, raised his family and would be able to leave his thriving jewellery business to his Grandson. Syria was like that: tolerant of people from all races and religions. It offered refuge and demanded in return only that you display a portrait of its ruler and never speak against him.

The young man brought out trays of Armenian jewellery fashioned from silver and semi-precious stones. He extolled the quality of the blue stone beads and silver-work and spread out the merchandise without reserve, each item carefully weighed on scales to determine its price. Every display was turned upside down to find the right item, or at least to encourage the travellers to buy something in compensation for the effort so obviously expended.

Whilst negotiations took place they sat on stools and were served glasses of pale yellow Armenian tea, made from dried flowers. Eventually they left, laden with compliments and free gifts of tea, their purchases and somewhat lighter purses. It seemed to have been a good day for the Armenian and his buoyancy cast doubt on how successful their efforts at haggling had been.

Meanwhile, in the coffeehouse, which was a few doors down from the jewellery shop, the storyteller arrived as usual to entertain the guests who had gathered there. He began as usual at nine o'clock:

"Has anything ever happened in the world that was not gossiped in the streets of Damascus?" he asked.

"No!" replied the listeners seated around him.

"And will anything happen in Damascus that will not get told across the whole world?"

"No, never!" came the reply.

"That's what they say about Damascus," he continued, "but sometimes news told in this city is easily missed, because it is told by the most unlikely of people. The smallest and least important of strangers in Damascus may have tales to tell that change the course of history.

"In the days when the great king Ben Hadad ruled, there was a young slave girl, in one of the big houses not far from here. One day she came to her mistress with a story."

He paused as a waiter brought him a glass of Armenian flower tea and the listeners settled themselves; then he went on:

"'My mistress,' she said, 'I hope you will not scold me for being too bold, but I know that the Master is not well. I have heard him groaning in pain and he hardly goes out these days. I know you are sad too, my Lady.'

'You are right,' the Lady replied, 'I don't know what will become of us now. Naaman was a great man; he could do nothing wrong. But now he is becoming a cripple. The physicians cannot cure him. He will die in shame, and I am afraid, child.'

The Lady's heart was stirred by the child's infectious faith. 'Is that so? What is his name and where would he find him?'"

The listeners' interest was aroused. So he told them how Naaman had thrown caution to the wind and set off, sick as he was, in search of the foreign prophet; and how he had eventually found him, and discovered that the child's story was true.

"The prophet told this great man to wash himself seven times in a local, muddy river; can you imagine!" the storyteller exclaimed. "His pride was offended and he protested, but his servants helped him see sense. He returned after a few weeks and all of Damascus came out to see what had happened. He stretched out his hands for them to see that his skin was totally restored. The people gasped. Could this have been the work of the god of their inferior neighbours?"

The listeners murmured. They had rather mixed feelings about this, but the storyteller pressed on:

"But the strangest thing of all was the two mule loads of earth he brought back with him. He had it spread out in the courtyard of his house and each morning he would kneel upon this earth to pray; not to his own god, but to the god of the prophet - the god of the slave-girl!"

There were more murmurs of disapproval, but there was an ending to the story he knew they would enjoy: "And sometimes in the afternoons, when the house was quiet and the lady of the house was sleeping, the young slave-girl would creep out into the courtyard, to where the soil was laid, and kneel on it herself. She would run it through her fingers and hold it up to her nose, stirring her memories with faint traces of a distant homeland. She had prayed to be reunited with the land she had been taken away from, but she had never imagined that the land itself would come to find her."

The audience applauded; their glasses were refilled and the waiters brought fresh lumps of apple and mint tobacco and red hot coals in swinging braziers to replenish their pipes.

On the third day the travellers felt the time had come to enter the great temple which, to this point, they had only skirted around. They joined the steady stream of pilgrims and visitors from all over the world who were converging on the south gate, the one through which entry for worshippers was permitted. There they removed their shoes and stepped into a vast carpeted hall.

Groups of people sat or lay on the rich red carpet reading, meditating or just sleeping. The travellers moved slowly along between two rows of enormous pillars, taking in the scene and craning their necks to see the arches and domes high above their heads. At the foot of the ninth pillar they sat down. Around three o'clock the faithful stirred themselves and moved to form long lines facing the southern wall. Old and young, rich and poor, well dressed and ragged stood side-by-side, with the women in rows well behind the men. Stewards patrolled the length of the temple, watching for any infringement of temple regulations; a child distracting attention; the offensive upturned sole of a foot; or the seductive bounce of a woman's tress escaping a veil.

Conscious that their difference might stand out, the travellers bowed down in a circle to pray. They were looking to the God who had led them safely thus far to fulfil the appointment they had come for. Surely here, at the ancient axis upon which world religions pivoted, they would be able to reach into the heart of a city that reached out to the whole world with it's messengers. But the rigours of the road over the past weeks had left them with few words.

As they prayed, grit from the road fell from the soles of their feet, tumbled down through the centuries of history and tinkled on a deep, stone floor. There, in a poorly lit under-layer of the city, a slumbering angel was awakened by its fall. Like the dirt Naaman had once laid down on a Damascus floor it carried the aroma of the faith; a faith that dares to challenge history's patterns and walks off the edge of maps in pursuit of unreasonable hopes. It called him up through the layers, from his chamber at the base of a city weary of struggle and sated with meaningless glitter, to stand by the ninth pillar. If the travellers had been able to observe him they would have seen a brilliant gold figure standing almost as high as the pillar itself. They didn't - but younger, keener eyes did. Three children, drawn by the glow that suddenly enveloped the strange worshippers, came over to stand in the radiance and, with shining eyes, introduced themselves. Afterwards, as they left, the travellers felt that, despite their poor prayers, their hearts had been strangely warmed and that the children were a good sign.

In her chamber, Great Mother Damascus stirred, disturbed by a dream in which a young man who had loved her many centuries ago came and stood beside her as she lay. He began to sing an old love-song that she hadn't heard in ages. "It's all coming back to me now," he sang, then reached down to touch her. She woke with a start.

Later that night, with some apprehension, she rode up the street and entered through the closed east gate of the temple to breathe deeply of the devotions of the day. She found she was not alone. There was an angel who had not been seen for a long time, standing by the ninth pillar. Things were happening today she did not understand. She paused and questioned him as to his business in the temple. He simply replied that he had been called for an appointment. This was now his position. Perplexed, she proceeded on, out of the west gate and into the streets.

The travellers felt that their visit to the temple had been significant, but that there was one further appointment waiting for them somewhere else in the city. So on the fourth day they headed in the direction of Straight Street. About halfway along that street they came across a deep excavation in the ground. A few metres down, the stones and arches of a much older street were plainly visible in the soil. They wondered: could this be a place to get under the skin of the city; the opening of another well? They sat on the nearby doorstep of a shuttered shop and closed their eyes. They explored the excavation with their imaginations and allowed themselves to sink back to an older layer of reality.

There was a well there; they drank deeply and splashed in its eternal waters. It chilled their feet, bathed their faces, soaked their clothes and went to their heads. There were no words spoken for a long time. After a while they found themselves sitting amidst the bustle of a more ancient marketplace, and the tales they had carried in their hearts lay before them on the ground, in a great leather-bound book.

The old man Ananias, whose house was in an alley not far from Straight Street, still liked to walk through the market whenever he could find someone to accompany him. He was older than anyone could remember, stooped and very unsteady on his feet. That morning gossip had trickled through the maze of narrow lanes that strangers from the north had appeared in the marketplace. A boy, the son of a neighbour, was called; and just after midday Ananias, wearing his white pilgrim's robe and skullcap, with his stick in his right hand and with the boy steadying him on the left, moved slowly out into the warm sunshine.

He recalled a time many, many years ago, when he had come this way to meet another visitor; a young, Jewish fanatic called Saul, who had come up from Jerusalem. Everyone had heard of him. He was intent on stamping out the followers of Jesus, or the 'Followers of the Way' as they were called. But just outside the city an explosion of light had knocked him down and he was led into the city blind. They had all been greatly relieved. Ananias wouldn't have gone near the man; he would have hidden or run like the others, had it not been for a vision in which Jesus himself had appeared and told him to go and pray for Saul. In the days that followed Saul completely turned the tables on the Jewish authorities. He ended up following 'The Way' himself - to the ends of the earth. It had all begun here. Damascus certainly had a penchant for stories with a twist in the tail. One never knew what might arise from an appointment on Straight Street.

"Take me to these strangers; I must greet them," Ananias said to the boy. As he got nearer to the marketplace the throng increased, but people stood aside to let him pass.

Now, stories were always highly prized here. The city had always had an insatiable appetite for them; but the 'Tales from the Margins' that the strangers had brought were an attraction quite out of the ordinary. To the travellers' amazement, offers were made for the book, and when the wealthiest merchants of the city joined the action its value climbed astronomically. Finally the city elders came and said that they would purchase it on behalf of the city, for the benefit of everyone. The book was entrusted to the storyteller so that its tales could be told in the coffeehouse by the east gate. The travellers then watched as the treasures of Damascus, given in exchange, were loaded onto caravans of camels. There was sufficient to furnish many houses and rebuild whole cities. The caravans were dispatched to the east and to the west, the north and the south.

At last Ananias arrived at where the travellers were sitting on the step. He surveyed them carefully. "Those tales have won these strangers far more than they hoped or imagined", he thought to himself. He wondered what would become of them, and if he would ever get to hear of it.

The travellers looked up, rather dazed by all that had happened. An old man, dressed in white and leaning on the arm of a child almost as tall as himself, had stopped in front of them.

"Peace be on you", he said, after observing them for a few moments.

They composed themselves and greeted him back. After a moment or two he turned and walked slowly on up the street. He was getting tired, and it would be unfair to detain the boy much longer.

The travellers felt that the 'Tales from the Margins' that they had set out to carry across the lands had now been deposited somehow in the heart of this ancient city. The city had been a delight and had enriched them far more than they ever expected; but they knew that their stories had to be dragged on to other places that needed to hear them.

Ahead of them lay mountains of offence that rose in defiance of all they believed Damascus should be, and beyond those a City of Peace. It was rumoured that if they could battle their way through those mountains an ageless king would come out of that city with bread and wine. By now the 'Tales' had a life of their own, and perhaps it was the Tales themselves now drawing the travellers back to the road and dragging them on to distant places. So on the fifth day they walked out through the city gates.

Later that night Great Mother Damascus rode up into the mountains outside the city. A warm breeze teased her hair as she looked down upon the place where the great square temple, gift of many lovers, squatted darkly amidst a sea of twinkling lights. It was there that the Barada River had first tumbled down the Anti-Lebanon Mountains and come to rest in a kindly oasis on the edge of the desert. It was where she had grown up; and where now, in the coffeehouse nestled next to its east gate, a flow of new stories was trickling down to the storyteller from some distant ancestral memory. The temple reminded her of the days when her power and beauty had been at its pinnacle and for ninety years she had been the heart and soul of an empire that grew to overshadow even Rome's, spreading its message from the Pyrenees in the West to Samarqand in the East. All eyes had been on the incessantly squabbling Persians and Byzantines, but she had seen the star rising in Arabia. She had given herself to the Arab tribesmen who followed it up into the spaces those empires left behind. They had found their way, through her, to fill the earth with their story, just as Saul and the followers of the Way had done in their time. Though she had enriched and entertained empires that rose and fell, and for a while built their thrones and filled her temple, she had other gifts reserved for poor, ragged strangers travelling new ways with world-changing stories.

She wondered if those travellers who had left that day had been humble forerunners of some new movement - or perhaps just laggards of an old one. Was true love coming back, as the song had said? Would she once again be romanced by bearers of a heavenly message on their way to the ends of the earth?

She could just make out the inscription carved in Greek above the southern entrance of the temple. It read:

'Your kingship, O Christ, is a kingship for ever; your reign lasts from age to age.'

It seemed to hint that there was something yet to come from those followers of the Way.

FACT FILE: DAMASCUS

The Spread of Christianity

"Paul's experiences in Damascus were to be primordial in spreading the new message... his Damascus conversion relaunched the new religion, removing it from an exclusively Jewish milieu into Rome's Hellenised world."

(Burns, Ross (2005) Damascus: A History, Routledge)

The Spread of Islam under the Umayyads

"...the transfer of the caliphate to Damascus... did launch the new faith in a form that it could never have achieved if it had remained based in the Hijaz... That impulse lasted only ninety years, but it was a period vital in spreading the new faith to a world audience."

(Burns, Ross (2005) Damascus: A History, Routledge)

In the ninety years that the Umayyad dynasty ruled from Damascus, the Islamic Empire doubled in size until it encompassed a territory more than twice the area that the Roman Empire had occupied at its zenith. It included Spain and Portugal in the west, and Pakistan and Tajikistan in the East.

(*To Rule the Earth* ... http://starnarcosis.net /obsidian/ earthrul.html, *accessed January 2008*)

Damascus Today

Damascus' population was 2.6 million in 2001. Syria is a secular state and whilst Islam is the religion of 90% of the population. Minorities, including Christians (5%), are accorded definite rights and privileges, with a measure of religious freedom.

(Johnston, Patrick and Mandryk (2001) Operation World, *Paternoster)*

Damascus has absorbed large numbers of refugees from wars in Lebanon and Iraq. Hospitable Syrians have attempted to integrate them, but the economy has come under increasing pressure as a result.

CHAPTER 26

The Road to Jerusalem
March 2008

REFLECTIONS FROM HOME

In shaping this team I had taken a number of risks which, given the nature of where we were going to be walking, left me slightly nervous. In all honesty, I would have preferred a much smaller team for all the unknowns that walking in the West Bank was going to present. Like-wise, there were three on the team that I had never met before. To be going into such a crucial leg of the walk with such questions was not the safest way of preparing. However, I had learnt over the years to trust the way teams seemed to come together without any real work from myself. I told myself to relax and waited with antic-ipation for what was to come.

I had often wondered whether there might come a point when I would find myself walking some of the most troubled spots of the world. No longer just an observer of the news on the TV, but able to go to these lands to call on the hand of the Maker; even if leading a team of thirteen through such a troubled part of the world was a big ask. As it turned out, every single person on this team played a unique part in seeing us through a number of challenging situations. Indeed, without Steve, Lucy and Nigel, three who had already spent a couple of months in the West Bank, we would not have made it. Our pathway was prepared, and whilst nothing prepares anyone for looking down the barrel of an Israeli high calibre weapon, I felt as ready as anyone could be for what lay ahead.

FINAL REPORT
Team: Vicki, Shelley, Chris S, Steve W, Nigel, Lucy, Mark, Paul, Richard, Dave, Val, Kathy and myself.

I'm sitting here in front of my computer, trying to find the words to encapsulate yet another incredible few days out on the road and the wonder of a journey concluded thirty two months on from setting out from Whitby. It's a walk that has taken us from the margins of the UK to the centre of three global religions, competing as they do for the attention and rights to the lands of Jerusalem. A walk, also, that has given me and many others the opportunity to journey with fellow adventurers who have wandered into the depths of the Middle East; picking up themes and fault lines that echo down the generations and continue to reverberate across the power systems of the world. How is it that we have been so privileged to go and sample such wonderfully diverse cultures; to see the hand of our Maker at work and to find ourselves wrapped up in a modern day story in the telling?

Walking down off the Golan Heights into Nazareth, through the West Bank and on into Bethlehem and Jerusalem, was as fitting a conclusion to this journey as anyone could hope to have. To walk the length of the West Bank was amazing. Many a soldier turned to us with a look of disbelief; one saying in complete astonishment, "What the hell are you doing here?" When we discover the doorway that is open to us, safe pathways can unfold.

I cannot in any way do justice to these few days in the brief lines here. However, let me highlight four places that might just give you a glimpse into some of the delights we encountered.

Nazareth

The place where the story of Jesus caught up and over-took the story of Israel. The place where Jesus, in the synagogue, announced that it was time to stop looking back to that which had gone before and towards that which is to come. Nazareth; the place where the living God underlined that homes and households in hidden places provide spaces for the kingdom. Nazareth; the place where Mary encountered the angels and found incredible grace for the most demanding of journeys that any mother-to-be could go on; a journey that we were about to embark on ourselves.

Nablus

The largest city of the West Bank; a seedbed of discontent and at the forefront of every uprising against the Israelis. Here, I leave Paul Wood to take up the most remarkable of stories.

Paul writes, "At the end of the day, we walked through a high pass overshadowed by mountains. I have rarely experienced land so cursed. The smell of death was over-powering; rotting rubbish, decaying corpses of animals and impoverished dwellings of a refugee camp on the slopes above us. Rocks had been hurled onto the road and fires had been lit. It felt overlooked by high places, ancient places of sacrifice and idolatry, a place of powers gloating over the cursed land and human debris. Our mandate was not to address any such places directly but to walk through. As the skies darkened and the clouds gathered, so we concluded the day on our knees, shedding ourselves of all pride in that place of gloating and death.

"We had finished on the outskirts of Nablus, known as Shechem in Old Testament times. The following day we realised that we had walked under the shadow of Mount Ebal, the mountain from which the curses for disobedience were proclaimed.

"Shechem was such a significant place for Israel and for covenant. It was the place to which Abraham came when he arrived in Canaan, the place where he first built an altar and where he was promised this land. Even further back in history, under the Canaanites, it was known for its temple to Baal Berit, the Lord of the Covenant.

"No surprise, therefore, that Joshua brought Israel there first, to renew the covenant on entering the promised land. In accordance with the instructions given by Moses, Israel gathered at Shechem, six tribes pronouncing curses from Mount Ebal to the north, and six pronouncing blessings from Mount Gerizim to the south.

"For a place that had been such a covenant marker for the land and the people that lived on it, it is easy to understand it being a fountainhead for cursing when covenant is broken and the alien and the orphan are not catered for. Israel's land was always meant to speak about their spiritual condition. This place shouts loud and clear."

The Mount of Olives

We concluded the walk here, wanting to gather in a place that man had not built on, and within which there lingered some of the olive trees from the time of Jesus. Walking into Jerusalem through the Dung Gate and out through the Lion Gate, we sat down on the slopes of the Mount of Olives. As we began to pray, a child of about ten years old started to throw rocks at us. The rocks bounced harmlessly as his range fell short, however, one of the team noted a connection with other moments in the walk when children had gathered around us, laughing and smiling as if they had sight of the angels that accompanied us. This time, the throwing of rocks seemed equally as appropriate, as if the city itself had come to give its own welcome to our small band of prophets. The words of Jesus echoed round our heads, "O Jerusalem, Jerusalem, who kills the prophets and stones those who are sent to her! How often have I wanted to gather your children together." Once more, in the most unlikely of circumstances, we knew we were on time, and in place. We drew encouragement even as the stones fell on the ground, a wonderful peace descending upon us.

A bus stop near the Dead Sea

The final memory, I give over to one of the team who took himself off to the Dead Sea for the last few hours of spare time. Getting into conversation with a fellow traveller, he discovered that he was actually a relative of one of the Jewish settler students who, just a week ago, had been gunned down and murdered. He found his heart touched as he began to connect with the other side of the story that our journey through the West Bank had kept hidden; that of the Jews. As I reflected on this, a quote came to mind of Prime Minister Olmert, "We are tired of fighting, we are tired of being courageous, we are tired of winning, we are tired of defeating our enemies. We want that we will be able to live in an entirely different environment of relations with our enemies."

Fear grips this land and only the shalom peace of the Master can break the cycle of victim and persecutor that torments Palestinian and Jew alike. Our hearts were tenderised therefore, to this most unique of tribes that live on the face of the earth.

This, then, is our journey. No earth shattering conclusions. No dramatic manifestos; rather just a simple dedication of prayer as we have risen to the sight of the open road and the faint whiff of adventure. Once more I find myself saying to all those who walked that we had no right to enjoy being together as much as we did, no right to travel as safely as we have done, and no right to pray anything other than the prayers of those who are not right.

Lingering in the airport at Tel Aviv, a smile came to my face as I lifted my head to the destination board. Directly underneath our flight back home to Manchester was a flight destined for Cairo. We had left behind a team already tracking south from Bethlehem to Hebron, then to the border and then on to Cairo. It seems there could be further adventures to follow!

CHAPTER 27

Destination Jerusalem: Inside the Muscle Museum

Chris Seaton

Chris lives on the south coast of England, is married to Loti and has three children. Founder of an organisation called Peaceworks he has given himself to active participation in conflict resolution in many situations around the globe. He joined us at the beginning of the walk in Whitby, once again in Rome, and for the final leg through the West Bank and into Jerusalem. In this the last city chapter he takes us inside the muscle museum that is this much scrutinised city.

When fair April with his showers sweet,
Has pierced the drought of March to the root's feet
And bathed each vein in liquid of such power,
Its strength creates the newly springing flower;

When the West Wind too, with his sweet breath,
Has breathed new life – in every copse and heath –
Into each tender shoot, and the young sun
From Aries moves to Taurus on his run,
And those small birds begin their melody,
(The ones who sleep all night with open eye,)
Then nature stirs them up to such a pitch
That folk all long to go on pilgrimage

And wandering travellers tread new shores, strange strands,
Seek out far shrines, renowned in many lands,
And specially from every shire's end
Of England to Canterbury they wend
The holy blessed martyr there to seek,
Who has brought health to them when they were sick.[15]

After two long years in the travelling, the company finally departs that most famed of little towns, Bethlehem, towards their final destination. It is a bright, clear day – warmer but not less hopeful than the spring morn when they had left their now far distant English homes. So much has befallen the band of pilgrims in these mercurial months. Some grew discouraged or quarrelled and turned back. Others suffered robbery, sickness and bodily assault along the way. The whole group was held captive for months. A new century has come along as if to exaggerate the passage of time. In short, each member of the fellowship has suffered countless hardships,

---

[15] Geoffrey Chaucer's General Prologue of Canterbury Tales translated into modern English by Tony Sewell http://www.bremesoftware.com/Chaucer/index.htm 1998

privations and trials. Had they known what lay ahead would any of them have set out so boldly and merrily that Pentecost day of our Lord's year 1598?

Yet for every one of these tribulations, every wanderer has also tasted in equal measure fare on these 'strange strands' so varied and so sweet to the body and soul that each one would say that they feel improved forever. Fare that has lingered longer in the heart than mere rich and novel victuals: the hope of a cool, clean dawn after an dreary, dusty day; the ferment and pace of a great city; the beauty of birdsong and of sunset in a strange clime; the kindness of a stranger sharing his bread, walking a mile with a weary traveller or merely offering a friendly smile.

Although we share the same noble theme, unlike Chaucer's tale ours is not one of medieval pilgrimage to the shrine of St. Thomas in Canterbury. Yet like Chaucer's tale ours also begins with the stirring of hearts and seasons in an English shire. The stirring was a call to travel towards that most renowned of all shrines – the Holy Land and particularly to its most Holy City, Jerusalem. The place of the death, resurrection and ascension of our Lord himself! The call came at a time of great turmoil and trouble at home and in foreign lands too, where the twin causes of religion and power once again made men to take up arms one against another. It was a most ambitious pilgrimage – and a story not yet told as the pilgrims took a vow to keep it to themselves. It was to be a journey sacred unto one another and unto God. To honour this vow, reader, my travellers' tale carries no names.

The author of this pilgrimage was a wise and generous lord of an English town that we shall call Wimcaster. Added to his other qualities, this lord was also a most devout Christian and a man deeply pained by the strife in our country between the Roman Church and the Reformers. At great personal effort and cost he refused to choose a religious party and somehow remained above the conflict between Catholics and the new Protestant Church. During his Lenten prayers he grew convinced that he must do something more than remain passive in the conflict. After making enquiries, he found a priest in a nearby parish who shared his sympathies and charged him to undertake a journey not attempted for many generations – a sacred pilgrimage to Jerusalem.

The nobleman supported his invitation to the priest with an offer to pay fifty sovereigns to enable the band of pilgrims to be equipped, clothed, fed and crossed safely to France. "Once this sum is spent, dear Priest, you must look to your wits and to the Lord, but if you are mindful this coin should take you well into Burgundy."

This "First Priest", was delighted with the lord's suggestion and with his benefice. A courageous soul and something of a mystic, he always sought to understand the mysterious and wonderful ways of God whether in human affairs, in places, nature or in the Scriptures. So cheerfully he accepted the challenge. Therefore, the Lord of Wimcaster commissioned him to gather together a band of pilgrims to this peregrination and to set off during Whitsuntide 1598. The two men had found a common mind: perhaps the spiritual discipline of a holy journey taken in humility and weakness could help some folk find a fresh understanding of true religion. Who knows – they dared to muse together – perhaps the prayers said on the way could even make a better way for this whole troubled world.

In quiet moments of preparation, the First Priest at times trembled as he wondered if his commission was indeed a foolish one. The group would be no Crusader army as in the old days, yet could be sure of many enemies on the roads they would travel. England was still at undeclared war with Spain, Spain itself was warring with France and the Holy Roman Emperor was failing to hold back the Turkish armies of the all-conquering Ottomans. In between these struggles lay the Italian States – a pawn in the games of empire played by the French and the Hapsburgs. If the First Priest and his troupe were to reach Jerusalem, they could only do so with the divine protection and gracious help of their heavenly Lord.

So on this 11th day of March 1600 the group sets out one last time with their faces set towards the goal, the Holy City. A 'shrine renowned' indeed, fought over for centuries and yet still a prize that draws the peregrine from his distant shore. By sunset they should be within the city itself.

The day begins in the company's time-honoured fash-ion. After breaking fast simply together they gather in prayer to invoke the name of the Holy Trinity. They ask for strength and bread for the day, to be kept and protected on the road and for care-taking of loved ones long departed from sight but never long gone from the travellers' minds. Then, in the way of so many days passed, the pilgrims that set forth from Bethlehem are led out by the First Priest. Today this sparkly-eyed plump man in his early 40s has a bounce in his gait. With him this morning is the Second Priest, a rather thin, sallow younger man for whom the pilgrimage is mostly a quiet, personal devotion. Bringing up the rear is the Third Priest, a kindly man in his 50s, now carrying a heavy limp after a sickness in the way. Yet despite his pain the Third Priest is always there with an ear for the troubles of his companions and with a ready wit to lighten the mood when the occasion requires it.

Some paces in front of the Third Priest are women from three generations of one family – the Daughter, the Mother and the Grandmother who have courageously faced lands and climates often hostile to women for the sake of the sacred journey. To offer some protection on the road, Lord Wimcaster has provided two military men, the Yeoman and the Captain, both seasoned in foreign campaigns. Two more women, both widows and sisters, also joined the pilgrims shortly before Dover and it is in no small part due to their means and their largesse that the party was sustained so well and so far beyond Burgundy. Finally, there is the Diplomat, a statesman who served our Queen across the courts of Europe. His good education in the classics (from which he has gained a rare and flexible talent with the Romance tongues) and his knowledge of German speech has brought the group through so many snares. What is more, his past experience in the East, where he learned a working command of Turkic and Arabic tongues and the ways of these peoples, has saved the pilgrims their very skins more than once.

With such a diverse fellowship and so many adventures, it is easy to see how the journey has taken twenty-two full months. From the crisp walk through Kent and across the choppy Channel to Calais, the pilgrims traversed the troubled Low Countries and with the growing heat passed into French lands, the Duchy of Burgundy then over the Alps to Savoy. Traversing the north Italian States, the pilgrims came at last to Rome in the late summer and moved from there south to the Kingdom of Sicily. Since the sea crossing to Ragusa in winter 1598, the pilgrims have spent all their days in countries of the Ottoman Empire. The Ottoman Turks rule all these lands, whether their people speak with Italian, Greek, Arabic or Turkish tongues. Passing through Athens and the Balkan lands to Constantinople, the journey reached a quagmire in that fabled city. The Diplomat's professional skills and his patience were tested to their very limits as one of the Sultan's viziers took a suspicion to the pilgrim's purpose and locked the group up in a tower overlooking the Bosphorus for four interminable months.

Since their imprisonment the group always seems to carry at least one member in ill-health and it has taken almost eleven months to travel from Constantinople around Turkey's coast to the Arab lands. Eventually the city of Damascus was reached. From the famed city of St. Paul's conversion, the way seemed quicker as the exhilarated pilgrims walked through the Holy Land at last, passing towns with such enigmatic names as Capernaum, Cana, Nazareth, Shechem, Bethel and now Bethlehem.

What a story; what a journey! All memories of loss and hardship along the way are forgotten this morning. The pure white almond blossom pleases the eye, the sun's warmth grows by the minute on each traveller's face and the strange, exotic sunbird delights every ear with its mimetic song. The talk among the travellers is an animated and excited bubble as they set out and the First Priest decides to set a focus for the day. His voice rings out over the laughter and chatter,

"Come now. We are full of joy, dear friends, as we tread the final path to the Holy City. But lest our minds run away on frivolous things, let's all take thought for our deepest impression of this last part of the pilgrimage. Who will first share with us their best remembrance of this Holy Land?"

A moment's silence then quietly but with passion the Grandmother speaks of the wonder of seeing Lake Galilee, recalling the peace that our Lord made there for his fearing disciples in the storm. "I felt my own heart stilled as we first encountered places where the Lord himself had walked, taught and shared friendship with his disciples." Her aged voice carries the warmth and love of a woman who knows him of whom she speaks.

The Third Priest is a faithful, celibate man. He has a love for children and secretly grieves that his calling means that he has never had the blessing of being a natural father. He speaks movingly about Nazareth, a place where Jesus was nurtured in childhood and learned the skills of human relations. The story he recalls is of the moment of their departure from that town when the pilgrim band had prayed their final morning prayers and a young child softly yet confidently joined their circle and freely offered them gifts of sweet-meats. The priest falls silent mid-sentence, choked with the emotion of that poignant memory. He is overwhelmed as he contrasts his own feelings of loss with the completeness of Jesus, the man from Nazareth who had no children of his own.

A hand gently touches the shoulder of the Second Priest, gingerly offering him some comfort, but he does not turn to see whose hand it is. Meanwhile, the Yeoman speaks up and strikes a different chord, "One thing puzzles me very much, Parson." He addresses his comments directly to the First Priest. "I had scarce thought that the Holy Land would be a place of such little peace between men." Some of the party murmur and *tut*, cross that the Yeoman has dampened the mood with his unhappy words. "Why we have seen three religions at war with one another and even fellow Christians at arms. I can't reckon why God let's that be." The Yeoman speaks his mind in the simple direct way of his kind. But for all his simplicity there dwells a true love for God in him. On the road deep thoughts have issued from his lips more than once that would shame any scholar.

The First Priest offers no response to the Yeoman. He has learned to leave space when controversial matters are raised. He wishes to watch how the group will manage such complex questions: for him this learning holds the essence of pilgrimage. Twenty awkward seconds of silent walking. Eventually, too embarrassed by the pregnant pause to endure the silence any longer, the Captain gruffly fills the gap in conversation, "Why it is the way of things, man. The heathen do not know godly ways and seek to force their religion on all the other people by the sword. The Turks rule all the people with an iron fist, whether Jews or Arab Christians. Jewish zealots break out from time to time to murder a few Mohammedans, and then the Ottoman defence forces make revenge attacks. And it is always the Christians caught in the middle here."

The usually quiet Second Priest is stirred to a sudden heat by the Captain's crude assumptions and responds curtly, "And do you think, sir, that King Richard and his Crusaders followed such a different path here in years gone by?" Before the Captain can rejoin and take the humour to a yet darker place, the First Widow speaks. To the relief of the company, her quiet manner and dignity changes the mood in an instant,

"Sirs, your discourse reminds me that we have often talked of 'right' and 'wrong' on our wanderings. I have become troubled in my mind over recent days. Before I left England I had thought that all Turks and Mohammedans were indeed lost heathen. I also thought secretly that Jews were Christ-killers who have deserved their sufferings down the ages. But in walking these lands we have met such love and hospitality from ordinary people of all kinds that I now question myself. Is it enough to be baptised and follow the rites of the church to please God and gain access to eternity?"

Again, a short silence and again no direct answer. Instead, the First Priest chooses to respond with a reflection of his own. "As we passed to the east of Jerusalem yesterday on our way to Bethlehem, I looked out to the Jordan Valley towards Jericho. I recalled the famed encounter that blessed Joshua had with an angel after he crossed the river. Joshua wanted to know if the angel was for his army or was against them." The First Priest draws himself up in a theatrical way to recite the biblical, "'Neither, but as the commander of the army of the Lord, I have now come.'"

The company listens on in wrapped silence for some application to the Widow's question, but the First Priest turns to another biblical tale. "My thoughts then went back to our walk through Samaria earlier this week. The Evangelist John tells us about Jesus' meeting with the Samaritan woman at the well in Sychar, the site of which we passed. She was amazed at the Lord's wisdom and with the love and respect he had shown to her. This woman wanted to know the 'right' place to worship God saying, 'our fathers worshipped on this mountain (by which she meant Mount Gerazim), but you Jews claim that the place where we must worship is Jerusalem.' His answer was similar to that of the commander of the Lord's armies." Again, the First Priest composed himself before delivering his line, "'Believe me, woman, a time is coming when you will worship the Father neither on this mountain nor in Jerusalem. For a time is coming and has now come when the true worshipers will worship the Father in spirit and truth.'"

The First Priest stops walking for a minute to withdraw the cork from his leather water-bottle and take a draught. One by one the other members of the fellowship also stop, impatiently waiting for the conclusion to the story. The storyteller, apparently ignoring his audience, looks ahead into the middle distance and says softly, "Perhaps, if our Lord was walking with us now and we asked him, 'Are you for us Christians or for these Mohammedans?' we might hear a similar reply to that heard by Joshua and the Samaritan woman. Perhaps he would say to us, 'Neither, but I have now come.'"

The whole company walks in silence for a while, carrying a mixture of confusion and inspiration at the First Priest's words. The Third Priest, always most aware of any anxiety in the group, calls out in his kindly but firm way from the rear,

"Brethren. Come, let's return to our happy theme and consider more of our learning in this Holy Land. I would like to offer my memory of that long hard walk up to Shiloh, the home of Eli the Priest. I know we bored some of you as the Second Priest and I discussed how Eli is like so many leaders of this world (not to mention those in God's house!) The Scriptures tell us that in Eli's day 'the word of the Lord was rare and there were not many visions.' Eli was an old leader growing blind. He was also too spiritually deaf to understand the Lord's word to him and the call to his young servant, Samuel, so his priestly family came under God's judgement."

At the mention of this last name, the Mother suddenly stops, turns and waits for the Third Priest, then walks closely alongside him. "I admit I was quite lost and frustrated when I heard you priests talking at Shiloh, but I did not hear you mention that name, Samuel. What of him?"

"Why Samuel represents true spiritual leadership," replies the Third Priest. "He understood that 'man looks at the outward appearance, but the Lord looks at the heart.'"

The Mother listens with great care. For she knows that back in England her son Samuel has a heard a call from God. She also remembers that she had a dream before she was even married where she was told that she should name her first son 'Samuel' and that he would hear God's voice himself one day. Today she understands more about her own story and that of her family but she does not share this with her fellow wanderers. Like the Virgin Mary, she hides these things in her heart, sensing that the Lord is looking there.

The Second Priest now takes his turn. "I fear I must again turn the humour of our talk to a more melancholy theme." His personality enables him to do this with effect. "Never have I known such a strong feeling of cursing as when we walked past the old city of Shechem. Do you recall? The stench of rotting animal corpses on the wayside filled our noses and made us wretch. The road had been made treacherous by huge rocks hurled from the mountains above. Beggars and vagabonds seemed to lurk behind every tree. The crops had seemed to fail and as we passed through this valley the sun was veiled by a gloomy canopy of cloud."

Different pilgrims nod in agreement, sobered by the memory. The Second Widow then takes up the story, addressing the Second Priest directly, "We all felt so downcast in our lodgings that night. You took us to the evening devotional reading, I believe that it was from the Book of the Law, and you read out a depressing catalogue of curses."

"Yes," the Second Priest picks up his story again with enthusiasm. "We realised that we had passed that afternoon beneath Mount Ebal and Mount Gerazim. These were the very mountains that Moses had the people of Israel climb to pronounce blessings and cursings when they entered the land. I then understood why the land felt so cursed. Indeed God's covenant God with the people in this land has been sorely broken."

A question rises from the front of the group. (Over the weeks and months even the youngest members of the band have gained confidence to enquire of one another). This time it was the Daughter who asked, "Why, Parson, did the Lord bring the Children of Israel to the Promised Land in order to curse them?"

340

"Surely this was not the Lord's purpose, my girl", the Second Priest took an unusually pastoral tone with the Daughter. "But as our Lord Jesus himself taught, the natural laws of sowing and reaping are reflected in the invisible ways of the Spirit. It is as if the very earth itself responds to the people to whom the land is given – whether in obedience and blessing or in rebellion and cursing."

The pilgrim's tale-telling is suddenly halted as the party passes over the small brow of a hill and the Daughter lets out a shrill squeal of joy and begins to skip. Soon everyone sees what her keen young eyes first spied – the gleaming and towering walls of the city of Jerusalem. Some let out an audible gasp; others cross themselves and mumble quiet devotions on the spot. One or two kneel in a posture of reverence and gratitude to God that they have at last attained their goal.

After several minutes of embraces and happy laughter, it is the Captain who encourages the party onwards, "Let us proceed, for we must conclude our journey well and safe and we are not in Jerusalem yet." The Third Priest is the quietest member of the group at this sighting of the city. Bearing a look of some disappointment, he speaks in hushed tones to the Captain by his side. "I had little thought to see such a fortress as the Holy City now seems." In truth, the structure of the walls is magnificent – overwhelming in its scale and strength. They are thicker than any walls seen in a European city and higher than a hundred feet with slots created for firing arrows and other missiles at would be invaders.

The Diplomat, who has overheard the Third Priest grunts, "Huh!" with an air of weary cynicism. "This place has always been a muscle museum – a city that seeks to control those within it and without it. Just think – Egyptians, Assyrians, Persians, Greeks, Romans, Crusaders and the Jews themselves – all have tried either to raze the place to the ground or to build it up impregnable. Suleiman the Turk was only the latest king to barricade the place. If you ask me great walls, gates and fences are no more than the last recourse of the bully and the tyrant who seeks to cling on to his power against the odds."

"A muscle museum, eh?" laughs the Third Priest, seeking to lighten the mood with his tone yet again. But in his heart, the words of the Diplomat ring true. This city does not feel to him like a benign place. And why should it? The place of the execution of the Son of God.

The group is hushed as they finally make entrance into the Dung Gate through the massive stone walls. Then, in a moment, they are inside and the bustle of the place filled with sellers, buyers and makers is all around them. Within a few yards they reach that last remnant of Herod's Temple known as the Western Wall. A number of Jewish men are gathered close to the wall mumbling their prayers. Behind the wall can be seen an imposing Mohammedan mosque with its golden dome.

Having arrived in the city, the travellers are now quite overwhelmed and confused. How are they to celebrate their arrival? Why had they not discussed this earlier? Should they try to find the Church of the Holy Sepulchre? The group begins to spread out as the weight and urgency of the city presses in on them. The narrow lanes with alleys here and there and sellers forcing their wares on the pilgrims make the First Priest afraid of losing someone. "Hi!" he shouts over the human din, "English pilgrims!" As the only English voice in the crowd he attracts attention from his comrades and the locals alike. "Quickly, come to me!" Still with his voice raised he says, "I think we must leave the city for now. Let's go now to the Mount of Olives where our Lord preached to his disciples and wept over Jerusalem."

Without another word, he turns and leads the ten pilgrims through the crowd and takes a turning right at a junction of narrow lanes. Unbeknown to the First Priest, he has taken what is known as the Via Dolorosa, what the Latins call Jesus' 'way of suffering.' Little also does he know that he is leading the fellowship a reverse route to that habitually trod by the pilgrim. That is, away from the Church of the Holy Sepulchre and towards the Lion's Gate. The throng subsides as they walk down towards the gate and the wanderers catch their breath.

Senses reel at the mixture of the intensity of the busy city and the elation at completing their task. The pilgrims almost stagger from the Lion's Gate towards the Garden of Gethsemane and on up towards the Mount of Olives.

As they walk past the Garden, some boys approach the pilgrims, begging for some alms. Suddenly wearied, overwhelmed and numbed by the event of their arrival, each one of the pilgrims gestures the boys away. The Diplomat speaks a few terse words of Arabic and they run on up the hill towards Bethany.

The Third Priest motions to the First Priest as they find a gap in the wall some 500 yards up the hill into the olive grove that gives the historic site its name. He nods and they lead the fellowship into a clearing for one final gathering overlooking the city less than a mile below.

Their gathering is informal. Prayers are said over the city and over the journey – simple thoughts and words of thanks. Not always very coherent, but every prayer is a holy moment. The women seem more eager to pray aloud than the men, who repose in quiet reflection.

The voice of the Diplomat has rarely been heard in prayer over all the thousands of miles and hundreds of days of walking. He makes a formal genuflexion on one knee and faces the city. "Lord. We know that you have promised to return to this world... to truly save it. We come to this most renowned and sacred spot and say we are yours. Even if the people of this city will not welcome you, we have walked here to welcome you... whenever it is that you will come." The sincerity of motive behind this stilted and inarticulate prayer touches everyone. "Amen!" calls the Yeoman, with a loud voice.

Scarcely has that word been uttered when a dull *thud* is heard and a stone, the size of an orange, bounces off the trunk of a nearby olive tree. Some fifty yards hence, back on the road the boys who had been begging earlier are calling to the pilgrims and one of them is hurling rocks from the wall in their direction. His arm is quite strong for a nine year old but he has left himself just out of range, no doubt expecting to have to run away at any minute. As his second and third stones bounce five or ten yards short of their target the Captain pulls himself up to his full height. The boy shouts more angry words as if to taunt him and the Captain makes a purposeful step towards the boy. "Wait!" cries the Diplomat. The boy hurls two more stones, the first of which lands only two feet away from the Captain, but he obeys the command he had been given. And then the boys are gone.

Another silence. No one could agree how long – two minutes or twenty. Then a familiar voice rings out. "O Jerusalem, Jerusalem." The First Priest fixes his eyes on the city and speaks with a greater authority than the pilgrims had yet heard. "You who kill the prophets and stone those sent to you. How often I have longed to gather your children together, as a hen gathers her chicks under her wings, but you were not willing. Look, your house is left to you desolate. For I tell you, you will not see me again until you say, 'Blessed is he who comes in the name of the Lord'"

His kind eyes filled with tears, he makes one final speech to the company of pilgrims. "That day will come, beloved, I'm sure." Then, with a voice breaking through weeping, he recites lines he had learned many years earlier, "'Yet it is not our part to master all the tides of the world, but to do what is in us for the succour of those years wherein we are set, uprooting evil in the fields that we know, so that those who live after may have clean earth to till.'" Another pause then, "What little we could do in this regard, I believe we have done."

With that, they turned and set off quietly up the hill to find lodgings in Bethany.

FACT FILE JERUSALEM

Pilgrimage

A pilgrimage is a religious or spiritual journey or search of great moral significance. Those who take part in such journeys, according to Psalm 84 are blessed and known as pilgrims. Members of every major religion participate in pilgrimages, often a journey to sacred place or shrine of importance to a person's beliefs and faith.

History of violence in Jerusalem

Jerusalem has suffered repeated traumatic episodes of massacre and destruction over its history. During the years of its role as the capital of the Kingdom of Judah, the city survived an Assyrian siege by Sennacharib in 701 BCE. This involved a miraculous deliverance according to the Bible where an angel slew 185,000 of Sennacharib's army. However, the Babylonians captured the city, took its inhabitants into captivity and partially destroyed it over the period of 597-586 BCE.

After restoration under Persian rule and successive conquests by the Greeks and then Romans, the Great Jewish Revolt of 66-73 CE saw over a million Jews killed in Judea as they rebelled against Roman rule. As Jerusalem fell after a long siege in 70 CE, tens of thousands of inhabitants were crucified around the city and both walls and temple were completely destroyed. This event is traditionally seen as a fulfilment of some of Jesus' prophecies, including those contained in Matthew's gospel.

Jerusalem then became a small town until the conversion of the Byzantine Emperor Constantine in the 4th century, when it was rebuilt as a centre of Christian worship. The period under the Arab Caliphates was generally calm and tolerant until the 11th century when one of the Caliphs ordered the destruction of churches and synagogues and there were reports of pilgrims being murdered. This triggered the First Crusade (see separate paragraph).

After the establishment of the Frankish Kingdom of Jerusalem in 1099, the city passed – often violently – between Crusaders, local Arabic sultans and emirs, Tatars and Egyptian Mamluks.[16] This combination of invasions and the Black Death meant that by 1500 the population of all Palestine had declined to barely 200,000 people.[17] In 1517, Jerusalem was captured from the Egyptian Mamluk Sultanate by the Ottoman Turks who ruled there until the First World War. The current walls of the Old City were built in 1538 by the Sultan, Suleiman the Magnificent. The walls stretch for approximately 4.5 kilometres, and rise to a height of 5–15 metres, with a thickness of 3 metres.[18] Altogether, the Old City walls contain 43 surveillance towers and 11 gates, seven of which are presently open.

The Crusades

The Crusades were a series of military conflicts in the high Middle Ages (roughly 1095-1291) of a religious character waged by much of Christian Europe against external and internal threats. Crusades were fought not only against Muslims but also pagan Slavs, Russian and Greek Orthodox Christians, Mongols, various 'heretics' and political enemies of the popes. Crusaders took vows and were granted an indulgence for past sins,[19] but the original goal of the Crusades was the recapture of

---

[16]See http://en.wikipedia.org/wiki/History_of_Jerusalem

[17]www.palestinefacts.org

[18]Zaun-Goshe, Heike Keys to the Treasure Trove - Jerusalem Old City Gates Jerusalem Post 2007

[19]Riley-Smith, Jonathan. The Oxford History of the Crusades New York: Oxford University Press, 1999

STEVE LOWTON

Jerusalem and the Holy Land from Muslim rule. This was a response to a call from the Eastern Orthodox Byzantine Empire for help against the expansion of the Muslim Seljuk Turks. The capture of Jerusalem in July 1099 was accompanied by the most appalling massacres of the Jewish and Muslim populations of the city, along with the pillaging of the city and the mosques.

Until recently the Crusades have been remembered relatively favourably as heroic acts in European countries which were, at that time, Roman Catholic. Nonetheless, there have been many vocal critics of the Crusades in Western Europe since the Renaissance, and latterly the church has joined these critics. According to one historian, the most devastating long term consequence of the Crusades was the creation of an Islamic mentality that sought a retreat into isolation. He says "Assaulted from all quarters, the Muslim world turned in on itself. It became oversensitive [and] defensive... attitudes that grew steadily worse as world-wide evolution, a process from which the Muslim world felt excluded, continued."[20]

The Suffering of Jews in the Middle Ages

It seems clear that Jews in the medieval Muslim world faced much less violence and persecution than the Jews of European Christendom. Jews of the Christian world were marginalized and excluded from the prevailing society in the Middle Ages; theological hatred and deeply ingrained anti-Jewish feelings led to massacres, restric-

---

[20]Peter Mansfield, A History of the Middle East, Second Edition, London: Penguin Books, 2003, p 21

tions on Jews' movements and expulsions from towns and countries.[21]

The Fate of Palestinian Christianity

Arab Christians are often seen as the real losers in the Israeli-Palestinian conflict. In seventh century Arabia, "...the true message of the gospel lay buried under a heap of senseless superstition. Many believers were more enthusiastic about fighting over doctrinal controversies than spreading the Word of God... The whole structure of church and empire was founded on a foreign hierarchy and an alien Greek philosophy. Christianity, as Mohammed encountered it, was born error-filled and without indigenous identity. It was no longer the religion of the people with God personified as one of their own; it had become the imposed faith of conquerors whose adherents were, all too often, rightly perceived as conspirators in the subjugation of their own people. This perception was scarcely lessened in later centuries by the Crusaders. They came into Arabia more zealous than any Muslim force to slaughter the infidels, to destroy homes as well as mosques, and to assume temporal as well as spiritual power. The chivalry of that most unlikely of conquerors, Salah El-Din, is not yet forgotten in the Holy Land, nor is the treachery and brutality of the Frankish Christians who opposed him."[22]

Today, Arab Christians in Palestine are seen by many as an endangered species. Facing animosity from Arab

---

[21]Cohen, Mark Under Crescent and Cross Princeton University Press 1995, editorial review

[22]Bishop Riah Abu El-Assal quoted in www.jerusalemites.org/jerusalem/christianity/2.htm

STEVE LOWTON

Muslim neighbours and Israeli occupiers alike, there is a constant exodus. In 1997 from an Israeli population of about 5 million, only 128,000 were Christian. In the Palestinian Territories the population was 2.5 million with less than 3% Christian, nearly all on the West Bank.[23]

The Protestant Western Church and Israel

Views within the Protestant Church in the West are often sharply divided on the theological and political issues surrounding Israel and Palestine. The movement known as "Christian Zionism" or "Restorationism" is based upon a belief among some Christians that the return of the Jews to the Holy Land, and the establishment of the State of Israel in 1948, is in accordance with biblical prophecy.[24] The idea that Christians should actively support a Jewish return to the Land of Israel, along with the parallel idea that the Jews ought to be encouraged to become Christian, as a means fulfilling a Biblical prophecy has been common in Protestant circles since the Reformation. It is often seen as a powerful view in the formation of Republican policy in the Middle East in the USA, which generally supports Israel in the Israel-Palestine Conflict. There is clearly a social dimension to this with large Jewish and Evangelical populations living side by side.

In contrast, a growing movement in the European (and to a lesser extent in the American) Church are becoming active for example in their advocacy of the claims of the Palestinian cause.

[23]Robert Fisk The Independent London, 24 September 1997, p.11

[24]See Oren, Michael Power, Faith and Fantasy: America in the Middle East: 1776 to the Present, W.W. Norton, 2007, p. 88

The Modern History of Israel/Palestine

This conflict is naturally told in different ways by different parties – most people have a position. It is worth noting that Palestinians have never enjoyed sovereignty over their territory. Here are a few landmarks over the past century:

1917 – British Government issued the "Balfour Declaration" supporting the creation of a national homeland for the Jewish people in the Holy Land.

1920 – Ottoman Empire dismantled under the Treaty of Sèvres and British Mandate for Palestine established over current Israel, West Bank, Gaza and Jordan. Jewish immigration increased rapidly over this period and Arab immigration soon followed.

1936 – The start of the Arab Revolt against the British, caused by the growing tensions in Mandate territory. Arab and Jewish "terrorist" atrocities (e.g. bus bombings) against the British and one another escalated and the British executed many offenders.

1939 – Because of these tensions, Jewish immigration was restricted by the British. This in turn caused great hardship in a period of extreme Nazi persecution of Jews and the holocaust in Europe.

1947 – Britain asked the newly-formed UN to help with its diplomatic problem and the UN proposed a partitioned 'two-state solution.' This was supported by the Jewish party and opposed by the Arab party.

1948 – Israel declared independence over its portion of land appointed by the UN for a Jewish State. The Arab League reiterated objections to partition and the armies of Egypt, Syrian, Jordan, Lebanon and Iraq invaded the territory partitioned for the Arab state and war with Israel began. Before and during this war over 700,000 Palestinians fled their original lands to become internal or external refugees.

1949 – An armistice was signed with the outcome that Israel controlled most Mandate Palestine west of the River Jordan. The 1949 armistice line, or the 'green line', is still the internationally recognised border of Israel.

1956 – Israeli-Egyptian war over the Suez Canal and Sinai.

1967 – Six-Day War occurred: Israel gained control of the Sinai Peninsula, the Gaza Strip, the West Bank, eastern Jerusalem and the Golan Heights. The results of this war affect the geopolitics of the region to this day.

1973 – Yom Kippur War: Israel resisted co-ordinated attacks from Syria and Egypt and began to take more territory until the USA secured a ceasefire.

1979 – Camp David Peace Accords returned Sinai to Egypt and Israel retained Gaza Strip.

1982 – Israeli invasion of Lebanon in response to Palestine Liberation Army (PLO) raids into Israel.

1987 – First Intifada (a combination of violent and non-violent Palestinian resistance to Israeli occupation) began and the influence of radical Islamic groups alongside the PLO became visible among Palestinians.

1993 – Israel and PLO signed Oslo Accords, their first face-to-face agreement, which established the Palestinian Authority (PA) over West Bank and Gaza Strip.

1994 – Israeli-Jordanian Peace Treaty signed, ending hostilities between these countries.

2000 – Israel withdrew from Lebanon.

2000 – Second Intifada began with both sides blaming the other for beginning the escalation, (e.g. Palestinians cite Ariel's Sharon's visit to the Temple Mount and Israelis claim it was planned by Yasser Arafat.) Unwelcome features like Palestinian suicide bombings and Israeli heavy armour, bulldozers and checkpoints within the PA territory have become enduring features of this Intifada.

2002 – Construction began of the Israeli West Bank Barrier, consisting of a network of fences and walls with vehicle-barrier trenches. It is located mainly within the West Bank, partly along the Green Line, but often well within PA Territory. As of 2006 the length of the barrier approved by the Israeli government is 703 kilometres and may not be completed until 2010. The barrier is a highly controversial project with supporters arguing that it is a necessary tool protecting Israeli civilians from Palestinian terrorism, including suicide bombing attacks. Opponents say the barrier has many negative effects on Palestinians including reduced freedoms, reduction of Israeli checkpoint closures, loss of land, increased difficulty in accessing medical services in Israel, restricted access to water sources, change in political tactics and strategy, and economic effects.

2003 – Israel began a policy of unilateral withdrawal of Jewish settlements from Gaza Strip.

2006 – In response to Hezbollah hostility from Lebanon, Israel invaded Lebanon destroying Lebanese infra-structure and creating one million refugees.

Further reading
- Geoffrey Chaucer The Canterbury Tales in Modern Verse (translated by Joe Glaser), Hackett Publishing Co. 2005

- Edward W Said Orientalism Vintage Books 1988
- JRR Tolkien The Lord of the Rings Harper Collins (first published 1935)
- Vaclav Vratislaw The Adventures of Baron Wenceslas Wratislaw Oxford University Press 1862 (digitised and available on http://books.google.co.uk 2006)

CHAPTER 28

Pawns or Players?

Steve Lowton

So the question remains, after thousands of kilometres and many wonderful memories: can cities and nations change through decisions made in our living rooms, or are we all pawns in the hands of the real power players?

Of course, there have been many amazing people who have risen to incredible significance from out of nowhere; Nelson Mandela, say, or Mahatma Gandhi. Others tell of heroes and heroines who come to the attention of a nation through wonderful acts of kindness or courage, often in terrible times of affliction. There is no doubt that a national conscience can be shaped by such people and that they find a place in the history of a nation that is totally fitting.

What, though, of those who have no great acts of courage to tell; people who have not captivated the heart of a nation through wonderful oratory or a life laid down in selfless service? Ordinary people, who stumble through life, seeking to do right and act right, but with no claim to greatness other than a belief in the power of prayer and the value of each life sown into the substance of the ground? Can we make a difference, or will any real change be down to the powers of military might and economic muscle; those who can bludgeon their way to the front of the queue?

Over the last thirty months we have journeyed our way from the edges of the north-east coastline of England, passing through the global gateways that surround the continent of Europe: London, Paris, Rome, Athens, Istanbul and Jerusalem. Each of these cities have shaped the history and the continent of which we are a part; and, indeed, the western world as a whole. During this time we have found ourselves tracking with incredible time scales, seen weather patterns change and found ourselves in a strange synergy with the events unfolding in the seven nations we have walked through. For others of us it has seemed as if the story line of our own lives was somehow wrapped up in all that we have been walking for. The grit off our boots has found its way back into the living rooms of our homes, or perhaps visa versa.

Yet has anything changed? The tensions in Israel and Palestine seem no different, if not worse, than when we set off thirty months ago. The genocide in Turkey continues to be written off by the Turkish government. Rationalist thought seems as strong as ever across the western world. The powers of economics continue to frighten and dictate. Meanwhile, the great religious institutions look on with just occasional words of comment. Are we deceived in believing something as simple as a few people walking and praying could make any difference at all?

Who knows what might unfold in the nations we have journeyed through and who can tell what contribution a few steps and prayers have made. What space might be found for justice to flow if Turkey is freed of its open wound of injustice and France come clear of the deep scars of imperialism, then? What treasures are there to discover when nations truly connect with their heavenly story line and how could righteousness flow when greed and self-interest drops to the ground?

Romantic nonsense, I hear you say; nothing can change patterns of imperialism established in human nature over many generations. Cities and nations are stuck in their ways and we are but pawns in the hands of a few.

Is that true? Or might there be ways by which we can connect with heaven and earth and see change come even to the heart of a continent?

Perhaps to get an answer we should return to the windswept cliff-tops of Whitby, and the lepers at the gates of the city of Samaria. Here do we not see a microcosm of all that this loaded question carries? In one, discussion unfurls around the table set deep in the heart of the Abbey, and something is set in motion that reverberates for centuries to come. A movement that had been borne along without brand name or corporate logo, like leaves dancing on the edge of the winds of time, suddenly encounters the rigidity of formality, power games and vested interest.

In the other, a few social outcasts abandon themselves to the most terrible of choices, and yet find liberation and life not just for themselves but for the city that has rejected them. Neither knew of the repercussions of their choices whilst events unfolded around them. They responded to the opportunity of the moment: one sensing the possibilities of power and personal gain; the other willing to gamble all on the hope of a better future.

We have walked and prayed in the footsteps of these early Celts and outcasts of Samaria. As a nation staggered from Olympic celebration to utter devastation within just twenty four hours in the summer of 2005, so decisions were made to go and pray for the continent of which we are part.

This is our offering.

Whether a whole continent is any different for our choices we will probably never know. One thing we do know, however, is that we have changed. No longer fearing the unknown, we have discovered the wonder of the open road and the quiet contentment and delight of companions along the way.

We have discovered that cities have personalities. Some welcome you with open arms; some resist and refuse to disclose even the shallowest of secrets. Still others seek to hold onto you when it's time to move on, seductively sowing doubts into the purpose of the new day.

We have laughed and cried at the delights along the way, finding the lands we have walked through rich in the wonder of humanity. No longer impressed by our own man- made ceilings, suddenly it's no big deal to walk through a nation, and to continue beyond Jerusalem seems at this moment, the most natural decision in the world.

We have marvelled at the wonder of our Maker, and known the deep assurance of his protection and provision. In so doing maybe just maybe pathways have been opened up from the shores of Galilee right back along the roads we have walked; paths that carry afresh the reckless wonder of those early disciples as they followed their Master from adventure to adventure.

This is our story, sown into the ground of the lands we have walked through, and captured in a thousand memories and moments of discovery. To you, the Ancient of Days, we do indeed offer up our prayer.

Echoes of the Road

Dave Herron

Here Dave leads the way in the first of four short appendixes that give another taste of life on the road. The memories we all carry are indelibly etched in all of our imaginations. Here Dave draws on some of those rich moments that will stay with him for ever. He lives in Leeds but was born in Scunthorpe, a steel town on the east coast of England.

In the early autumn, if the winds blow south over the Crimea from the freezing Steppes, then the summer warmed Sea of Marmara can steam for days. Walking east out of Istanbul I saw this and felt myself to be a long way from Scunthorpe!

Only days earlier I had walked alone in a blizzard through eight lanes of hooting traffic up to the walls of old Constantinople; to the very gates where the besieging Ottoman armies had breached the defences of the eastern bastion of Christendom and begun a new era. I sang praises to the God who had led me there and, momentarily, Leeds could have been an echo of a former life.

Some months before, on a day of deluge, I walked with a monk called Amstel through the streets of ancient Thessalonica. Knee deep in water in the underpass we dodged the heavy lorries which threw water six feet up the concrete walls. At the change of the lights we raced and splashed and hooted with laughter to the shelter of the next buttress. Life seemed to be calling and we were giving our answer.

In the pre-dawn moments of an earlier spring I walked strongly along the Loire valley with a friend who had dragged me onto the road with his desire to 'awaken the dawn.' Side by side we ate up the kilometres and sang and shouted to open fields, impassive woodlands and the curious sunrise. Nature needed to respond and there at our side, thirty metres into the riverside scrubland, appeared a wild boar... then two, a dozen, twenty, or more! Large tuskers, females and adolescents; racing and rampaging through the bush in startled abandon with four or five little squeakers scurrying behind. I glanced back, hoping to catch a glimpse of old Obelix pursuing his breakfast, and then turned back to the road with awakening thoughts of coffee and croissants.

How do you decide to take part in a walk across a continent? By what process do dozens of people come to the conclusion that it is reasonable to buy in to at least a part of such craziness – to walk and pray from northern England to Rome and, having reached there, on to Jerusalem and beyond?

I can have a stab at explaining for myself but only speculate for others. My guess is that, to some extent, there are as many explanations as there have been participants – and each comprised of a mixture of components. Some theological; others intensely personal; some to do with friendship and loyalty; others a breaking out and lust for adventure; some a launching out into adulthood; others a final fling in late middle age; perhaps for some a pursuit of God - or even a pursuit of self; possibly a combination of some or many of these.

At one level my own decision was lightly made. I would join in just one stage of this bizarre trek to Rome. I would walk in the beautiful Loire valley in central France for ten days. I had the time, I had the money, I was curious and I had permission from my wife! I missed the banter and camaraderie of office life now that I worked alone and ten days of intense travel, prayer, walking and living together might satisfy even my craving for the herd.

At another level, deeper and more enigmatic, I wanted to express my commitment to and value of both prayer and that prophetic realm where God may speak if we show any inclination to believe it and listen up. I figured that leaving the comforts of home, sleeping and eating in strange places with odd companions, embracing sore limbs and blistered feet - and both paying for these privileges and also forgoing my income - all of this might indicate, if only to myself and to God, that the value I purported to place on prayer and the prophetic went at least slightly more than skin deep.

For me the verdant road along the Loire valley turned into the rolling hills of Southern Italy, storms around Mt Olympus in northern Greece, blizzards on the way to Istanbul, trying to eke a welcome from the grudging impassivity of hard faced Ankara, a robbery on the road to Antioch and the joys of drinking beer in a Syria wreathed in welcomes, Ramadan and the exotic fragrances and sights of Damascus.

The Beauty of Breakdown

Sharon Cooke

Sharon is in her early thirties and walked with me all the way to Rome. Without her I doubt that the walk would have happened. Living in Preston she is a gifted musician and cannot settle for the ordinary. A radical adventurer in her choices and priorities she helped carry the walk the full distance.

Over the last year or so I have had a lot of time to reflect. I was given this time, as well as many broken bones, by a drunk driver. I'm not grateful, as you can imagine, for the broken bones, but the other gift has been priceless to me.

So many times, I know I pass through life in a hurry, always looking to the next big event, and forget to drink in the moment in which I find myself. And sometimes those moments are vivid, intoxicating, those moments when you really know you're alive. As I've lain in a hospital bed, surrounded by the unrelenting blandness of ward decor, I've realised how many of those vivid snapshots I have been given through the years.

Many happened on the road to Rome.

Just for the sheer fun of it, walking to Italy was a great idea, but even from that first point, when I looked back and saw Whitby Abbey disappear into the distance, I got the feeling that we were part of something that God was a part of too. I would soon become overwhelmed by the new friends I would make on the road. There are landmarks I would remember for their stunning beauty: Paris stretched out below us as we stood at the Sacre Coeur, or the first sight of the majestic French Alps. But there were also those ordinary places that would become landmarks to me personally, etched in my memory as the backdrop of another significant moment of connection with another significant person.

Then there were those places that have a bittersweet memory attached to them: four of us having bread and wine together in a tiny basement apartment as a storm raged outside in the port of Genoa. The weather seemed to mirror the particularly difficult week experienced by each of us, yet my abiding memory is the haven which that little room became as we remembered Jesus together.

But there were also those spaces that were filled with just flat out wonder. I'll never forget one winter night in the ancient Italian city of Lucca, stepping into the silent beauty of a courtyard twinkling with tiny white lights. At times like that, it seemed so crazy that I had arrived in such an otherworldly place through the simplicity of just putting one foot in front of another.

As Bilbo Baggins says in 'The Lord of the Rings':

"It's a dangerous business... going out your door. You step onto the road, and if you don't keep your feet, there's no knowing where you might be swept off to."

I think my most treasured memory of the walk though, is that final moment of reaching St Peter's

Square. Surrounded by the fortress walls of the Vatican City, a song by the band Frou Frou rang in my heart, a song that seemed so appropriate to Rome and all that it stood for:

'Let go, let go...
Well what you waiting for,
It's alright 'cos there's beauty in the breakdown.'
(Imogen Heap/Guy Sigsworth)

I could almost hear in that moment Jesus singing it over Rome, over us, reassuring us that our destiny doesn't lie in the monotony of simply building and maintaining our own 'empires', whatever form they might take. Maybe true beauty really is in the breakdown, that scary letting go of our own agendas to run after the ultimate adventurer, the God of the open road.

APPENDIX 3

Tears of Laughter and Tears of Pain

Andrew Crump

Andy is a good friend to many and a wonderful companion of the road. A gifted painter he works part time as an architect, making room in his life for adventure and fun. Just turned forty he has been one of the core walkers through the past few years.

I have loved taking part in the prayer walk; which isn't something I would say about praying in a room. When you mix walking, praying, friends, purpose, adventure and God, then it's an awesome thing and something I was able to live to the full as I spent five separate weeks walking in France, Italy, Greece and Turkey.

I love the contrast and inter-weaving of the big picture and history, together with the small picture; the detail, each step, each blister. It's the big purpose and small details I love so much.

So, I remember now a few of the small picture times which ran within and alongside the big picture, some of the real life not so glamorous 'in between the lines' of the 'official' walk reports.

On arriving in Calais, mainland Europe, the prospect of life, adventure and mission was breathtaking in all it offered. My spirit soared as I realised we were on our way to Paris, with angels walking around us and the sun on our backs. After a few miles, reality set in and the prospect of the walk became anything but breathtaking. The spirit is willing, but the flesh is weak. My flesh, including my large belly, aching feet and unfit body, was about to go on strike. On asking my bionic partner how he was feeling, he told me "marvellous, I'm riding a wave of prayer". I felt like I was riding a bag of potatoes. And it didn't help as our support car was lost and wouldn't return before I nearly broke down. Any angels that may have been with us went heading out of the way of one unfit prayer warrior.

Things picked up and my body got used to walking (even if I didn't mutter many prayers), and we arrived in Paris, where I literally walked along the banks of the Seine with my arms held out, trying to catch every ounce of atmosphere that hung heavy in the Parisian evening air. What a prize after so many miles.

The beauty and deep, tangible history of resting in Paris took a turn for the bizarre further in to the city. We headed back to our 'digs' after a day on the road and took the Metro. As usual, we were all packed in and I paid little attention to the Frenchman sat next to me. That was until I became aware of his hand next to my leg. Well, it is rush hour, but I am wearing shorts, so don't be over sensitive Andrew. As the journey progressed, the Frenchman took a shine to me and started to tickle my knee and leg! Normally, I would have quashed the unwelcome advances, but I actually laughed, then felt embarrassed. Fortunately, ours was the next stop and a bit of knee tickling from a Frenchman didn't do me any harm apart from dent my masculine ego. I suspect I need to get out more often. Any of my friends who say I actually enjoyed the leg tickling incident had better look out.

I love the laughs, camaraderie, fun and many highs out on the road, especially in a foreign land, but the lows can be deep at times and affect you to the very core of your being.

On walking through Italy towards Brindisi, I took some time to walk alone through the lush, green pastures along a winding road that revealed amazing new horizons at every turn. As I walked I could soak up some sunshine, talk with God, pray for the land and get some space. I was amazed at how subtly the beauty of the day turned in to fear, anxiety and a sense of aloneness, which shouldn't be a surprise when wondering what we were walking for and the spiritual battle raging all around.

The further I walked the deeper my heart sank, and I was glad to then walk with someone else after a two hours or so by myself. With a brave face I managed to push down the fear rising inside of me until it was no use. I burst in to tears, as sobs of pain and trauma came spewing out. I was shocked at the depth of the garbage coming from inside me. Not as shocked as my walking companion. He looked at me in horror, then bewilderment and then fear. After a few expletives he mustered up all of his pastoral gifting and compassion and asked me if I was alright! As soon as I had gained some form of composure, we were off again, striding out the miles.

I look back now and smile at what a bizarre situation it was and actually a good place for a meltdown. I suspect it may be some divine humour as a year or so earlier, one of our young walking friends had a meltdown on the A1 in the middle of the night. We told him to get back in the support car and left him with a Bruce Springsteen CD for company.

I love God's purposes, His plans, His calling, Him using me to pray for nations and their history, but I also love His intricate working and fun amidst all the depth.

APPENDIX 4

Assorted Comments and Memories

These are the unsung heroes or the 'chuffers' as we affectionately called one another. Each and every one put finance, time and energy into the weeks of walking, yet to a person all said that they came back the richer for the experience. These are just some of their comments, or at least those that are printable!

"One abiding memory of the start of the walk to Rome was the wind that froze our bones as we stood at Whitby Abbey atop the huge cliff overlooking the sea. Despite trying to stand in the lee of the ruins to deflect the onslaught, it always seemed to find us"

Jane Almond, age 52, Teacher; Whitby to York.

"Driving over the purple clad moors was amazing, then dropping down into Whitby took my breath away. However dropping down meant a long climb back up! Despite the hills and sore muscles I made it to York with connections created, friendships forged and a hunger to keep on journeying"

Mel Holloway, age: mid forties, Educational Support Worker, Whitby to York.

"My memory surely attests to the grace of God. We completed the walk at the Tower of London, with all that that signifies of power and empire. It was a holy moment of making a stand against so much of what our society implicitly admires, in a place where you can literally feel the weight of history all around you. And then the first thing our group leader does is to crack open a can of Coke and sup from the teeth of corporate empire! Despite that, and despite the beautiful weather that had accompanied us all day long, it seemed like God responded to the completion of that stage with interest. No sooner had we got up off our knees in that place and the said cola had be downed did the first cloud appear in the sky. A matter of minutes later we were experiencing a heavy downpour. By the time we reached the M25, we were navigating our way through flooded roads that demonstrated to me the complete fragility of everything that our society is built around."

Tim Jones, age 26. Liason Officer. Into London.

"The brief part I took in the walk was both a milestone for me personally and had a significant effect. I was recovering from major illness and managed about 12 miles in total."

Rob Dicken, age 51. Administrator, London and Greenwich.

"As the Marseille sleet slowly soaked its way into my undergarments and my wife looked at me with a 'help me!' expression, I decided that this walking malarkey was not always the most glamorous of activities. However, the next morning creation blew my mind - all was forgotten."

Chris Swan, age 29. Housing Support Worker. Marseille.

"It was amazing to walk through France - from flat vineyards as far as the eye could see, up through the hills on the edge of the Alps, and then down to the Mediterranean coast - impossible to choose a favourite bit!"

Hannah Swan, age 25 Ass Psychologist; Into Marseille and along Med coastline.

"Some memories: praying along the coast in glorious sunshine; walking the length of Genoa in torrential rain and lightening storms; shopping down the market, knowing only 20 words of Italian; walking a mile long coastal tunnel, pitch black due to maintenance work on lights! Awesome week."

Justin Thomas, age 34. University Administrator. Genoa.

"Nice to Genoa will always be the sun shining off the Mediterranean sea, Justin's masterchef cooking, being stuck in tunnel traffic for three hours and managing not to kill each other, driving, driving, driving, losing Steve and receiving the text 'I'm on the road to Rome'. Duo cappucino per favore!"

Sally Ann Dyer; age 50. Professors wife. Genoa.

"Walking on the road to Rome in the most beautiful scenery I was heard to say,
The reply was,
'Val you are in Tuscany!'
Oh! Maybe in the future it would help to know where I'm walking."

Val Bruce, age 63, retired, on the road through Tuscany.

"It was raining. I was not happy. Text home 'Why am I here exactly?'

The reply 'Get your butt out on the road and start walking!'

I did. I laughed, a lot. I didn't want to come home. I know why I was there."

Deborah Robinson, Age 42. Teacher. Northern Greece.

"To Athens and Syrian border; these were times where my heart was stretched and captured as we walked the roads. I just loved those moments such as passing women in black and seeing those faces crack open into the biggest heart warming smiles. If eyes are the window to the soul then smiles are a great way to break down the walls and sow a seed of prayer. The spontaneous greeting at the Syrian border by a local grandad, father and son and the wild roses they gave us were such a treat and made it for me."

Helen Anderson, age: mid forties, Graphic Designer. West coast of Greece.

"Hearing of the 3 murdered missionaries really shocked me. One of them was a German. I could never imagine that they would kill a German."

Martin Eller, age 51. Mechanical Engineer from Germany. Konya, Turkey.

"For me, the walk as a pilgrimage encapsulated what it is to live as a pilgrim. When others have different agendas, personalities and even spirituality, it is easy to feel squeezed and to want to travel alone. However, acknowledging differences, and actively choosing to journey together anyway is a very real blessing."

Nigel Hodder, age 25. Graduate. West Bank.

"Putting my feet on the 'no-go area' that is the West Bank with such a diverse group of people who had chosen to journey together will remain with me for a long time. Deciding to walk somewhere and pray is such a simple act, but at times can feel so profound."

Steve Watters, age 26. Mechanical Engineer and Nomadic Wanderer; West Bank.

"The friendship and laughter, the highs and lows, an aching body, physical and mental exhaustion, the blisters and needles, getting lost, looking for bushes for potty stops.

The freedom of praying out on the road, the encouraging texts from friends back home and the amazing cultural differences. The most challenging, exciting, fulfilling and releasing adventure of my life."

Val Bruce, age 63. Retired. Paris, Rome, Athens, Istanbul and Jerusalem.

www.storiesfromthestreet.com

Stories from the Street is an online space created to give room for stories to be told; extraordinary stories from ordinary people. It is your opportunity to tell your story, or that of someone you know, and in so doing have the chance to see your work published alongside that of others.

Stories from the Street offers the facility for audio or video blogging, with the opportunity to post live stories in the making. It is for writers and actors, storytellers, adventurers and those who just love to read stories; stories that are authentic, that dignify and inspire others.

Stories from the Street is not for professionals! We are a growing community of writers and actors who believe in the power of story. Whilst wanting to develop our skills to the highest levels, it is the stories themselves that really matter. Anyone is invited to have a go at the ancient art of storytelling.